学术顾问／张宪文　朱庆葆

哈佛燕京图书馆文献丛刊第三十种
南京大学人文基金资助项目
南京大学“双一流”建设文科卓越研究计划资助项目

美国哈佛大学哈佛燕京图书馆藏
中国科学社北美分社档案

The Documents of the American Branch of the Science Society of China in the Harvard-Yenching Library, Harvard University, U.S.A.

主编／姜良芹　郭　洋

1

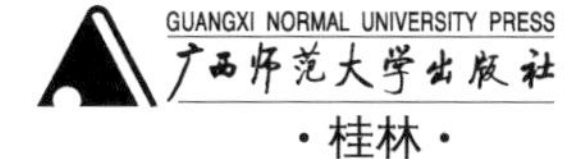

GUANGXI NORMAL UNIVERSITY PRESS
广西师范大学出版社
·桂林·

MEIGUO HAFO DAXUE HAFO YANJING TUSHUGUAN CANG
ZHONGGUO KEXUESHE BEIMEI FENSHE DANG'AN

图书在版编目（CIP）数据

美国哈佛大学哈佛燕京图书馆藏中国科学社北美分社档案：全3册：汉文、英文 / 姜良芹，郭洋主编. —桂林：广西师范大学出版社，2020.10
ISBN 978-7-5598-3274-0

Ⅰ. ①美… Ⅱ. ①姜… ②郭… Ⅲ. ①社会科学－学术团体－档案资料－汇编－中国－近代－汉、英 Ⅳ. ①C262

中国版本图书馆 CIP 数据核字（2020）第 188179 号

广西师范大学出版社出版发行
（广西桂林市五里店路9号　邮政编码：541004
网址：http://www.bbtpress.com）
出版人：黄轩庄
全国新华书店经销
广西广大印务有限责任公司印刷
（桂林市临桂区秧塘工业园西城大道北侧广西师范大学出版社集团有限公司创意产业园内　邮政编码：541199）
开本：880 mm × 1 240 mm　1/16
印张：93.25　　　字数：1 492 千字
2020年10月第1版　　2020年10月第1次印刷
定价：2800.00元（全3册）

前　言

在探寻历史真相、还原历史事实的过程中，过去所遗留的痕迹，是后世史家书写历史倚靠的重要内容。形式多样的痕迹中，文字史料的价值得到古今中外史家的认可。而在文字史料中，档案更扮演着独一无二的角色，其真实性相对可靠，蕴藏着丰富内容，吸引着众多学人去阐释与解构。拓展新史料，是史学创新的重要途径。因此，档案史料的发掘与整理工作当是史学工作者的职责所在。美国哈佛大学哈佛燕京图书馆典藏的"中国科学社北美分社"档案，已沉睡多年，现终于可以影印出版，惠及学林。为方便读者更为深入地了解该档案的相关情况，仅就中国科学社北美分社的人与事，这批档案的主要内容与史学价值等做简要介绍。

一、中国科学社北美分社的兴衰(1922—1936)

中国科学社是近代中国最有影响力的科学团体组织，其发展历程是近代中国科学史的重要组成部分。中国科学社北美分社(The American Branch of the Science Society of China)则是中国科学社在民国时期唯一的海外分社。

1915年10月25日，由胡明复、邹秉文、任鸿隽三人起草的《中国科学社总章》得到社员赞成通过，标志着中国科学社成立。此后其社务不断扩展，并得到了蔡元培、黄炎培、张謇等社会名流的支持，连续召开三届年会，于1917年正式向中华民国北京政府教育部申请注册，成为合法的社会团体。1918年开始，由于社员流动，中国科学社社务转移到国内。1922年5月，美国社员代表向董事会来函请求设置分会。8月，中国科学社决定进行改组。此次改组正式提出创办"分社"，"凡国外重要都市本社社员在三十人以上，社务发达，经理事会或该地社员半数认为有设立分社之必要者，得有理事会之提议，经常年会过半数之通过，设立分社，管理该地及其附近地方之社务，名曰中国科学社某地分社"[①]。后经过董事会商议，决定设置理事长—书记—会计—编辑的组织架构，正式组建北美分社，中国科学社北美分社由此成立。[②] 有资料显示：截至1924年，中国科学社共筹建了北美分社、欧洲分社、日本分社三个分社。但据笔者考察，实际发展起来的其实只有北美分社。初创时期北美分社理事会成员有7人，分别是：社长顾毅成，书记钱昌祚，会计丁绪宝，分股委员长程耀椿以及三名驻美编辑。[③] 1923年，据报道北美分社计有社员39人。社员们热心社务，积极向中国科

---

① 《中国科学社修改总章草案》(1922年10月)，载林丽成、章立言、张剑编注《中国科学社档案资料整理与研究：发展历程史料》，上海科学技术出版社，2015，第38—39页。1929年修订的社章相关条款改为："凡国外相宜区域内，本社社员人数在四十人以上，社务发达，经理事会或该地社员过半数认为有设立分社之必要者，得由理事会之提议，经常年会过半数之通过设立分社。"具体参见《中国科学社总章》(1929年9月)，载林丽成、章立言、张剑编注《中国科学社档案资料整理与研究：发展历程史料》，第50—51页。

② 《董事会1922年5月26日会议记录》，载何品、王良镭编注《中国科学社档案资料整理与研究：董理事会会议记录》，上海科学技术出版社，2017，第6页。

③ 《中国科学社概况》(1924年)，载林丽成、章立言、张剑编注《中国科学社档案资料整理与研究：发展历程史料》，上海科学技术出版社，2015，第214页。

学社社刊《科学》杂志投稿。[1] 这年夏天,驻美临时执行委员会委员长叶企孙向总社报告,他希望北美分社每年能够负责编辑《科学》三期,并在分社设置分股委员会。[2] 年底,北美分社还制定了《中国科学社驻美分社章程》,总共十章二十六条。但或许由于组织力与联系度不够,这些条款日后未能落实。

随着一批在美核心社员的归国,北美分社在1920年代中后期的发展不尽如人意。[3] 1929年,总干事杨孝述对分社的状况有如下总结:“美国分社,久已无人负责,本年曾由理事会指定留美社员数人,请其重行组织,亦无消息,本社留美社员无从联络,极感困难。”[4]北美分社业务荒废的原因在于,中国科学社的发展重心在国内,而且自身发展尚且困难重重,无暇料理美国分社的业务,对分社的支持不够;在美社员分散各地,联系不易,缺乏一个威望高、号召力强的组织者。

1926年,中国教育文化基金会开始定期补助中国科学社生物研究所。次年,南京国民政府财政部拨付国库券四十万元作为基金,以后按月取息,作为中国科学社的经常费。[5] 至此,中国科学社有了充足的经费,迎来社史上的黄金时期。与此同时,重组北美分社也成为一项紧要之事,毕竟中国科学社是在美国诞生的,且在美国度过了最初数年。再者,美国作为科学技术迅猛发展的发达国家,中国海外留学生的重要聚集地,也是中国科学社了解国际前沿科学信息的重要来源地。鉴于北美分社涣散已久,之前尝试的整顿,效果均不佳。新上任的总干事杨孝述决定委托梅贻琦来主持重组事宜。梅贻琦在教育界赫赫有名,威望高,号召力强。他是第一批庚子赔款留美学生,毕业于美国伍斯特理工学院,回国后担任清华大学教务长。1919年他加入中国科学社,是《科学》杂志的编辑员,热心社务。1928年11月他卸任清华大学教务长,赴美任清华大学留美学生监督处监督。留美学生监督处负责管理分散在全美各地的清华留学生,特别是管理他们的经费。此时对于业务停滞、组织涣散的中国科学社北美分社来说,需要一位能够广泛联系在美留学生、号召他们团结在一起的名流,梅贻琦可谓是不二人选。

1930年1月30日,梅贻琦为重组之事向约40名在美中国留学生写了一封公开信,呼吁大家积极宣传,把北美分社重新组织起来。[6] 很快,同学们的反馈接踵而至。留学生周田回信说他收到了两个入社申请,另外他自己也希望入社。[7] 两个月后,梅贻琦再次发出一封公开信。据他介绍,目前已经收到31份入社申请,他建议把大家组织起来,选举一个理事会(社长、书记、会计)为大家服务。[8] 本次选举由梅贻琦把候选理事名单、选举票随信附上,然后依据社员的回信进行统计。1930年7月,梅贻琦向总干事杨孝述报告,经过初

---

① 《中国科学社纪事:美国分社之新气象》,《科学》第8卷第9期。

② 《叶企孙1923年夏初致函中国科学社》,载叶铭汉、戴念祖、李艳平编《叶企孙文存》,首都师范大学出版社,2013,第183页。

③ 叶企孙于1924年3月回到上海,任东南大学物理学副教授,同时成为《科学》杂志的编辑。《叶企孙年谱》,载钱伟长主编、虞昊副主编《一代师表叶企孙》,上海科学技术出版社,2013,第172页。美国分社书记钱昌祚于1924年8月归国。钱昌祚:《浮生百记》,传记文学出版社,1975年,第22页。会计丁绪宝于1925年回国在东北大学任教。孙文治主编《东南大学校友业绩丛书》(第1卷),东南大学出版社,2002,第138页。

④ 《总干事报告》,载中国科学社编《中国科学社第十四次年会纪事录》1929年10月刊,出版地不详,第29页。

⑤ 《中国科学社三十六年来的总结报告》,载林丽成、章立言、张剑编注《中国科学社档案资料整理与研究:发展历程史料》,上海科学技术出版社,2015,第281页。

⑥ 《梅贻琦就中国科学社美国分社重组之事致全体在美社员(1930年1月30日)》,*Documents of the American Branch of the Science Society of China*, Harvard-Yenching Library, Harvard University, Cambridge, Massachusetts. Box6, File1, p.6.

⑦ 《周田致梅贻琦告知新收到两份入社申请(1930年2月12日)》,*Documents of the American Branch of the Science Society of China*, Box5, File1, p.13.

⑧ 《梅贻琦致中国留美学生告知中国科学社美国分社最近情况(1930年3月20日)》,*Documents of the American Branch of the Science Society of China*, Box5, File1, p.19.

步选举,33 位社员推选梅贻琦为社长,吴鲁强为书记,黄育贤为会计。① 这次临时选举,是中国科学社北美分社开启重组工作的标志性事件。

刚刚走上正轨的北美分社,开始谋求与中国工程学会北美分会召开联合年会,以进一步扩大影响。梅贻琦写信给时任中国工程学会北美分会年会主席张贻志,表达了合开年会的诉求,并获得同意。随后两人以书信方式交换意见,商讨年会的具体议程,商定于 1930 年 8 月 30 日至 9 月 1 日召开联合年会。北美分社派遣王德郅、胡竞铭作为代表,与来自中国工程学会北美分会的两位代表组成年会执行委员会。8 月 9 日,年会执委会向北美分社全体社员发出通知信函,告知年会具体议程。通知中就举办年会的目的列出了三点:第一,增加社员间联系;第二,交流学术,分享最新科学知识;第三,讨论学社事务。② 此时,北美分社的社员总人数已经达 40 人,发展迅速。学社总干事杨孝述也致函梅贻琦,祝贺北美分社重行组织。③ 中国科学社总部第十五次年会闭会后,8 月 26 日,杨孝述致函梅贻琦,告知其国内同仁闻北美分社业经重组情形,"莫不欣慰鼓掌"。杨孝述希望梅贻琦尽快安排美国编辑员及通讯员,每月寄回国内几篇科学文稿,以帮助《科学》杂志的刊行。④ 8 月末,重组后召开的第一次年会顺利召开,标志着北美分社正式完成重组。⑤

1930 年 10 月,初步完成重组的中国科学社北美分社进行了理事会正式选举,由梅贻琦、张洪沅、王德郅三人组成司选委员会,向全体社员发出通知。社长、书记、会计三个职务,每个职务推出三位候选人。最终收到有效选票 40 张,新当选的理事为梅贻琦、张洪沅、王德郅,具体票数是:社长梅贻琦 39 票,书记张洪沅 26 票,会计王德郅 18 票。⑥从这次选举结果可知,梅贻琦得到了北美分社同仁们的高度认可与支持。对于中国科学社北美分社而言,1930 年是一个关键的转折点。这一年 5 月,中国科学社北美分社进行了临时选举;8 月末,与中国工程学会北美分会合办了年会,拓展了业务;11 月底,完成了正式选举,开启了一个新时代。

北美分社经历了 1930 年的重组,在 1931 年进入常态化有序发展,各项具体事务均有条不紊进行,与国内总社的联系也愈发密切。鉴于北美分社得天独厚的条件,《科学》杂志编委会请求分社能够定期向国内传递最新的科学信息,以充实杂志的新闻栏目。⑦ 1935 年,时逢中国科学社成立二十周年。这年的联合年会于 9 月 12 日在纽约召开。大会的主题是"工业化——科学应用对于中国经济发展和国家重建的作用"。裘开明代表中国科学社北美分社做题为《中国科学社二十周年以及未来计划》的报告。⑧ 原计划出席之重磅嘉宾——中国驻美大使施肇基,因事未能到场。在裘开明的主持下,大会特别召开了题为"中国工业化的意义"的专题研讨会。本次年会结束后,在时任北美分社社长裘开明的协调下,华美协进社社长孟治同意把该

① 《梅贻琦致杨孝述报告美国分社新一届理事会成员:理事长梅贻琦、书记吴鲁强、会计黄育贤(1930 年 7 月 9 日)》,Box5,File1,p.2. 本次临时选举,收到有效选票 30 张,梅贻琦以 24 票当选为社长。《梅贻琦关于临时选举情况的声明》(1930 年 5 月 30 日),*Documents of the American Branch of the Science Society of China*, Box5, File1, p.30.

② 《中国科学社美国分社 1930 年度年会委员会致全体社员的通知(1930 年 8 月 9 日)》,*Documents of the American Branch of the Science Society of China*, Box1, File1, p.18.

③ 《中国科学社总干事杨孝述祝贺美国分社重行组织致梅贻琦(1930 年 8 月 10 日)》,*Documents of the American Branch of the Science Society of China*, Box1, File1, pp.22-23.

④ 《杨孝述致梅贻琦(1930 年 8 月 26 日)》,*Documents of the American Branch of the Science Society of China*, Box1, File 1, pp.33-36.

⑤ 本次年会的具体情况,国内有一简单概述。参见《美国分社消息》,载《社友》1931 年第 16 期,第 2 页。其实,两个社团联合召开年会早已有之。1919 年 9 月,两组织就曾于美国纽约召开过一次联合年会,只不过后来因为组织关系,这种合作方式未能持续进行。关于此次年会的具体情况参见吴承洛编《中国科学社、中国工程学会联合年会纪事录》,出版地不详,1919。

⑥ 《1930 年美国分社选举情况》(1930 年 11 月 30 日),*Documents of the American Branch of the Science Society of China*, Box5, File1, p.29.

⑦ 《〈科学〉杂志编辑部致梅贻琦科学新闻栏目扩充请求美国分社新闻通讯员惠赐最新科学研究状况(1931 年 1 月 20 日)》,*Documents of the American Branch of the Science Society of China*, Box3, File1, pp.10-11.

⑧ 程焕文编《裘开明年谱》,广西师范大学出版社,2008,第 141 页。

社总部办公室当作中国科学社北美分社的永久办公室,以便收发信件与保存文件。① 中国科学社北美分社的办公条件得到较大改善。

1932 年至 1936 年的中国科学社北美分社社务,基本上是"萧规曹随",将 1930 年至 1931 年确定的发展模式延续下来,每年都在纽约与中国工程学会北美分会召开联合年会;定期向社员收取年费;按时从总社接收《科学》杂志月刊并及时向社员分发以及定期向国内报告最新的科学信息等。从笔者目前阅读的文献可知,北美分社的此种有序发展模式,可以确定延续到 1936 年。这之后的情况有待今后进一步考察。

二、中国科学社北美分社档案的主要内容

美国哈佛大学哈佛燕京图书馆藏中国科学社北美分社档案,经详细整理共有十余大盒,经整理选编为三大册,主要为相关人士的往来书信及各类报告、名录等,此外还有相当数量的《科学》杂志(不全)。经整理选编的书信涉及的各界人物有胡明复、邹秉文、任鸿隽、叶企孙、杨孝述、梅贻琦、吴鲁强、黄育贤、汤佩松、王德郅、吴大猷、熊学谦、裘开明、陈世昌、高尚荫、万绳武、冯汉骥、赵不凡等数十人之多。他们当中,有的早已为学界深入研究,如任鸿隽、梅贻琦等,有的则较少为人所知,相关研究还很薄弱。

具体而言,本书的第一册,主要收录的是中国科学社北美分社相关人士的往来书信,以及记载了北美分社社务活动的相关文献。书信内容主要是 1930 至 1936 年间北美分社的社长、书记、会计与分社其他社员、国内总社间的往来通信,内容丰富。此外,第一册还收录了许多记载社务活动的文件,也弥足珍贵,如中国科学社北美分社与中国工程学会北美分会合办年会的手册、部分在年会上宣讲的论文以及详细的社员名单等。这些文献揭示了北美分社重建前后的面貌,甚至具体到换届选举细节事务上。

第二册,收录的是中国科学社总社文献。在制度上,总社与分社之间保持着业务联系,北美分社由此能够不定期接收到国内邮寄的文献。这些文献直接记录了当时活跃在国内的中国科学社的活动,反映出总社与分社的良好互动。这些文献中较有代表性的如《中国科学社总章》《中国科学社概况》《中国科学社年会纪事录》等。《年会纪事录》尤为珍贵,记录了当年年会召开的详细情况,包含了总干事、会计、生物研究所、图书馆、《科学》杂志编辑部等所做的报告。

第三册,收录的是 1915 至 1950 年间《科学》杂志登载的较有代表性的文章。此杂志创刊于 1915 年,为月刊,前后出版了 32 卷,总发行量达 76 万余册。在抗日战争的艰苦岁月中,《科学》杂志仍坚持以毛边纸印行。1951 年,该杂志与《自然科学》合并,不久停刊,后于 1957 年至 1960 年间短暂复刊。1985 年开始,《科学》杂志办刊至今,由上海科学技术出版社出版,成为一份兼具学术性与科普性的期刊。

三、中国科学社北美分社档案的史学价值

近代以来,资本主义所取得的成绩,为人类社会带来的改变,相当程度上得益于 17 世纪以来的自然科学革命。一般而言,科学,指的就是分科而学,后指将各种知识通过细化分类(如数学、物理、化学等)研究,形成逐渐完整的知识体系。它是关于探索自然规律的学问,是人类探索、研究、感悟宇宙万物变化规律的知识体系的总称。著名的"李约瑟之问",折射出中国长期以来有技术而无科学。到了 19 世纪后半叶,在内忧外患中,中国人方才意识到近代科学的重要性。1919 年的五四运动,新式知识分子们更是大声疾呼民主与科

① 程焕文编《裘开明年谱》,广西师范大学出版社,2008,第 142 页。

学。时至今日,欲实现中华民族伟大复兴,更加离不开科学。

近代科学怎样来到中国,到来之后的发展命运又是如何?长期以来,中国近代科技史的研究不被重视。中国科学社作为民国科学社团之母体,历经北京政府、南京国民政府和中华人民共和国时期的风风雨雨,算得上是观察中国近代科技发展历程的重要窗口。早在1960年,任鸿隽便撰写了《中国科学社社史简述》,留下了弥足珍贵的第一手资料。[①] 后我国台湾学者郭正昭与美国学者戴维·雷诺兹均对中国科学社进行了专题研究。[②] 1980年代以来,海内外学界对中国科学社的研究日渐升温,成果颇丰。[③] 21世纪以来,冒荣所著《科学的播火者——中国科学社述评》一书,是国内第一部关于中国科学社社史研究的专著。[④] 2005年,范铁权出版了《体制与观念的现代转型:中国科学社与中国的科学文化》(人民出版社),张剑出版了《科学社团在近代中国的命运——以中国科学社为中心》(山东教育出版社)。二者的研究对象虽相同,但侧重点各有不同。前者聚焦于中国科学社的组织沿革与具体活动,后者专注于中国科学社如何推动科学观念与事业在近代中国的发展。近年来,在张剑先生的主持下,"中国科学社档案资料与整理"丛书诞生,目前已经出版了三本。[⑤] 该课题所依托的,主要是馆藏于上海市档案馆的中国科学社档案,其重要性自不待言。在此基础上,张剑出版了巨著——《赛先生在中国——中国科学社研究》。[⑥] 近900页的篇幅,全面翔实地研究了中国科学社的兴衰,可以说是此领域研究的集大成之作。

美中不足的是,中国科学社北美分社,作为中国科学社发展史上的重要一环,理应是中国科学社研究不可或缺的部分。然而,截至目前,除了美国学者王作跃,再未有人对此有所探讨。遗憾的是,王作跃的研究,仅仅是揭示了中国科学社北美分社的一角,还远远不够。上述张剑团队的一系列工作,均未能攻克此领域。2017年,张剑写道:"哈佛大学燕京学社图书馆和康奈尔大学东亚图书馆相关史料留待机会成熟再行整理研究。"[⑦]现如今,这个遗憾可以部分弥补了。

通过对相关研究学术史的大概梳理,哈佛燕京图书馆所典藏的中国科学社北美分社档案的价值已经无需多言。随着这批档案的影印出版,今后中国科学社社史的书写,将更加丰富圆满,更多历史细节将得以揭示,这也有助于中国近代科技史研究。此外,相关人物研究也能得到补充,如梅贻琦研究。[⑧] 若将视野进一步放宽,中国近代留学教育史、中国近代社团发展史等课题均可受益。时至今日,中国在美留学生与学者数以万计,他们在求学、求知之余,又该发挥怎样的能量?中国科学社北美分社的学人们,八十多年前的实际行动,当有一些启发意义。

---

① 任鸿隽:《中国科学社社史简述》,载《文史资料选辑》第15辑,中华书局,1961。

② 郭正昭:《"中国科学社"与中国近代科学化运动(一九一五——一九三五)》,载"中华民国"史料研究中心编印《中国现代史专题研究报告》第1辑,1985。David Reynolds, *The Advancement of Knowledge and the Enrichment of Life: The Science Society of China Understanding of Science in the Early Republic 1914-1930*, Ph.D. Dissertation of University of Wisconsian, 1986.

③ 相关著作的梳理,参见张剑《科学社团在近代中国的命运——以中国科学社为中心》,山东教育出版社,2005年,第3—7页。

④ 冒荣:《科学的播火者——中国科学社述评》,南京大学出版社,2002年。

⑤ 分别是《中国科学社档案资料整理与研究:书信选编》《中国科学社档案资料整理与研究:发展历程史料》和《中国科学社档案资料整理与研究:董理事会会议记录》。由上海科学技术出版社在2015年至2017年陆续出版。

⑥ 张剑:《赛先生在中国——中国科学社研究》,上海科学技术出版社,2018年。

⑦ 何品、王良镭编注《中国科学社档案资料整理与研究:董理事会会议记录》,上海科学技术出版社,2017,"前言"第9页。原文中所言"哈佛大学燕京学社图书馆"应为"哈佛大学哈佛燕京图书馆"。

⑧ 梅贻琦与中国科学社北美分社的关系,历来不为学界所知。

总目录

第一册

书信选编

集最近之科学教育资料(1930 年 8 月 28 日)

16. 留美中国工程学会书记黄学诗致梅贻琦,愿与贵社加强联系便于互通信息(1930 年 10 月 1 日)
17. 杨孝述致梅贻琦,对北美分社之重整表示认可并指导今后工作方向(1930 年 10 月 3 日)
18. 厉德寅、杨俊阶致梅贻琦,请求加入北美分社及入社手续已经托人在国内办妥(1930 年 11 月 26 日)
19. 《科学》杂志编辑部致梅贻琦,科学新闻栏目扩充请求北美分社新闻通讯员惠赐最新科学研究状况(1931 年 1 月 20 日)
20. 顾毓珍致梅贻琦,希望中国工程学会北美分会能与中国科学社北美分社继续合办 1931 年度年会(1931 年 6 月 16 日)
21. 中国工程学会北美分会年会主席致梅贻琦,咨询其对 1931 年合开年会之态度及建议(1931 年 6 月 24 日)
22. 梅贻琦致中国工程学会北美分会年会主席,同意两社继续合办年会(1931 年 7 月 7 日)
23. 梅贻琦致汤佩松,请其担任年会委员会主席并负责整理在年会上宣讲的科学研究论文(1931 年 8 月 3 日)
24. 梅贻琦致汤佩松,商讨年会具体细节问题(1931 年 8 月 22 日)
25. 陈友松致梅贻琦,将在考试结束后参加年会并展示科学电影放映技术(1931 年 8 月 31 日)
26. 赵廷炳致梅贻琦,表示愿意积极参加社内活动并附上通讯地址及履历(1931 年 9 月 3 日)
27. 梅贻琦致汤佩松,约定本月十日或十一日见面(1931 年 9 月 4 日)
28. 梅贻琦致汤佩松,对其继续留美还是回国之事提出建议(1931 年 9 月 22 日)
29. 1931 年中国科学社北美分社与中国工程学会北美分会合办年会之主席报告(1931 年 10 月 17 日)
30. 杨孝述致梅贻琦,感谢其为学社之奉献并就北美分社今后发展问题提出建议(1931 年 10 月 28 日)
31. 杨孝述致任之恭,就几名新社员的入社志愿书问题提出疑问(1932 年 2 月 8 日)
32. 中国科学社北美分社 1932 年年会主席团向社员告知下届学社领导人候选名单(1932 年 9 月 15 日)
33. 赵元任致汤佩松,以选举委员会主席身份告知其当选为 1932—1933 年中国科学社北美分社社长(1932 年 10 月 15 日)
34. 杨孝述致赵元任,告知顾毓珍等九人入社申请已经通过(1932 年 10 月 26 日)
35. 杨孝述致任之恭,收到北美分社第三届年会纪事与论文稿并请北美同仁多给《科学》杂志投稿(1932 年 11 月 21 日)

社务文献

10. 中国科学社北美分社年度财务报告(1934年4月30日)
11. 中国科学社北美分社选举委员会关于新一届领导人选举情况的说明(1934年9月28日)
12. 丁燮林、赵元任订购丁在君讲演录音的材料(1936年4月7日)
13. 北美分社1934—1935年度财务情况
14. 裘开明等十二位中国科学社北美分社社员1935年社费收据
15. 陈励刚、熊廷柱、谈家桢的入社志愿书
16. 柏林大学医学博士刘绍光提交到1930年年会的研究报告《化学动力学的新进展》(1930年8月31日)
17. 波士顿大学医学博士陈耀真关于治疗青光眼的报告

第二册

中国科学社总社文献

1. 中国科学社总章(1929年9月)
2. 中国科学社总章(1932年10月)
3. 中国科学社概况(中英文,1931年1月)
4. 中国科学社社员分股名录(1933年1月)
5. 中国科学社第十七次年会纪事录
6. 中国科学社第十八次年会纪事录
7. 中国科学社第十九次年会纪事录
8. 中国科学社第十九次年会论文题及提要

第三册

《科学》杂志选编(1915—1949)

1. 发刊词(1915年第1卷第1期)
2. 杨铨:战争与科学(1915年第1卷第4期)
3. 任鸿隽:科学与工业(1915年第1卷第10期)

4. 任鸿隽:科学与教育(1915 年第 1 卷第 12 期)
5. 中国科学社社友录(1916 年第 2 卷第 1 期)
6. 中国科学社总章(1916 年第 2 卷第 1 期)
7. 新入社员(1916 年第 2 卷第 4 期)
8. 董事会决议(1916 年第 2 卷第 5 期)
9. 新入社员(1916 年第 2 卷第 7 期)
10. 成立二周年纪念会(1916 年第 2 卷第 9 期)
11. 分股委员会章程(1916 年第 2 卷第 9 期)
12. 本社致留美同学书(1916 年第 2 卷第 10 期)
13. 预备常年会(1916 年第 2 卷第 11 期)
14. 驻美经理易人(1917 年第 3 卷第 1 期)
15. 常年会干事部报告(1917 年第 3 卷第 1 期)
16. 任鸿隽:外国科学社及本社之历史(1917 年第 3 卷第 1 期)
17. 茅以升:中国圆周率略史(1917 年第 3 卷第 4 期)
18. 杨铨:中国实业之未来(1917 年第 3 卷第 7 期)
19. 美国各地之社友谈话会(1917 年第 3 卷第 12 期)
20. 1918 年常年会之盛况(1918 年第 4 卷第 4 期)
21. 杨铨:中国科学社、中国工程学会联合年会记事(1919 年第 4 卷第 5 期)
22. 美国新社员——去年八月至十一月在美洲入社之新社员名单(1919 年第 4 卷第 7 期)
23. 杨铨:詹天佑传(1919 年第 4 卷第 10 期)
24. 任鸿隽:何为科学家(1919 年第 4 卷第 10 期)
25. 南京社友会近况(1919 年第 5 卷第 1 期)
26. 尤乙照:铁路在战争中之价值(1919 年第 5 卷第 1 期)
27. 杨铨:中国科学社第四次年会记事(1919 年第 5 卷第 1 期)
28. 北京社友会近状(1920 年第 5 卷第 3 期)
29. 今年年会筹备情形(1920 年第 5 卷第 3 期)
30. 美国社友会筹备之经过(1920 年第 5 卷第 12 期)
31. 中国科学社第七次年会记事(1922 年第 7 卷第 9 期)
32. 美国分社之新气象(1923 年第 8 卷第 9 期)
33. 中国科学社年会纪略(1924 年第 9 卷第 7 期)
34. 中国科学社驻美分社章程(1925 年第 10 卷第 5 期)
35. 驻美分社消息(1925 年第 10 卷第 5 期)

《科学》杂志选编(1950 年第 32 卷)

6. 张孟闻:科学工作者的联合阵线(第 3 期)
7. 竺可桢:中国科学的新方向(第 4 期)
8. 卢于道:科学与政治斗争(第 4 期)
9. 周谷城:科学的新生(第 5 期)
10. 李四光:欧美自然科学界向的现状(第 5 期)
11. 李四光:读了“欧美自然科学界向的现状”讲词记录以后(第 6 期)
12. 刘咸:建设与科学的人力(第 6 期)
13. 土地改革与农村建设第 6 次座谈会(第 6 期)
14. 郑集:新中国科学发展的途径(第 7 期)
15. 怎样做好科学普及工作座谈会纪录(第 7 期)
16. 胡永畅:和平,科学,与科学工作者(第 8 期)
17. 工人业余技术教育座谈会记录(第 8 期)
18. 张孟闻:团结与建设(第 10 期)
19. 卢于道:治淮是计划科学的革命工作(第 11 期)

目　录

书信选编

社务文献

书信选编

本册所收录的文献为中国科学社北美分社相关人士的往来书信以及记载北美分社社务活动的相关文献，这些文献收藏于美国哈佛大学哈佛燕京图书馆的中国科学社北美分社档案中。本册选编之书信，主要是1930—1936年间北美分社的社长、书记、会计与分社社员、国内总社之间的往来通信，内容十分丰富，揭示了北美分社从重建至正常发展过程中的大致面貌，涉及梅贻琦、竺可桢、杨孝述、刘绍光、张贻志、赵元任、裘开明等知名人士。“社务文献”包含北美分社比较完整的社员名单、换届选举的记录、年会手册等内容，与“书信选编”一起为学界了解鲜为人知的中国科学社北美分社提供了一手资料，价值重大。这些文献对于中国科学社社史研究及中国近代科学史研究均大有裨益。

孝述先生大鉴：日前接来示及附件各种，敬悉一一。近来美科学社，社务竟至衰废，诚属可惜。理事会诸公要将以重组分社之职责对于科学对于本社皆素所注意，今承委托，不敢不勉。惟旧社员在美者似已甚少，即尊处开来名单中之廿人，亦尚有数人亦已回国。现方设法与诸君联络，并设法征集新会员。社员及其他社务以后有何进行，当随时报告，并希尊处不时赐教，俾收多所商讨之利，幸甚盼甚。专复，顺颂

陈[illegible]

Chinese Educational Mission,
2645 Conn. Ave., N. W.,
Washington, D. C.
January 30, 1930.

To Members of the Science
Society of China in U.S.A.

Dear Fellow-members:

I have recently been asked by the Board of Directors of the Science Society of China to see what could be done to revive and reorganize the American Branch of the Society among its members here. The American Branch as you know, used to be very active and give considerable support to the activities of the Society in the years past; but lately, on account of the small number of members remaining, the organization has not accomplished much and has almost been forgetten in the minds of many. However, there now seems to be an increasing number of our students engaged in scientific studies in this country, and surely such an organization as the Science Society will serve a very useful purpose here in uniting the kindred spirits for mutual fellowship and to promote projects of common interest.

So, there should be no question that we ought to organize, or rather re-organize, the American Branch of the Science Society among our students specializing in the field of science in America. And the first thing for us, the old members,to do would be to re-cruit new members so that when we have got a larger number, old & new, together, we can proceed with the election of officers and the mapping out of activities we like take up. For the time being, I am glad to offer the servise of my office for carrying on our correspondence until the regular officers are elected.

Under separate cover, I am sending you a few copies of the constitution of the Science Society, and of a pamphlet describing its present state of development, and some membership cards. I understand you are already a member of the Society, but if not, I think interested as you are in science you certainly ought to be one. And I wish to ask your help in distributing these pamplets and cards among the Chinese students in your city, who are pursuing scientific studies and who would be interested in joining the Society.

I hope to hear from you soon, say before the end of February, about the result of your recuiting (please just send the cards to me, - the question of fees etc. can be attended to later).

With kind greetings and best wishes, I am,

Yours sincerely,

Y. C. Mei

Y. C. Mei.

THE YOUNG MEN'S CHRISTIAN ASSOCIATION OF CHICAGO
WEST SIDE PROFESSIONAL SCHOOLS DEPARTMENT
L. Wilber Messer Memorial
1804 WEST CONGRESS STREET
PUBLIC CORRESPONDENCE

Feb. 12, 1930.

My dear Mr. Mei:

Thank you for your circular letter of Jan. 30th on behalf of The Sciece Society of China and also for the literature of the same. I have only received two membership cards which have been properly filled out and herewith enclosed. The item under 介绍人 is left blank since neither I myself nor Mr. Li is a member yet. Therefore we beg you to supply the signifure if you please. Very much obliged.

That The Science Society is worthy of support should be obvious to us students. It would be indeed an honor as well as a pleasure to be able to participate in the activities of such an organ which is the outstanding factor in present China for the promotion of scientific knowledge. I am sorry that I live so far away from the South-side Campus. However if I may have a few more blank membership cards, I shall try to approach some of our science students in case I have a chance to go to the South-side.

Respectfully yours,

Chi C. Wen

11

孝、述先生大鉴：兹奉上科学社新社员入社願书三十三件，照章请君交次待经理事会选决后方为正式社员。惟因时间短促，又查诸君之履历似无问题，故即认为社员，以便从事组织分社事宜。目前分社职员业经推定如下：

理事长　梅贻琦

书记　吴鲁强

会计　黄育贤

现分社拟与社员商量，于夏间召集开会，惟候筹备未就，结果如何，或须与此间工程学会或他学会联合举行，应较便利。一切候将来再为报告可也。专此顺颂

学祉

琦名具

附入社願书33件
社员总名单一件

JUL 9 1930

育贤
会阳两君惠鉴：月前阅于科学社美洲分社职员选举结果之报告，知已达览。
两君被推任会计、书记之职，将来于社务发展，[illegible]较实。兹上新旧社员总名单一份，即希詧收（请多留一份）备用。再上次选举票亦寄存两君参阅，阅毕存吴君处可也。社员收费事，或可待夏间年会集讨论后再行征收。至本夏年会筹备事宜，拟请二君与裴鉴、胡竞铭、[illegible]为委员，请王君任主席，筹划办理。其地点与时间，如能与工程学会或化学会联合举行，较为便利。一切务请分劳负任，感荷之至。专此顺颂
公祉

[illegible]

✓分致 胡竞铭、裴鉴、王任郅

迳启者：科学社美洲分社自重组以来，同学加入者已有三十余人，可谓盛矣。以兹当夏间假中正宜大家聚集商讨学问，惟关于年会之时间地点、问题与论文之征集不可不先期筹备，以便进行。以兹请

先生担任年会委员之一（其他委员为王任郅（主席）、胡竞铭、裴鉴、黄育贤、吴鲁强），一切印布，费神筹划，无任感荷之至。再本社重组伊始，诸事布置未完，仓促本年年会或以与工程学会或他学会联合举行，较为便利，如何商酌办理可也。此致

——君

JUL. – 1930

Mr. Waling: Herewith Mr. Chang to reply. Please return to me after reading. Y.C. M

Apt 4-c
548 Riverside Drive
New York City, N.Y.
July 27, 1930

Mr. Y. C. Mei
Chairman, American Section
of The Science Society of China.

Dear Mr. Mei:

Thank you for your letter of the 24th. in bringing up the matter of having the conventions of the Science Society and the convention of the Engineering Society together and also having some meetings in common.

Science and engineering are so inter-related that no other two societies can hold their conventions more appropriately together than the American Section of the Science Society of China and the American Section of the Engineering Chinese Society. Both are Chinese and are of American Section. Many of the members are as much interested in the Science Society as they are in the Engineering Society, for many of them are members of both organizations.

Though I have not yet had the chance of bringing up the matter before our Committee of the Annual Convention of the Chinese Engineering Society, I am sure that the members of the Engineering Society will be as happy as the members of the Science Society in having the Conventions of the two Societies together.

I may say that our program is almost in its final shape and we are anticipating sending it to a printer in the latter part of this week. We shall be very glad , if you wish, to have your program printed together with ours.

We shall be glad to hear of any arrangement you have already made or you are anticipating to make, relative to the Convention.

Sincerely yours,

E. Y. H. Chang

July 31st, 1930

My dear Director Mei:

This is to inform you that I want to present two papers in the Chinese Scientic Congress held in New York on Aug. 3rd this year by the members of the National Scientic Association together with the members of the Engineering and Mining Association. My Subjects will be:

1) The New Development of Chemical Dynamics

2) The Development of the Electro-chemical Dynamics

It deals with the establishment of new fundamental laws in Chemistry. I like to present the theories before our scientists before I shall publish my work in Europe. Herewith I send you a copy of the outline of my work. After you are through with it, please send it to me per post. I hope, you will accept my application as a deliverer of research work in name of the National Scientic Association or under the program of the said association. With best wishes and highest regards,

I remain,

respectfully yours,

Shao-Kwang Liu Shao-Kwang Liu

Dr. Shao-Kwang Liu
361 W 119th Street, N. Y. City.

9

Mr. Y. C. Mei
Chinese Education Mission
Washington, D. C.

Dear Mr. Mei;

In my last letter of July 27th, I expressed to you that the Chinese Engineering Society-American Section appreciates and welcomes your suggestion of having the Convention of the Science Society of China and Convention of the Chinese Engineering Society together this year.

Our program is in its final shape . We are waiting to hear from you about the program of the Science Society before we send it to the printer. We shall be glad to modify ours, if necessary, to fit in for the program of the Science Society.

Early reply would greatly oblige.

Sincerely yours,

E. Y. H. Chang

548 Riverside Drive
New York City, N.Y.
August 2, 1930

P.S. The program of the Engineering Society announced in its circular remains unchanged.

10

ANNOUNCEMENT

The Science Society of China - American Branch

Dear Members:

The American Branch of the Science Society of China under the able leadership of her new president Mr. Y. C. Mei was reorganized in the early part of this year. Up to the present time, the membership has been increased to about forty. There is every prospect that it will be continually growing!

In view of the fact that the members are scattered at the various places in this country which presents a great handicap for the carrying out of many important activities of the Society, the president sometime ago appointed the undersigned committee to arrange for and to take charge of an Annual Convention in the summer for the members.

The purposes of the Annual Convention are three-fold; namely, to offer the members an opportunity:

(1) To get acquainted with each other;
(2) To exchange technical knowledge on the various specialized fields of their scientific pursuit; and
(3) To discuss the business of the Society.

With deep appreciation of the cooperation of the Chinese Engineering Society, the committee is glad to announce that our Annual Convention will be held jointly with the latter organization, from August 30 to September 1st inclusive, at the International House, 500 Riverside Drive, New York City. The following is our tentative programme:

Saturday, Aug. 30,	7:30 p.m.	- Opening Session and Smoker*
Sunday, Aug. 31,	2:00 p.m.	- Presentation of papers
	6:30 p.m.	- Banquet*
	8:30 p.m.	- Social*
Monday, Sept. 1,	10:00 a.m.	- Presentation of papers
	12:00 m.	- Luncheon and Business Meeting

You will please note that the items marked with (*) will be held jointly with the Chinese Engineering Society. Your attention is also called to the fact that our Convention will be closed half a day earlier than the latter so as to give ample time to those members who have to go to their works the next day, as well as to enable those who are members of the Engineering Society also to join their excursion trip in the afternoon and their farewell banquet in the evening.

The total expense of the Convention to each member will be about $4.00. Two dollars of which go to the registration fee which entitles you to participate in the Sunday banquet and social, and the other $2.00 will furnish you a nice pleasant room in the International House for a couple of nights.

PLEASE NOTIFY C. M. HU, 226 S. 38th STREET, PHILADELPHIA, Pa., AT ONCE OF YOUR INTENTION TO JOIN THE CONVENTION AND OF THE RESERVATION FOR YOUR LODGING ACCOMODATION. WHEN YOU ARRIVE AT NEW YORK CITY ON AUGUST 30th, GO DIRECTLY TO THE INTERNATIONAL HOUSE AND REGISTER WITH MR. GEORGE T. C. WANG.

Looking forward to seeing all of you in the Convention and with best wishes to you all for a pleasant summer vacation,

We remain,

Yours faithfully,

George T. C. Wang (Chairman)
Lu Chiang Wu
Yu Hsien Huang
Ching Ming Hu
Committee for the Annual Convention

August 9, 1930.

18

中國科學社用箋

貽琦先生大鑒：頃奉

手教並入社證卅三張，敬悉美國分社業已重行組織，熱忱毅力，欽佩莫名。國內年會將於下星期二在青島開幕，可有組織貴處分社經過事，當于大會中詳為報告也。康南耳大學之劉錕君大函及顧毓琇君(美東社) Y.T. Ku 302 Mitchell St. Ithaca 討論分(美中社)大學之張春霖君 T.L. Tchang 威斯康新大學之厲德寅君 Teh-ying Li, 813 W. Johnson St. Madison 對于推

總辦事處 上海亞爾培路三〇九號 電話三六五五一號

中國科學社用箋

廣社員、徵集著作等事均曾与本社有所接洽，務望

先生与彼等加以聯絡，對于分社社務積極進行，定有良好之結果也。分社社成立，所有費用可在所收社費內支用，惟請（社費收入）會計隨時報告總社。又新社員須于繳納入社費後方可得科學及論文專刊等印刷品，並請轉告會計注意。弟即須搭輪赴青，不及縷述，匆復，順頌

道安

弟楊杏佛啓 八月十日

總辦事處 上海亞爾培路三〇九號 電話三六五五一號

August 16, 1930

Dear Mr. Wang:

I have received your letter of August 9th. and was glad to hear that things were getting in shape for the meeting. And I trust you have received the circulars which were mimeographed in my office and sent out early this week.

Regarding expenses for the meeting, I think we ought to spend a few dollars to share the cost of printing the program with the Engineering Society, and for postage and other incidentals. Only the treasury has not got any money as we have not collected the membership dues but will have to od so during the meeting.

I have received a request from Dr. Shao-Kwang Liu, (Graduate from P.U.M.C. and M.D. from Berlin, now at Chicago) 361 W. 119th. Street, New York, to present a paper on his recent research on Chemical Dynamics. He has sent his outline to me, which, though I can not understand it very much, looks like good solid stuff. So I have answered him ~~and~~ assuring him of our welcome of his presentation at the meeting. I think he will need at least half an hour for it. Will you please notify him when the list is made out. As to the other papers, I am writing to Chai-han Kiang and Tung-ching Chow to urge them to prepare something for the meeting in the fields of Mathematics and Physics. Too bad Pei Chien will be gone by that time. But I think we should get a number of others to present short papers or reports on the progress of their research. I will try and see if we can not get a few more.

I am planning to come up for the Annual meeting, and will be at the International House Saturday evening, unless something unexpected should detain me here. And also I will prepare a talk for the genral session that night.

With best wishes,

Sincerely yours,

P.S. Shao-Kwang Liu has just joined the Science Society as a new memebr, and also Chai-han Kiang whose address is c/o Department of Mathematics, Princeton University Pri[illegible] N. J.

August 16, 1930

Dear Mr. Chow:

I presume you has received the announcement of the Annual Meeting of the American Branch of the Science Society of China, to be held from August 30 to September 1, at the International House in New York. Are you planning to gttend it? I hope you are, if you can do it at all.

I am planning to go up also. As I shall be driving up in a car, if you are going, I can stop at Princeton and pick you up on the way. So I am wriitng to urge you to go and also to ask to urge Dr. Kiang, in the Department of Mathematics, whom you must have got acquainted with already, to go, too. If you both can go, let me know as soon as possible so that we can arrange about the trip together. By the way, I shall have room for one or two more in the car, and if Mrs. Kiang, whom I have heard of though not met, can come along, I shall be glad to have her company also. The International House has accommodations for both men and women.

Then another thing I wish to ask you and Dr. Kiang to do, i.e. to present a paper, long or short, at the meeting. The committee have got a few papers in the fields of biology and chemistry, but nothing in physics and mathematics. So, I think you and Kiang should help out in making the program a balanced one. Of course, the timre is too short to get anything elaborate. But you may have written something on some subject you have been interested, or you can make a brief report on the progress of your research on hand, which will also be very interesting to the other memebrs. Perhaps Dr. Kiang will have a number of topics to present, and in that case, he can present two or three papers. But I hope each of you will at least give one. You can let me the topics later when you have them ready.

Please convey my good wishes to Dr. Kiang as I shall not have time to write him a separate letter, and I hope to see you both soon.

Yours sincerely,

Mr. Tung-ching Chow,
Princeton, N. J.

30

焕琦先生：

同学王恒守（学物理）朱熙人（学地质）二位志愿入科学会。入会手续，请函知为盼。

九月月费请仍寄（至）剑桥。

在纽约开科学会时，当往会晤。

陈[illegible]敬上。八月十六日。

王恒守 H.S. Wang 77 Sacramento Street, Somerville, Mass.

朱熙人 H.Y. Chu 57 Gorham Street, Cambridge, Mass.

中國科學社用箋

月涵先生大鑒：美國分社經先生屬力提倡，得重新組織，業將經過情形代為報告于十五次年會，同者莫不欣慰鼓掌。寄來之入社願書三十二人，業經第九十次理事會正式通過，並已專函分別通知。美會計黃君育賢處曾有三聯社費收據簿寄去，囑其向在美新舊社員照章收費，以資分社費用。書記吳君憲張處亦有十四卷十期科學三十五冊寄去，囑其轉贈

總辦事處　上海亞爾培路二〇九號　電話三六五五一號

中國科學社用箋

新社友 美國分社現宜推定編輯員及通訊員如能每月寄回科學文稿二三篇对於科學刊行大有稗益也本社現方致力於科學教育並已成立委員会從事討論以期對於中等學校之科學教育有所指導而資改進用故特托分社代為搜集最近美國關于科學教育之資料及書籍並乞代索各著名中學校之科學課程寄社以資研究在美同人如有

總辦事處 上海亞爾培路三〇九號 電話三六五五一號

37

中國科學社用箋

關于科學教育之論文尤所歡迎　本屆新選出之理事高君珊女士現已至美國攻博士學位務請代為調查其住址示知俾對於本社自當竭誠贊助也　專此順頌

著祺

弟楊孝述謹啟

十九　八月廿六日

總辦事處　上海亞爾培路三〇九號　電話三六五五一號

38

THE CHINESE ENGINEERING SOCIETY
AMERICAN SECTION

敬啟者中國留外學生歸國後往々苦無机會用其所 30
學而同時國內需用人材時亦往々患不得人此種缺
病皆原於國內外消息不通致供求不能呼應棄才
不用良可惜也敝會有鑒於此故擬進行調查在美
中國專門人材編訂通信錄以爲應用惟茲事重大
且專門人材除工程學生外科學學生亦佔一大部份故
特上函要求點々
貴社合作編輯在美中國科學工程人材錄如
蒙概允請與敝會職業介紹委員會主席李嗣
綿君商量進行方針不勝感禱之至此致
科學社社長
梅月涵先生 台鑒

（李君通信處爲 Mr. S. M. Lee, c/o Waddell's Hardesty, Cons. Engrs. 150 Broadway, N. Y. C.）

留美中國工程學會分會記黃學詩 啟
[illegible]

中國科學社用箋

分社方始重组 兹得有力如 先生者起而响应此举鼓励分社同人之兴趣也社友通讯录正在印刷中一俟出版即可寄奉 至于缴费问题依向例为入社费美金五元常年费二元此次曾通知分社会计入社费四元常费仍收二元 兹合纸币确较国内为大但分社收费亦得提出四成为分社自己经费总社仅收六成且邮费甚大每期寄报须费一角二分至一角五分故纳费不能过减也

總辦事處 上海亞爾培路三〇九號 電話三六五五一號

31

國科學社用箋

先生努力科學，熱心社務，曷勝欽佩。所述發展美國分社計劃，尤見肯要。查美國分社久已無人負責，周茲緒君亦早經回國，故社中曾分函囑託留美友人重組分社。近據華盛頓梅貽琦君報告分社業已成立，有新社員約四十人，其中以哈佛M.I.T.學生占多數。後據

總辦事處　上海亞爾培路三〇九號　電話三六五五一號

32

中國科學社用箋

康南尔大學顧毓琇劉錫二君報告彼方所徵得之社員約有二千餘人並定（經李榕君聯絡）于八月間在紐約城與中國工程學會合開年會 聯並且實業健聯絡是在美社員已有六十人以上今示得 先生再在詩家谷方面主持到在美分社可有三個中心點於社務發展大有裨益 茲另紙抄錄分社職員及康校顧劉二君住址以便 先生與彼等通訊討論

總辦事處 上海亞爾培路三〇九號 電話三六五五一號

33

中國科學社用箋

撰文投稿分佈著作悉在美同人中願負此
責任惟本社尚有所希望于分社者以本社近來欲注
意于改進中等學校科學教育在美同人必能以美
國中等學校科學教育狀況詳細見示者尤所歡迎
也此外尚望時
賜教言爲幸　專復　順頌
學祉

弟楊孝述啓　十月三日

總辦事處　上海亞爾培路三〇九號　電話三六五五一號

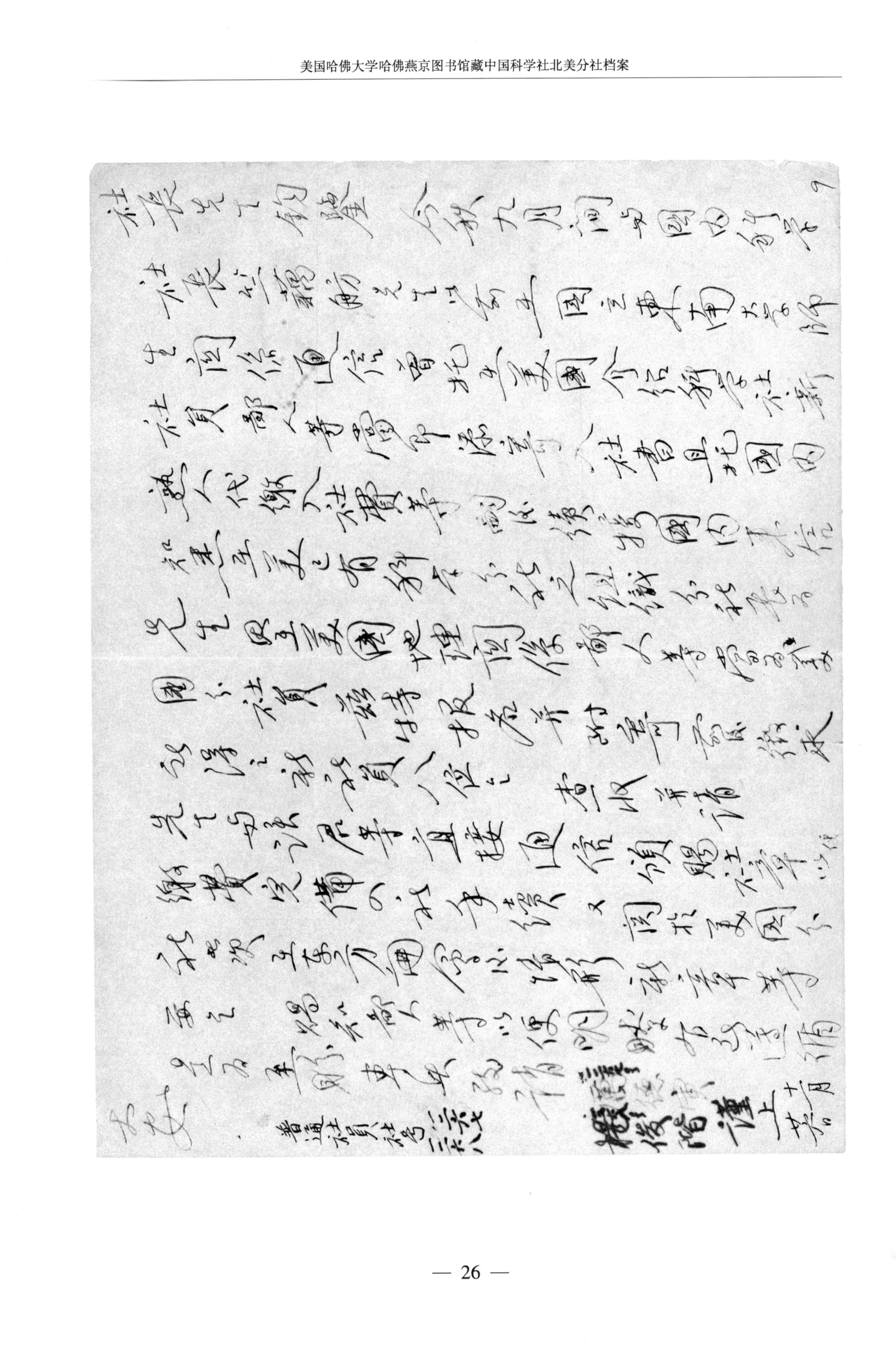

中國科學社用箋

月涵先生大鑒敬啓者學術研究貴乎切磋各地消息尤須
靈通本社出版科學中向有科學新聞一欄現擬加以擴
充國內外科學消息莫不爭先刊載惟是地限一隅見聞
有涯爰懇
台端擔任
貴處科學新聞通訊員關于各研究機關工作狀況以
及最近書報摘譯均祈隨時賜寄素仰
先生提倡科學不後他人諒必樂於惠稿也專懇祇頌

總辦事處 上海亞爾培路五三三號 電話三六五五一號

10

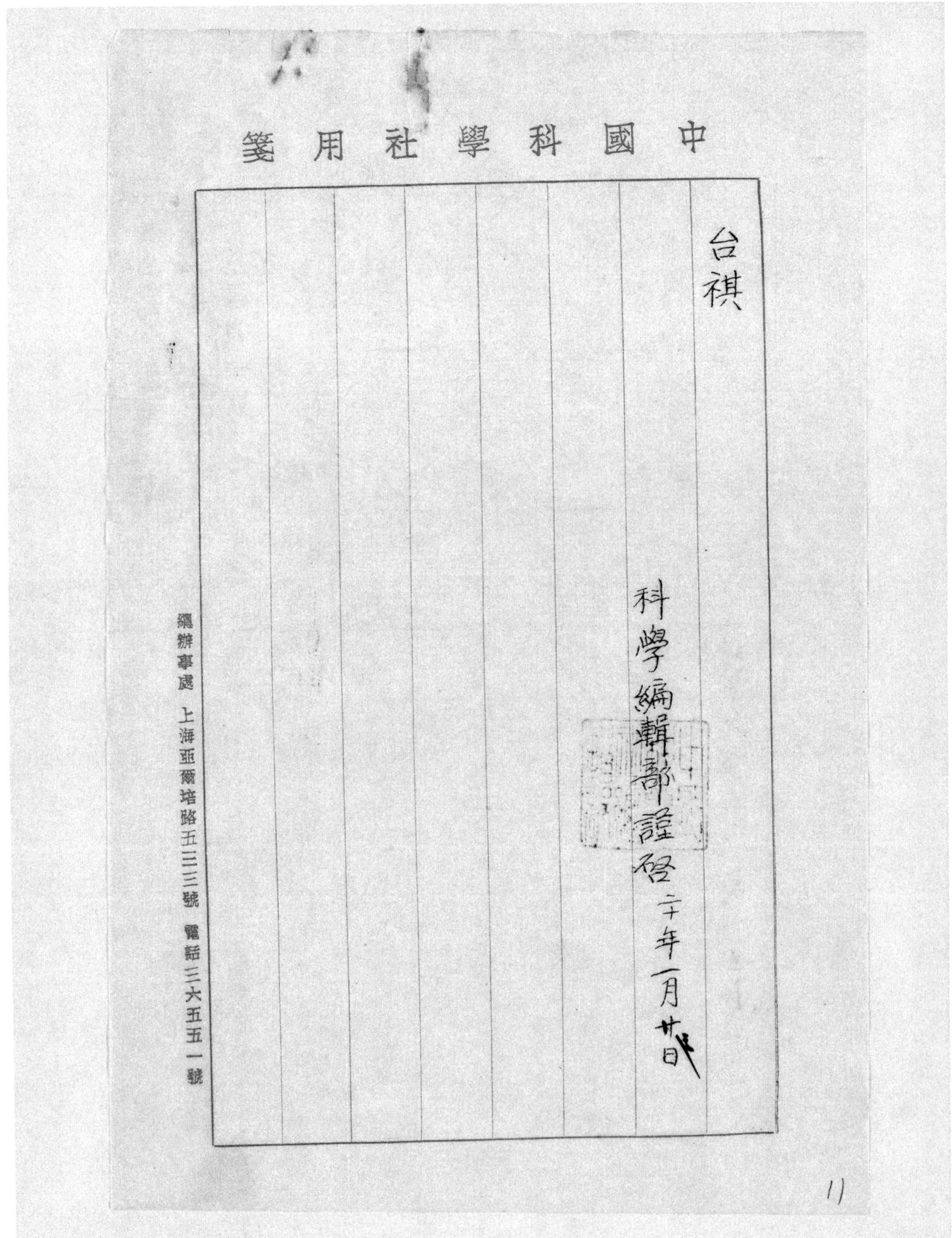
中國科學社用箋

台祺

科學編輯部謹啓 卅年一月廿日

總辦事處 上海亞爾培路五三三號 電話三六五五一號

11

THE CHINESE ENGINEERING SOCIETY
AMERICAN SECTION

二十年六月十六日

月涵會長先生台鑒敬啟者工程
学会留美分会將於本年九月初
舉行年会曾憶去歲
科学社留美分会曾与敝会
同時合併舉行成績斐
然不識
貴社此時曾否籌備年会
定否与敝社合併舉行如
有接洽請逕与敝会年会
籌備委員会主席李嗣綿接
洽可也(Richard S. M. Li, Room 905, 150 Broadway,
N. Y. C.)特此奉聞敬請
公安　　　　　會長顧毓琇謹啟

20

Room 905 I50 Broadway,
New York City, N. Y.
June 24 193I.

Mr. Y. C. Mei, President,
Science Soceity,
American Section.

Dear Mr. Mei:

A year ago, the Chinese Engineering Soceity and the Science Soceity had a joint annual convention together in New York City. The satisfactory result of that Convention must be still vivid in your mind. The Chinese Engineering Soceity is going to have its annual convention next September in New York City. The place will be probably in the International House, and the time the second week-end of September. We have not definitely decided anything yet, because we like to know if you would jion us in this Convention like last year. Mr. E. C. Koo, a member of your Soceity andour own is in charge of securing persons to present technical papers. I understand that he has already written you about the same subject.

Kindly let me know your opinion as early as you can. If this proposal should meet your favor, it will not take us long to have all the details worked out.

Yours very sincerely,

Richard S. M. Li

Richard S. M. Li
Chairman, Annual Convention Committee,
The Chinese Engineering Soceity,
American Branch.

21

July 7, 1931

Mr. Richard S.M. Li,
Chairman Annual Convention Committee,
Chinese Engineering Society, American Branch,
New York City.

Dear Mr. Li:

I have the pleasure to acknowledge the receipt of your letter dated June 24th. which has been forwarded to me from Washington.

Yes, I have also received a letter from Mr. Koo suggesting the holdinh together again by the Engineering and Societies Science in America their annual meeting in New York this fall. I think it will be very good for us to do so. The result of the joint conference we had last year was more than encouraging, and this year we can perhaps make it even more interesting and successful.

I am writing to Mr. George T.C. Wang, at Sewaren, New Jersey, to be chairman of the committee for the Science Society to make arrangement for the annual conference. I shall give him your address so that he can get in touch with you in order to draw up plans for the conference very soon.

With best wishes, I remain,

Yours very sincerely,

24

August 3, 1931

Dr. Pei Sung Tang,
Marine Biological Laboratory,
Woods Hole, Mass.

Dear Dr. Tang:

Very soon we shall have our annual meeting of the Science Society. This year we have made arrangments again to have the meeting held jointly with the Engineering Society. The date is temporarily set on Sep. 12-13, and the place, as no other place is as good, is again New York.

I like to ask you to serve as chairman of the Committee for the Annual Meeting, particularly to have charge of the scientific papers for presentation. George T.C. Wang is another member on the committee, who will attend to business arrangements at the International House. And I am writing to Chih-kung Jen and Y.C. Yin asking them to be on the committee with you. I trust you will be willing to assume this task which is really the most important feature of the conference.

Dr. Shao-kuang Liu has sent from Europe a supplementary section to his paper on Chemical Dynamics which he read last year. I will communicate with you about other papers which will be available to my knowledge.

With sincere regards to Mrs. Tang, I remain
Yours sincerely,

28

August 22, 1931

Dear Dr. Tang:

Thanks for your letter and your good suggestions. Enclosed is a program T.C. Wang has worked out jointly with Mr. K.S. Lee representing the Engineering Society. It embodies the points that you have mentioned. Only about the meeting for presentation of papers, I am not clear whether they meant to have the two groups meet separately or together. There seems to be advantage in either plan. What would be your idea? Perhaps we can decide when we know the number of papers available and the the nature of their contents.

Did I tell you in my last letter that Dr. Shao-Kwang Liu has sent over from Europe a second report on his Theory of New Chemical Dunamics? We shall have to get one to read it for him. If you like to look it over yourself, I will send it to you next week. Beside this, I think one man can present a paper on 'science teaching by motion pictures'. I will write you again when it is definitely arranged. Then I hope Jen can present something in his field of research.

Would your whole family be coming down to New York next month? If you are I hope you can take a side trip after the convention and visit Washington for a few days. Then you will give us the pleasure of meeting Mrs. Tang and the baby here.

Yours sincerely,

31

Box 368, Teachers College,
Columbia University,
New York City,

August 31,1931

My dear Mr. Mei:

Many thanks for your kind answer and your invitation to a chance of expressing my ideas. I am taking four points in the Intersession Period and much burdenned by research work . The examination will take place on the 11th,Sept. Will you kindly leave my place in the program optional . When I talk anything I must make good or not at all. I will prepare my best after examination is over.

I have a 16mm projector at your free service for showing any scientific films which can be loaned fromm the museums.

I shall pay the fee when you come. The flood catastrophe has put us in the deepest sorrow. All may be said to be result of the poverty of scientific knowledge. Now every loyal son should do his best to promote science.

Very respectfully yours,

弟 陈友松

Ronald Y.S. Cheng.

38

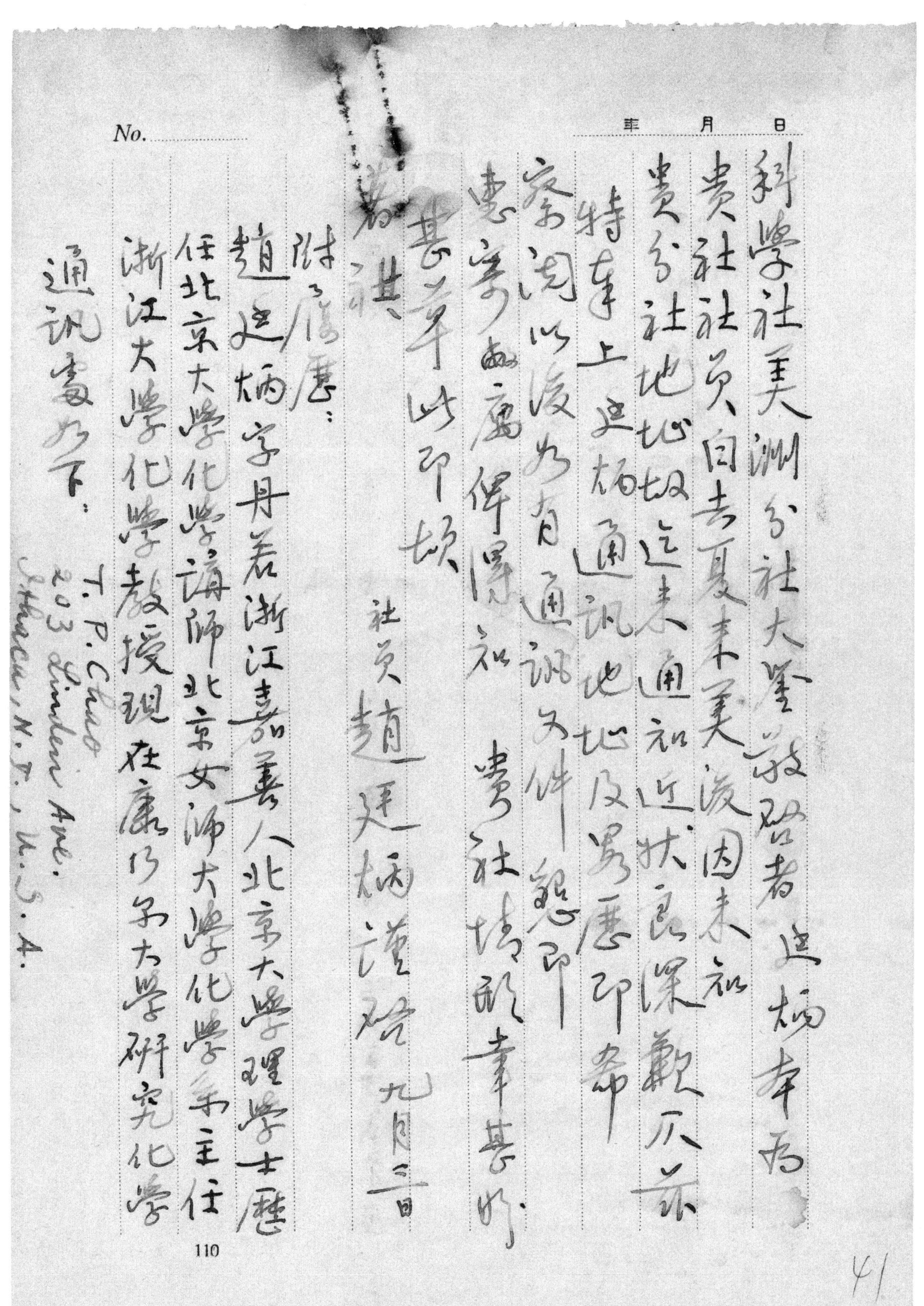
No.　　　　　　　　年　月　日

科学社美洲分社大鉴：敬启者，廷炳本为贵社社员，自去夏来美后，因未知贵分社地址，近未通知近状，良深歉仄。兹特奉上廷炳通讯地址及略历，即希察阅。以后如有通讯文件，恳即惠寄为感。俾得知贵社情形，幸甚盼甚。此即颂
暑祺

社员 赵廷炳 谨启 九月二日

附略历：
赵廷炳，字丹若，浙江嘉善人，北京大学理学士，历任北京大学化学讲师、北京女师大学化学系主任、浙江大学化学教授，现在康乃尔大学研究化学。通讯处如下：

T. P. Chao
203 Linden Ave.
Ithaca, N. Y., U. S. A.

110

41

September 4, 1931

Dear Dr. Tang:

Yours of the 25th. of August was duly received. Herewith is Dr. Liu's paper on New Chemical Dynamics.

The enclosed letter from Mr. Richard S.M. Li, chairman of the committee for the Chinese Engineering Society, I think you would like to read over as it mentions several things connected with the program. It seems that all are in favor of having the meetings together for the presentation of papers. Mr. E.C. Koo, now at 34 Mass. Ave. (Apt.6), Cambridge, Mass., who is Chairman of the Chinese Engineering Society, American Branch, has charge of the technical papers from the Engineering members. So, will you try to see him about the program for these meetings.

It seems that all the other arrangements are all right. I am planning, if nothing unexpected happens, to go up on the 10th. or 11th. So we shall meet again there.

Yours sincerely,

P.S. C.K. Jen's latest address is 201 Oak Avenue, Ithaca, N.Y.

43

September 22, 1931

Dear Tang:

Many thanks for your letter about the Convention. I was only sorry that something developed quite unexpectedly just at the time I was to go up for it. However, it is very gratifying to ehar of its being such a success, which was largely due to your good efforts. Will you send back to me Dr. Liu's paper so that I can sned it to "Science" together with the other papers. I am writing to Mr. Hu and Mr. Chao about the new election.

Under separate cover I am sending you the application forms for research fellowship from the China Foundation. My advice would be that if you can get the fellowship, it will be better to stay for another year, but otherwise, return home. Of course, there may be other position available by next sring.

About Jen's case, my feeling and my judgement are against each other. I should like to give relief to their what I understand to be a difficult financial situation, though last July I was told by Jen that they would be quite all right this year, b but drawing from his reutrn passage will be only to increase the burden for next year. The hardship will be felt much more then than now. However, if he must have some assistance now, I will send him a hundred dollars and hope that he can get along all right with it.

Yours sincerely,

Dr. Pei Sung Tang.

61

JOINT ANNUAL CONVENTION FOR 1931

By The Chinese Engineering Society, American Branch, &
The Science Society of China, American Branch.

PROGRAM

Sept. 11 - 7:00 P.M. Registration.
(Friday) 7:30 P.M. Opening Meeting.
Greetings by Chairmen of the TWo Societies.
8:30 P.M. Address (Speaker to be announced).
9:30 P.M. General Discussion.

Sept. 12 - 9:00 A.M. to 12 Noon. Presentation of Technical and Scientific Papers.
(Saturday)
2:00 P.M. to 5:00 P.M. Inspection Trip - to places of interest in New York, details to be announced later.
7:00 P.M. to Midnight. Dinner, Social & Dance - at Chin Lee Restaurant, 48th Street & Broadway.

Sept. 13 - 9:00 P.M. to 12 Noon. Presentation of Technical and Scientific Papers.
(Sunday)
2:00 P.M. to 5:00 P.M. Program to be announced.
6:30 P.M. Farewell Dinner at China Garden.

Time: September 11 - 13, 1931.
Place: The International House, 500 Riverside Drive, N. Y. C.

Important - A fee of $2.00 will be charged to each member to cover all expenses of the Convention including the cost for the dinner and dance party. Outside guests are welcome to the meetings, especially to the dinner and dance party. Members are expected to invite their lady friends; an additional fee of $1.25 will be charged to the member who invites a guest to the dinner and dance party.

Members are urged to prepare papers for presentation at the Convention. For scientific papers, please send the title and abstract of your paper to Dr. P. S. Tang, Marine Biological Laboratory, Woods Hole, Mass.

For room reservation please write to Mr. K. S. Lee, c/o Purdy and Henderson, 45 E. 17th Street, New York City

59

Joint Annual Convention
of
The Chinese Engineering Society, American Branch
and
The Science Society of China, American Branch.

General Report.

The purpose of this report is to set forth all the events and proceedings of the 1931 Annual Convention as a matter of record. It is also hoped that for the benefit of those members who could not attend the Convention in person, this report may describe the things to them, which they otherwise would have missed entirely. To those who rendered service, facility, or any form of assistance to the Convention, this repott is intended to express our thanks and appreciation.

As in previous years, the preparation of the Convention began with the organization of a committee to handle its affairs. This was done by Dr. Y. T. Ku, former president of the Chinese Engineering Society, who appointed the writer as Chairman of the said Committee with four members namely: E. C. Koo of M. I. T., T. H. Chen of Cornell, S. C. Kao of Ill., and C. T. Liu of Ind. These members were wisely chosen to represent as many localities as possible. It seemed at first that this advantage would be offset by the fact that the Committee-members would have difficulty to get together in order to decide a definite program for the Convention. However things could be discussed by mail just the same. It was through this procedure and with the good cooperation of theCommittee-members, a definite outline was agreed and then the details were sarried act accordingly. The outstanding accomplishment was the participation of the Science Society of China in oder to make this Convention a joint affair for these two sister Societies. Such precedent was established in 1930 and its repetition was not only logical but also desirable.Mr. Y. C. Mei, President of the Science Society appointed Mr. Geroge T. Wang as their chairman to cooperate with us. Thus we were able to organize several sub-committees to take care of various responsibilities. First we had the Committee in charge of technical and scientific papers, which was entrusted to E. C. Koo of the Engineering Society and Dr. P. S. Tang of the Science Society. The second was a Social Committee headed by Geroge T. Wang and assisted by Mr. C. L. Hsiong. Mr. Wang is a member of both Societiez. Then we had K. S. Lee, member of the Engineering Society to take care of accommodation matters. Then the writer with the suggestion of our Committee-members went ahead to find a speaker for the opening session and the dinner party and places of interest for the inspection trip. The time for the Joint Convention was decided on September 11 to 13 inclusively, and the place in New York City. The meeting rooms of the International House were used for all the meetings, and Chin Lee Restuarant was chosen for the social and dinner party.

63

The opening session of the Joint Convention was held in the International House Sept. II at 7-30 P. M. 38 members registered, of which 8 came from Ithaca, 9 from greater Boston, 2 from Ann Arbor, 3 from Illinois, 2 from Baltmore, I from Baffulo, I from Lowell, and the rest I2 from greater New York City. Outside guests in that meeting numbered more than ~~twi~~ twice as many as our members. The writer as Chairman of the Joint Convention presided, made a brief remark and greetings to the members, and then introduced the speakers. E. C. Koo, President of the Engineering Society for the year I93I to I932 made a short address about the aims and activities of his Society Dr. P. S. Tang did the same thing for the Science Society in place of Mr. Y. C. Mei, President of that Society, who was unable to come in person on account of urgent matters in Washington. The next speaker was Mr. Thomas H. Wiggin, Chief Engineer of the Federal Water Service Corp. " Mr. Wiggin, who for two years was chief engineer of the Grand Cannal of China Board of Improvement, spoke on various flood control measures now being adopted to prevent a repetition of the disastrous floods which have played such a tragic part in China's history" This is quoted from the New York Times on Sept. 12. Our last speaker was Judge Paul Linebarger, legal Adviser of the National Government at Nanking. His subject was "From Literati to Scientists through the SanminJui" It was a very impressive speech pointing out the responsibilities of the Chinese Literati. We were fortunate to have those speakers in addition to several press agents to give us some publicity. Refreshments were served shortly before mid-night and the meeting was adjourned without further discussions.

The inspection trip was made in the morning of Sept. I2. A group of about 20 members with a few guests went to the Geroge Washington Bridge accroes the Hudson River between New York and New Jersey, the longest single span bridge in the world at present. The writer secured permission from The Port of New York Authority to visit the said bridge and obtained a guide to show us the points of interest, when we arrived there. The weather was fine and we all had a nice walk over the bridge. The fact that the Convention was held in a week-end made it hard to obtain entrance into other places. Nevertheless arrangement was made to visit the Bell Telephone Laboratoryies and this had to be done in the morning of Sept. I4. I5 members went there, and I was told that they enjoyed the visit. This was the first time in our Convention history where an inspection trip was actually made. The writer hopes that in the future better and more interesting places can be arranged for this purpose.

There were two sessions for the presentation of scientific and technical papers, one in the afternoon of Sept I2 and the other in the morning of Sept. I3. P. S. Tang presided the first session and E. C, Koo the second. The name and subject of those speakers are shown in the following list prepared by E. C. Koo, who was in charge of that matter. All the speakers demonstrated splendid learning and

64

-3-

preparation. Time and space do not permit the writer to give you any summary or comment of the various papers presented. But it is understood that if the papers are put into written shape and sent to the secretary, they would be published in the Engineering Journal in Shanghai.

The dinner and social party was by no means an unimportant part of the Joint Convention. The interchange of knowledge is desirable, but the acquisition of friendship among the members is equally important. Besides everybody likes to have some pleasure and recreation. The dinner party was therefore designed to fulfill that requirement. It was held at 7-0 P. M. Sept. 12 in Chin Lee Restaurant, where dinner was served and music provided for the members to dance with their fair ladies. The party was attended by more than 50 persons including the guest speakers namely Judge Paul Linebarger, Prof. C. H. Robertson, and Mr. Y. T. Ling, the members, and their guests, mostly lady guests. Geroge T. Wang in charge of the Social Committee was the Toast Master and introduced the guest speakers. We all had an enjoyable evening, and were glad to have Judge Linebarger with us. His enthusiastic personality impressed us very much. He introduced some resolutions for the members to adopt, but it was thought best to have them considered in the business meeting in the following day. The party then continued to enjoy themselves with dancing and getting aquainted with one another.

A farewell lunch was served at noon Sept. 13. Then Judge Linebarger's resolutions were brought up for discussion. These resolutions called for a vote of thanks to President Hoover for his "Wheat loan to China" and another to the China America Union for its valuable service to China. It was thought that the wheat loan was more or less a business proposition, and much as we appreciated the generous attitude of the American government toward China, President Hoover probably is too busy to mind our thanks. The writer was unable to furnish any information concerning the activities of the China America Union, so the members could not offer any official expression. However we all appreciated Judge Linebarger's effort and wished him all success in his service to China. The Joint Convention was thereby adjouned.

The report will not be complete without a word of thanks to those who helped in one way or another to carry out the Convention's program. The splendid support and co-operation given by all the members were very gratifying to the committee members. It is the writer's hope that that spirit will be maintained and increased for all the future scientific and engineering undertakings and developments. Thanks are also due to those fore mentioned speakers for their kind effort and intention to talk to us. We want to thank Mr. C. L Hsion without whose valuntary assistance our dinner party would not be as satisfatory and enjoyable as it had been. A word of gratitude is hereby expressed to the officials of the International House , who gave us the liberty to use their qmarter and other facilities for our Convention withour charge, and who gave reduced rate to our members

65

-4-

who stayed there during the Convention. Mr. Y. C. Mei contributed us $20.00 to meet the expences of the Joint Convention. He did so in his capacity as Director of the Chinese Educational Mission in Washington. His generous and thoughtful contribution was very much needed and therefore appreciated. Mr. E. C. Stone rendered many valuable assistances to the Convention without taking any specific post. He deserves a word of thanks here. Others who helped us greatly but whose names are not mentioned here are equally thanked. Finally the writer wishes to thank all the Committee members for their highly appreciated co-operation and support. It is remarkable that this Joint Convention finished its task as it was without having had a single plenary session of all the Committee members.

Mr. K. S. Lee, Treasurer of the Engineering Society was also Treasurer for the Joint Convention. He has already given me his statement which shows a total reciept of $122.25, a total expences of $II2.83, and thus leaving a balance of $9.42. The balance, according to past practice was turned over to the account of the Engineering Society. Mr. Lee's statement is herewith enclosed. I want to thank him for taking all the trouble in that matter.

If the writer has failed to mention any particular event that should have been mentioned or express a word of recognition and appreciation to any particular person, that should have been expressed, it is done through oversight but not intentional neglect.

Very respectfully submitted,

Richard S. M. Li

Richard S. M. Li.
Chairman of Joint Annual
Convention, I93I.

October I7 I93I.
Room 905 I5o Broadway,
New York, N. Y.

66

中國科學社用箋

月涵先生道鉴：接来示知美洲分社自任先生主持以来，社務日見發展，不勝欣慰。入社願書与章程業于昨日寄出，又有新辦之社友錄亦同附付郵，即煩尊處代為分送在美各社友。為此辦法至尊處或多一番麻煩，但藉此与各社友間增多一份聯絡，並可驗在社友住址之確否，亦稍有用處也。本社概況已在重印，此次報告較舊本為詳，而英文之部与中文之部同一詳矣，一俟出

總辦事處 上海亞爾培路三〇九號 電話三六五五一號

二

中國科學社用箋

版印當寄奉並擬請代為分送美國各學術團體也分社收費問題前曾函令計黃育賢君入社費收美金四元（以前規定為五元）常年費收美金二元由近接威斯康辛厲君德寅等來函云從入社費三元常年二元但此問所發新社員社費單代說明入社費華幣十元常年五元者收美金若干於年問題三元二元之數之目前見匯原無不可也但社費必須盡力收取一則可以表明社員能盡其義務一則總社分社均須賴社費為之

總辦事處 上海亞爾培路三〇九號 電話三六五五一號

64

三

中國科學社用箋

惟事務所囑會計注意此點，收到社費提出四成為分社之用，並請其將收款名單隨時報告總社會計以資查考。科學十二卷十二期，除東南百名社友交顧毓琇君代送外，其餘新舊社友仍由書記吳魯強君接任分送。自十五卷一期起，即由總社直接分寄，惟上屆年辦法凡新社友未繳入社費之先，認為尚未為正式社員，其姓名不列入郵寄科學名單，故務必請會計將收款名單寄來，以符手續。但國外相遠，情形不同，一期寄後以

總辦事處 上海亞爾培路三〇九號 電話三六五五一號

65

四

中國科學社用箋

弟仍當繼續分送，不致實無停止也。諸美社友住址近已發見數人移改，將全件退回，以後兄如有所知者，即來函改正為荷。又英文論文專刊現擬擴充贈閱名單，兄如有意見，請代擬一名單。現每年改為分四期發行，或可得到若干交換品也。社友中如有從事職業著事，可請其開一學歷，以便在「社友」內發行，必有極大效力于

此頌

旅祉

弟 楊孝述 啓

十月廿六日

總辦事處 上海亞爾培路三〇九號 電話三六五五一號

66

中國科學社用箋

求社員函啓及社章願書等項計六色一併交郵寄
奉另附在美社員通訊處（比較準確者）抄錄一份至祈
詧照分寄刊物為荷嗣後每期「科學」及「社友」出版後
即郵寄六十份請代分送如不敷用　來示照郵總
社不再另寄如此辦法雖消耗郵資幾至加倍但使
在美社員與美分社多所接觸精神　亦屬貫注免致
散漫不過有瀆
清神耳專復即頌

總辦事處　上海亞爾培路五三三號　電話七一五五一號

68

中國科學社用箋

著祺

弟楊孝述謹啓 館

附名条一份印刷件六包另郵

總辦事處 上海亞爾培路五三三號 電話七二五五一號

69

1360 Madison Street, N.W.
Washington, D. C.
September 15, 1932.

Dear Fellow Members:

At the business meeting of the Third Annual Convention of the Science Society of China, American Branch, held on August 29, the undersigned were elected Election Committee for the Officers of 1932-33, to proceed as follows:

The method of election is to be the same as that of the Home Society for the election of Directors, namely, making a multiple list of candidates and sending it out for supplementation by members and then submitting the list with supplementary names for final voting. Owing to the comparatively small number of members here, it was decided that a minimum of five members should be sufficient to nominate additional candidates.

The list of candidates we submit for your consideration is as follows:

Chairman:	Ting, Supao	丁緒宝
	Chow, Dr. Bacon Field	周　田
	Jen, Dr. Chih Kung	任之恭
Secretary:	Jen, Dr. Chih Kung	任之恭
	Wang, Sherman R.	王慎名
	Chao, Ting Ping	趙廷炳
Treasurer:	Chow, Dr. Bacon Field	周　田
	Hsiung, Sherchin C.	熊李謙
	Wang, Pao Ho	王葆和

Additional nomination signed for by more than five members at the Convention:

Chairman: Tang, Dr. Pei Sung

If five or more members wish to nominate additional candidates, please send signatures in so as to arrive at the above address by September 26, at which date we shall send out the ballots.

Faithfully yours,

Election Committee

Y. R. Chao
P. S. Tang
C. Y. Hui

Encl. Directory of members.

Following is a supplement to the directory:

Chiu, A. Kaiming	c/o Chinese Library, Boylston Hall, Cambridge, Mass.
Djang, G. F.	Rockefeller Hall, Ithaca, N. Y.
Feng, H. Y.	351 Harvard Street Cambridge, Mass
Koo, E. C.	M. I. T. Dorms, Cambridge, Mass.
Hui, Ching Yeung	Cornell University, Ithaca, N. Y.

83

1360 Madison Street, N. W.
Washington D.C.
October 15, 1932

Dr. Pei Sung Tang
Laboratory of General Physiology
Harvard University
Cambridge, Mass.

Dear Dr. Tang:

We take pleasure in informing you that you have been elected Chairman of the Science Society of China, American Branch, for the year 1932-33, during which we look to a year of great progress.

Faithfully yours,

Election Committee

By Y. R. Chao
Chairman

74

中國科學社用箋

元任學兄大鑒前承
寄來顧毓琇等入社
願書九份除蔡鎦生早已入社無庸再提外其餘八人
均經通過并分別函知矣社費已請其就近交于
尊處藉資分社開支分社新職員曾昭掄君尚希
示知俾資接洽且「科學」中分社職員表內至今仍列
楊孝述名字殊屬不妥也分社社員留美之期既暫
且往來時有變更關于通訊送報收款等事據本社已
往經驗若匯由總社辦理實感散漫不如由分社集

總辦事處 上海亞爾培路五三三號 電話三六五五一號

75

中國科學社用箋

中辦理即可有一批函件雜誌包送達分社負責人再由分社分送各社員，俾分社與在美社員之間隨時之密切聯絡，而總社亦可隨時得分社之消息。如此辦法尊意如何，如以爲然即可照辦也。

本社創辦之中國科學圖書儀器公司自遷入特建之新屋后業務益能發展，現專力于出版事業，茲擬請求我兄二事：(一)我兄本人如有通俗(或半通俗)性質之著作，請交本公司出版；(二)前擬編譯一種近世科學的叢書

總辦事處 上海亞爾培路五三三號 電話三六五五一號

中國科學社用箋

其性質最好合于大学初级生及中学教员参考之用我

兄在美对于新出版物見聞較廣請介紹一二種俾此間

得請人分譯等此奉懇尚祈

不吝賜教為幸　順頌

公綏

弟楊孝述頓　十月廿六日

寄允中

總辦事處　上海亞爾培路五三三號　電話三六五五一號

中國科學社用箋

之恭先生 大鑒 美國分社第三屆年會紀事暨論文稿二篇均經收悉紀事原文已附入總社年會紀事中不日即可出版論文稿亦已付印將來原作者每人可得單行本四十份也此次分社年會到會人數雖不甚多而全體精神煥發辦事秩序井然諸位司事者賢勞可想也所示議決案四則關係於國內外社員溝通消

總辦事處 上海亞爾培路五三三號 電話三六五五一號

中國科學社用箋

息有裨于國内學術之發展總社方面定當設法逐項辦理留美社員中新著作定必不少本社科學雜誌月出一期發行已及十七年在國内已有相當地位尚望于留美同人中隨時徵集文稿在科學中發表倘能一次集成一期則可發行留美社員編輯專號每年有一二期亦甚相宜本社另有「社友」一種為刊布社務及社友消息之惟一機關留美同人之近況亦望時々

總辦事處　上海亞爾培路五三三號　電話三六五五一號

81

中國科學社用箋

惠登以資聯絡為幸專復順頌

旅社

弟楊孝述謹啓 十一月廿日

又啓者最近分社社員姓名住址單亦已收登嗣後本社刊物當

照分社書記來單證實之住址按期分送茲又附奉新通過之

留美社員名單一份除已分函分社會計外即希

詧登

總辦事處 上海亞爾培路五三三號 電話三六五五一號

82

致中國科学社總會(社)幹事楊孝述先生書 — 存稿

允中先生大鑒 前接来函内情均悉 所述留美同学投稿「科
学」雜志事 弟極願代理徵集文稿 并將發信與在美社員 結
果如何 隨後再報 「社友」到弟處者已有三期，内容豐富，留
美同人特别歡迎 前趙元任博士查出入社願書七[illegible]想未經
總社通過 并奉上趙博士原函(中有弟之附註)請總社理事會
斟酌辦理 此外有鄧振先及寥溫義兩君請求入社 鄧君之
願書已由趙博士直接寄回 寥君之願書附此奉上 又聞趙
博士言 先生希望分社辦理分發函件雜誌 敝分社同人

96

對此提議十分贊同，如總會欲如此辦理，請將下期科學雜誌

整包寄至中處為要。再者，分社會計周田居現正徵收會費，俟

收集完畢後，將抽出十分之六寄回總會，俾容再報。即頌

公祺

中任之恭謹啟

廿十二年一月九日

Circular No. 1

The American Branch of the Science Society of China

Feb. 22, 1933

Dear Member:

I am transmitting to you a recent letter from Dr. P.S. Tang, the Chairman of our Branch, with the suggestion that a symposium on the "Industrialization of China" be held in our coming annual convention. You are requested to examine the suggestion and turn in your answers to me (on the enclosed post card) as soon as possible.

I have received a letter from Mr. S.Z. Yang, the Secretary General of the Science Society of China, asking the members in America to contribute articles to the "Science" magazine. He mentioned the possibility of publishing a special issue for the articles from our Branch if there is sufficient number of them. We think best advantage may be had by the latter offer at our coming annual convention, when we expect to collect many papers worthy of publication. To this end we wish to urge our members to prepare their articles at an earlier date.

Dr. B.F. Chow, our Treasurer, thanks our members for the prompt remittance of the fees. If you have not paid the annual dues ($1.50), please remit to Dr. Chow, address: 24 Chauncy St., Cambridge, Mass.

Please return promptly the enclosed post card with answers.

Yours very truly,

C. K. Jen Secretary
Research Laboratory of Physics
Harvard University
Cambridge, Mass.

100

Dear Fellow Members:

It has been suggested that in the coming annual meeting of The American Branch of The Science Society of China, a symposium be held in which a topic of common interest may be discussed. The subject for discussion, as tentatively planned, is that of the "Industrialization of China". We believe that such a subject should be of interest to every Chinese scientist--"pure" or applied"--and it is our hope that scientists, engineers, economists, and students of business administration may all have a chance to contribute their knowledge to such a question.

Roughly, there are two parts to this symposium. First, before planning for the industrialization of China, it is our task to gather and present data on the natural resources and the economic geography of our country; second, the problems relating to the utilization of these resources towards industrialization. It is our hope that the coming meeting will be held jointly with The Chinese Engineering Society.

Part I of the symposium may be subdivided into the following divisions:

1. Mineral Resources
   A. Metallic B. Non-metallic
2. Power and Fuel
3. Agricultural Resources
   A. Animal husbandry B. Farm and Forest Products, etc.

Part II may be subdivided into:

1. Problems in engineering (in relation to Part I)
2. Transportation and communication
3. Marketing
4. Foreign trade
5. Monetary problems

101

致欧阳藻石函—存稿

藻兄：来示敬悉。工会既请张光华君为主席，王藻松君为论文主任，可称得人，且王君为多年熟友，可就近磋商，会作当不成问题。所择日期（八月廿五、六、七）似于参观不便，而颇有"周末"之利，弟拟如参观移在第一日举行，则可两全矣。兹拟下列拟会序，求兄指正：(1) 廿五日下午双方在万国分寓注册及共同参观 (2) 廿六日上午双方宣读论文，下午各自讨论会务，晚间聚餐（共同）(3) 廿七日上午会同"讨论会"，午后散会。关于以上"讨论会"须加解释。四五月前科学社杨君佩松曾提议在年会中举行一种"讨论会"Symposium，题目为发展中国实业问题，其讨论目的及范围已

105

THE CHINESE INSTITUTE OF ENGINEERS

AMERICAN SECTION

之恭我兄：

關於年會事，工程科學兩會合作似早已得我兄同意。工會年會主席至今尚未聘定，緣以人選問題頗難。弟意倘科學會負責人選決定在紐約或在波城，能以就近辦事便利起見，由本會聘定。迄今未聞科學會有何消息，工會主席似不能久懸，是特函請我兄在波城物色科學會負責人選，請兄商定地點日期及科學會負責人選，迅速通知，以便早日組織聯合委員會，從速徵文，請科學家演講等事。暑假已迫，此事似宜早日籌備，用特函達，尚祈賜覆是幸。此請

研安

弟歐陽藻

四、五日

105

致工程師学会会長歐陽藻君關於年会書—存稿

藻兄惠鑒：前書以年会事相問，因科学社尚未確定計劃，未能即時答覆，抱歉之至。今科学社同人皆以為芝加哥城為本届年会之最適當地点，因工会及科学社会員在此城附近者想不下二十人，他地会員欲參觀世界展覽会者想為數亦甚夥，如能乘此良機合開年会，可收一舉多得之效。社要社在確定之前當須請吾兄等之同意，而為免除遲延起見，已致函趙君以炳，請其代表科学社籌備一切。如工会表示同意，務望能早日派定負責人員，而會令作急速籌備。年

117

会時間尚未確定，而目暫時預定為八月二十四五日左右，若此時間，舟上会有不便處，尚可更改。兄等決定结果，請賜覆為禱

即頌

学安

弟 任之恭 上

廿二年五月十二日

118

致趙以炳君請其負責芝加哥年會——存稿

以炳学兄：去歲林陰城（Woods Hole）别後，不覺又將一載，不識近况如何？啟者，科学社（美洲分社）同人以為芝加哥城為本屆年會之最適当地点，因社員在芝城附近者不下八人，他地社員欲參觀世界展覽会者必想為數甚夥，如乘此良機舉行年會，可謂為一舉兩得。因知吾兄在芝資格高大，特請兄主持籌備年會，諒必能應允，就委員会主席，與芝城及附近諸君（如張宗漢，袁翰青，曹簡禹，馮德培諸君）接洽共同籌備。現工程師学會亦擬與科学社合開年会，弟亦當能與工程師学会諸君接洽，請其籌備委員会與吾兄諸方合作，以收互助互益之效。現時科学社社中

118

為湯兄佩松主席，周兄田及弟為會計及書記，弟今代表湯周二兄特請吾兄先生為主持一切。決定結果請即示知。尚此敬請

學安

弟任之恭謹上 廿二年五月十二日

附：年會時期預定為八月廿四五左右，如有不便，當可更改。

120

Dr. Chih Kung Jen
Research Lab of Physics
Harvard Univ
Cambridge Mass.

中国科学社美国分社书记任之恭博士

之恭学長：

接奉廿一，五，十七赐书，以筹备今年分社年会見嘱，

敬悉。頃查在美社员（據去年印的在美社员錄及今年印的中国科学社社员分股名錄105、106頁）

大约在 Cornell 者十六人

在 Michigan 者十一人

在 Harvard 及 M.I.T. 及波士顿市者九人

在 Chicago 者五人

他处不及五人。Rochester 現僅一人。鄙人意分社社長將離哈佛，

而仍在美，当继续多勞。会址似宜向前三处社员

接洽，而由該地社员中請人負責籌备，庶易观

130

成。大约地址选择，期能合于下之条件

一、本地社员多，

二、他处去的社员常讯能多，

三、加入数望最大处。

四、与中国工程师学会联合。

宝因欲专其所能。惟年会筹备委员长则不胜任，其他一例如收集论文——如有所命，当效棉薄也。

去年（廿二、八、廿九）宝曾向年会提议函贺廿二、九、十至十二开之中国工程师学会年会并提议今年之会合开会。不知讨论结果如何，曾有函来往否？

专复敬请

研安

弟中 储宝人敬启 廿三、五、廿一 17:40

去秋以来，在美社员有若干增加否？

131

復丁居緒寶函，存稿

廿六，五，廿一

緒寶學長：賜書敬悉。前次請學長主持年會係完全根據最適當人選，未曾顧及各地社員人數分配。茲學長提議以會址本地社員負責籌備，用意極善，唯有時難請適當負責人，每人負責也困難耳。今按最近社員名單社員之分配大概如左：

(1) Ann Arbor：十一人

(2) Boston 九人

(3) Chicago 及其附近 八人

(4) Ithaca 六人

(5) Washington 及其附近 五人

(6) New York 四人

(7) 其他各地 十九人

總共四十九人（此因去秋後新加入者約有八人）

135

學長提出之年會地址選擇條件與弟所擬大致相同。本屆年會由工程師學會合開，早有此項同意，故此條已成必須。前者工程師學會會長歐陽藻居多次通信，咸以為New York為最集中地點，因該城人數無不多，而Ithaca，Boston，及Wash. D.C.等地之社員可望有一部分到會。因此現已決定紐約為年會地址，並已致書該地社員許禎陽君請其負責籌備，如彼不肯，尚須另請其他社員，直至請到妥當負責人為止。學長既肯担任收集論文，特請俯就。將來確定紐約負責人時，即刻奉聞。為此敬請

研安

學弟 任之恭謹啟 廿六年五月廿五日

附：湯佩松學長之計畫尚未確定，聞彼或將回國。弟將於六月十七日離紐約由歐洲回國，擬赴山東大學（青島大學）授課。拙作四本已由另封寄上，望指正。弟之恭附白

Drs. Pei Sung Tang, C. K. Jen, Bacon F. Chow
Lab. of General Physiology
Harvard Univ.
Cambridge, Mass.

中国科学社美国分社
社長湯佩松
书记任之恭 博士：
会计周田

佩松
之恭学長：
周田

關于分社事，頃想及三点，敬陳其意見如左：

一、劍橋同学素多績学深思之士，必多徵請入社。擬請于
佩松之恭学長離劍橋前特別徵求一次，或由
学長等就同学錄中名單共同磋商一次，然後分别詢洽，
則社員人数可增一倍，例如若請于哈佛麻工各增二十人——
庶
学長等去後，可以繼起有人也。

二、請
学長擔任為今年社中年会备論文一篇，
中英文及長短性質不拘。

三、請
学長費神向哈佛麻工同学徵集分社年会論文。

141

徵集社友及論文，均以分別就地進行為易有效果，且時近暑假，亦徵文求友之好時機。特述管見，以備參考採擇。專請

研安

弟丁緒寶敬啟 廿二，六，二一

MR. TING SUPAO
INSTITUTE OF APPLIED OPTICS
UNIVERSITY OF ROCHESTER
ROCHESTER, N. Y., U. S. A.

致中國工程師学会会長歐陽藻兄函存稿

藻兄惠鑒：前月廿四曾奉上一函，討論在紐約今明年年会事，諒已登覽。近復弟等又商請負責東部籌備年会事務，現弟等已請定科学社美東分社社長湯君佩松為主席，丁緒寶君為論文委員，及正商請熊君学謙為總幹事，諸事似有頭緒。關於時間，弟等仍以八月廿四五六七日為最合宜。不識工会對人選及會期有何決定？故時間急促，弟因擬於本月十七日乘Europa船赴歐，甚望於離美前對年会籌備有所確定，並希於十三日前覆告，望兄撥冗賜復為幸。即請

研安

弟 任之恭 啟

廿二年六月五日

致熊學謙君請其担任年会總幹事書

學謙學兄：前次未能前往 Baltimore 開說，遺憾莫銘。先生近來有否大致？暑中是否仍留巴城？茲啟者，科學分社擬於本夏八月廿五六左右在紐約城舉行第四屆年会，現已請定湯君佩松為籌備主席，丁君緒寶負責收集論文，現弟等公舉先生為委員会中之總幹事，所需職務並不繁重，因開会前之一切準備如發通告已由弟等担任，開会地點及一切庶務併由工程師學会会辦，会費此事概由周君負責，先生之責任不過僅限於總指揮而已。素知先生對会務熱心，故敢請勞，望能俯允為禱。即請

研究

弟任之恭謹啟
廿二年五月
五日

155

致丁绪宝君函

绪宝学长：前示（六月一日）敬悉。弟曾经多次函请年会筹备委员会主席而远未致，兹请因筹备事势难延迟，分社长湯君佩松自身已允兼任此职，若湯君决定（离美）时，必请適当人材充满其职位。弟個人將於一週內離劍橋，故年時撰作论文，唯在途中（航海途上）或可抽作一二，如有即（快郵）寄奉。前曾收廖温义君论文一篇，現將其原函一併寄上，（於分討內）为時震函，已应许在年会中发表，请学长收存，如有其他问题（关於发表），请学长與廖君直接商議。兹特奉上学长所需之大波士頓同学録及年会討論会回元二十二張，收後請於用後寄還。即請

研安

学弟
文蔡 謹上
廿二年六月七日

151

Circular No. 2

The American Branch of the Science Society
of China

June 12, 1933

Dear Fellow Member:

In the last circular we submitted to you a proposal to add on the program of our Fourth Annual Convention a symposium on "The Industrialization of China". We are very glad to announce that the answers sent back by our members were unanimously affirmative. As the coming Convention is already within sight, we take this opportunity to make the following announcements:

(1) The coming convention will be held jointly with the American Section of the Chinese Institute of Engineers. The time and place of the Joint Convention are fixed by mutual agreement as follows:

Time:
Aug. 25 (afternoon)--Registration, Excursion, and Socials
Aug. 26 -------------Technical papers, Business meetings, and Banquets
Aug. 27 (forenoon)---Symposium on the Problem of China's Industrialization

Place:
New York City: The International House
500 Riverside Drive

(2) We have invited the following members to form a Committee in charge of the Annual Convention:

Mr. Ting Supao--in charge of the Technical Papers and the Symposium
Dr. Bacon F. Chow and Mr. Sherchin C. Hsiung in charge of all General Managements

The committee is charged with full power in managing the Convention, supervising the election for

8

the officers of the succeding year and making a final report of the Convention to the Science Society in China.

(3) Every one of our members is urged to make early studies on his speical topic chosen for the symposium. He is requested to search for accurate data and thoroughly digest them to find a workable solution. The presentation of technical papers will be conducted entirely apart from the symposium. Every paper should contain results of an original investigation of a certain special problem. Papers may be written in Chinese, English, or any other foreign language (chosen for convenience by the author) accompanied by a short abstract summarizing the essential points. It will be acceptable for special publication by the Science Society. Please send all finished papers to:

Mr. Ting Supao
Institute of Applied Optics
University of Rochester
Rochester, New York

For other particulars about the Convention please communicate with:

Dr. Bacon F. Chow
c/o China Medical Board, Inc. 61 Broadway
New York City

Rooms at reasonable rates may be had at the International House.

Yours very truly,

(signed) C. K. Jen (Secretary)

9

大猷兄：四兄：子谦兄：

在车上不好写，到Seattle以来保写。

现船将开。

在Chicago社员：

1. 陆志韦 Dr. C. W. Luh 心理 旧社员
International House.

2. 赵修鸿 S. H. Chao 物理
Intl Ho. 旧 " "

3. 魏培修 Pei Hsin Wei 物理 新
交6元 5515 Woodlawn Ave
Chicago Ill.

4. 杨汝楫 Ju Chi Yang " " "
5738 Drexel Ave
Chicago, Ill.

5. 熊子璥 D. S. Hsiung " " "
交6元 Intl Ho.

6. 褚圣麟 Chü Sheng-Lin " " "
交6元 Ryerson Phys Lab
U of C.

(3—6：物理)

7. 张鸿德 Dr. Stephen Chang 新
Dept of Physiology
U of C.

8. 臧玉洤 Y. C. Tsang 心理 新
5738 Drexel Ave, Chicago, Ill.

13

9. 黄汝琪 Wong Yue Kei 数学
上海中央研究院
廿十，十同船回国

10. 新社员 10. S. C. Chen 陈世昌 物理
Phys Lab, U of Pennsylvania,
Phil., Pa.

11. S. T. Chen 陈世骧
12. Y. Chen 陈义
Zoological Lab
U of Pennsylvania
Phil, Pa.

附上 18元 美金是 熊子璥 6元
顾皓修 6
褚明麟 6
入社费
廿三年：费

请转 熊先生
多谢，
小蔡。

学弟 绪宝 廿，十，十.

14

5M-1-34

CABLE ADDRESS
ROKSTITUTE

THE HOSPITAL OF THE ROCKEFELLER INSTITUTE
FOR MEDICAL RESEARCH
66TH STREET AND YORK AVENUE, NEW YORK

Feb. 26, 1934

Dear Sherchin,

I am today forwarding your "autobiography" to the Science Society of China and hope they will publish it soon. I am indeed sorry that I did not attend to this matter at an earlier date, but I have been exceedingly busy.

About 10 days ago I had the opportunity of writing to one of the professors at Nankai and mentioned that you were looking for something in China. When I hear about it from him, I will let you know. Have you made any connections yet?

I wish you would try again to collect more dues. I know that members are slow in paying, but perhaps if you would remind them again, you may get some more money.

Please tell me how much you have already collected as I agree with you that we should send some of it to China. The two life-membership payments which you spoke about must certainly be remitted to China but wait and see how much more we can send in the way of the other collections.

Am returning the slips from the Shanghai Commercial and Savings Bank, Ltd., because if they want them they can write us for them. In the meantime, you can keep them on file.

I cannot say now just when we will be leaving for China. In fact, I have a possibility of staying at the Institute another year, but that is just between you and me. Nothing definite yet to speak about as I must have correspondence from China also. Am glad that you have delayed your trip until later so that you will be able to attend the convention. I hope that I may be able to go this time wherever it may be.

Idellajoins me in sending regards. The baby is very big now and you must come over and see her when you are in town.

Sincerely yours,

Bacon F. Chow

P.S. Consider Dr. Eugene Chan as a member as I am sure he will be O.K. by the main office. You asked me in your letter of Dec. 12, and I do not remember if I told you or not. Collect his dues if you can.

33

漢和圖書館用箋

CHINESE-JAPANESE LIBRARY

HARVARD UNIVERSITY
BOYLSTON HALL

CAMBRIDGE, MASS., U. S. A.

美國哈佛大學校

November 7, 1934

Mr. Harry Gaw
Department of Zoology
Yale University
New Haven, Connecticut

My dear Mr. Gaw:

I understand that Dr. Bacon F. Chow has written to you about the affairs of the Science Society, and he has also sent you the balance of the Society's fund.

Will you kindly start at once the process of collecting the membership fees for the present year? According to the Constitution the membership due is Mex. $5.00 but at the present fluctuating rate of exchange and in order to cover heavy postage from China to America, we better collect $2.00 gold from each member. Sixty per cent of all membership fees shall be remitted to China.

Please mail out your letters according to the new directory which Dr. Chow sent to you. The following members left for China according to my knowledge:

Dr. Wu Ta-you, Dr. Li Chen-nan, Mr. Sherchin C. Hsiung, Dr. Y. P. Liu, Dr. Chenfu F. Wu, Dr. Samuel H. Zia, Dr. C. W. Luh, Dr. Wong Pao-ho and Mr. Robert Chao.

Sincerely yours,

A Kaiming Chiu

裘开明

AKC:MMA

92

中國科學社用箋

尚蔭先生大鑒：逕復者，十月十三日

大教奉悉。美國分社事宜多荷

公等備勞，同人極為贊佩。惟查本年度分社社

務及會計收支各情尚未蒙

見示，頗以為念。緣分社每年度歷有報告并稍

通消息，尚希于課餘之暇，將分社情形、新選職員

及前任會計出納一併報告，以慰翹企。茲另郵社

費收據簿、在美社友名條各乙份，至乞

總辦事處　上海亞爾培路五三三號　電話七二五五一號

96

中國科學社用箋

……答入若有社友未曾繳過入社金與本年年度常年費者請代為收取名条中如有變更住址或已回國者統乞　隨時見告以便據寄刊物瑣瀆清神無任心感耑此敬復順頌

籌祺

中國科學社總幹事楊孝述

附名条一份　收據簿乙本　空白入社願書三十份　社章十份均另郵

二十三、十二、十八

總辦事處　上海亞爾培路五三三號　電話七二五五一號

97

17/1/35

中國科學社用箋

来字第一〇二三号

世昌先生大鑒接奉
台函承示美洲分社新任職員名單並擬為科學雜
搜集稿件足徵
貴分社之熱心至深欣慰關于科學名詞已經教育部
頒布而印行者僅有天文物理及化學命名原則三種其
餘多散見各處且亦不易收集茲將該三種名詞先
行奉上各一冊即希
台收嗣後關于編輯事務可逕與本社編輯部主任

總辦事處 上海亞爾培路五三三號 電話七二五五一號

27

中國科學社用箋

劉咸博士接洽本社前社長兼編輯部〻長現任理事王季梁先生近亦在美國彼主持編輯達八九年對于社務十分熱心茲將王君住址另單附奉俾便分社與彼通信茲有下列諸事委託分社辦理

(一)本年四月間美國費城將舉行美國政治及社會科學會議来函敦請本社派員参加茲將原函奉上請即由分社推舉代表就近前往参加並請先函復該會議

總辦事處 上海亞爾培路五三三號 電話七二五五一號

28

中國科學社用箋

(二)美洲分社近三年来收支欵項僅去年有收入一表寄社而無支出報告以致總社無法登賬務請分社會計就可能範圍加以整理製成報告寄來以後並將所收社費之六成照章滙寄本社藉資彌補一切刊物之郵寄費

(三)分社為美國與祖國科學者之聯絡機關凡留美同人之近况及住址更改等務請隨時調查報告以便刊入「社友」互通聲氣

總辦事處 上海亞爾培路五三三號 電話七一五五一號

29

中國科學社用箋

（四）本社近二年来努力于科學化運動頗著成效所出科學畫報半月刊一種以極淺顯之圖文紹介于一般民衆每期銷數逾萬又圖書館方面近亦擬收集大批通俗科學書籍雜誌俾使一般人之閱讀留美同人對于新出通俗科學書報方面見聞較切尚望隨時調查　見示以資採購為幸

美國為本社之發源地留美同人向来對于發展國内科學十分熱心現由分社諸位職員領導社

總辦事處　上海亞爾培路五三三號　電話七二五五一號

30

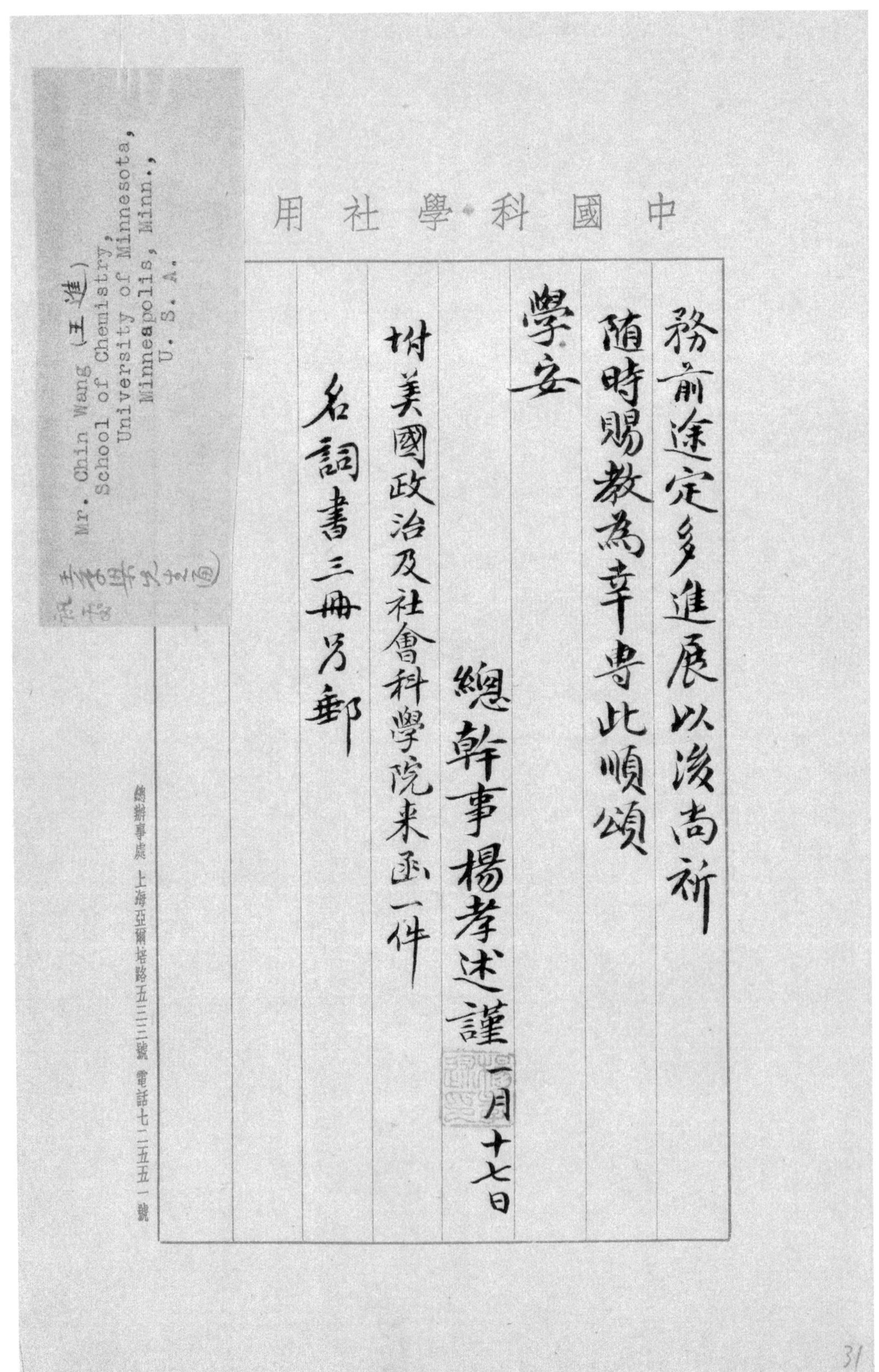

Mr. Chin Wang (王進)
School of Chemistry,
University of Minnesota,
Minneapolis, Minn.,
U. S. A.

中國科學社用

務前途定多進展以後尚祈
隨時賜教為幸專此順頌
學安
總幹事楊孝述謹 一月十七日
附美國政治及社會科學院来函一件
名詞書三册另郵

總辦事處 上海亞爾培路五三三號 電話七二五五一號

31

漢和圖書館用箋

CHINESE-JAPANESE LIBRARY
HARVARD UNIVERSITY
BOYLSTON HALL
CAMBRIDGE, MASS., U. S. A.

美國哈佛大學校

February 14, 1935

Dr. Henry S. C. Chen, Secretary
Science Society of China in America
Physics Laboratory
University of Pennsylvania
Philadelphia, Penna.

My dear Dr. Chen:

In reply to your letter of February 11 I would suggest that you, Mr. Harry Gaw and Mr. Han-yee Feng of your University be asked to serve as our delegates to the thirty-ninth Annual Convention of the American Academy of Political and Social Science. If time permits, I may be down there too in order to talk over with you about the plans for our annual convention in the summer. Meanwhile please let me have your suggestions about our convention which will be devoted to another session on the Industrialization of China, that is, the application of science to the economic development of our country. This year will be the 20th Anniversary of the founding of our society, so we have to put up a good program.

I have written to ask whether Mr. Gaw could be in Philadelphia about that time so that we three could discuss our affairs together.

Very sincerely yours,

A. Kaiming Chiu

A. Kaiming Chiu

35

漢和圖書館用箋

CHINESE-JAPANESE LIBRARY
HARVARD UNIVERSITY
BOYLSTON HALL

CAMBRIDGE, MASS., U. S. A.

February 14, 1935.

Mr. Harry Gaw, Treasurer
Science Society of China in America
Osborn Zoological Laboratory
New Haven, Connecticut

My dear Mr. Gaw:

According to a letter received from China office, we have to remit to the main office 60% of our total receipts for the current year. Will you kindly let me know (1) the balance left over from previous administration (2) total receipts for the current year up to date and (3) number of members who have failed to pay their dues.

Could you go to Philadelphia about April 5-7 so that we three could talk over the plans for our annual convention in the summer which will be devoted to another session on the Industrialization of China, i.e. the application of science to the economic development of our country. This year will be the 20th Anniversary of the founding of our Society, so we have to put up a good program. Meanwhile please let me have your suggestions about the coming meeting.

Very sincerely yours,

A. Kaiming Chiu

A. Kaiming Chiu

AKC/B

102

Secretary
S. C. Chen,
Physics Laboratory,
University of Penn.,
Philadelphia, Penn.

President
A. Kaiming Chiu,
13 Boylston Hall,
Harvard University,
Cambridge, Mass.

Treasurer
Harry Gaw,
Osborn Zoological Lab.,
Yale University,
New Haven, Connecticut

The American Branch of
THE SCIENCE SOCIETY OF CHINA

Feb. I8, I935

Dr. A. K. Chiu
Chinese-Janpanese Library
Harvard University
Cambridge, Mass.

Dear Dr. Chiu:

Your letter of Feb. I4th. received. I am glad to inform you that I have remitted to the main office 60% of our total receipts for the current year and year I934 by the request of Mr. Chow, treasurer at the main office. The balance left over from previous administration is $I37.53. The total receipts up to date are $30.50. Only eleven members have paid their dues. I have sent out another announcement asking for dues.

I think I could arrange to go to Philadelphia about the time you suggested, but if you could make it some time around the end of March, it will suit me better. I know Dr. Chen won't have any objections as he has no official duties.

For the occasion of our 20th. anniversary, I wish to suggest that we should combine our efforts to publish an anniversary special containing articles of original researches. What do you think of this plan?

Let me hear from you. With best wishes,

Sincerely yours,
Harry Z. Gaw
Harry Zanyin Gaw

19/2/35

38

中國科學社用箋

收社费按常105—136每五元 $160.00

收 〃 〃 〃 入44—63每十元 $200.00

收 〃 〃 〃 永9 原照按合作社 60.00

收 〃 〃 〃 永10 〃 〃 〃 〃 $74.75

$494.75

收社费按常128-136九人每人五元汇水0.26 $2.34

$497.09

收美社汇余先还前代华物理名词审查费之一部 $0.22

$497.31

支社费按常105-127廿三人每四五元汇水1.055 $24.26

$473.05

支社费按入44-63廿人每四十元汇水3.425 $68.50

$404.55

支社费按永9/10四原照按合六十元/七十四元七五汇水6.216/9.000 $15.22

$389.33

支社费按常105-127廿三人除去5%缴分社经费每1.578 $36.29

$353.04

支社费按常128-136九人加汇水除5%缴分社经费每2.104 $18.94

$334.10

支社费按入44-63廿人除5%缴分社经费每2.630 $52.60

$281.50

支社费按永9/10除5%四成分社经费21.514/26.300 $47.81

$233.69

收黎行照按周32D.D.Vong美金四元六成每2.63合 $6.31

共国实通银行汇京149911# $240.00

三

總辦事處 上海亞爾培路五三三號 電話七二二五五一號

105

Secretary
S. C. CHEN,
Physics Laboratory,
University of Penn.,
Philadelphia, Penn.

President
A. KAIMING CHIU,
13 Boylston Hall,
Harvard University,
Cambridge, Mass.

Treasurer
HARRY GAW,
Osborn Zoological Lab.,
Yale University,
New Haven, Connecticut

The American Branch of
THE SCIENCE SOCIETY OF CHINA

March 11, 1935

Dear Mr. Gaw,

I have the pleasure to inform you that you have been requested to serve as delegates of the Science Society of China to the thirty-ninth Annual Convention of the American Academy of Political and Social Sciences, to be held on April 5th and 6th, 1935, at the Bellevue-Stratford Hotel in Philadelphia. I believe that you will receive further details directly from the Academy.

Trusting that we shall have your co-operation, I am,

Yours very truly,

Henry S. C. Chen

(S. C. C. , Secretary)

108

元任先生惠鉴：顷奉

手教，敬谂一是。承　示科学社选举两种办法，

惟吴君汝麟现在是否仍在纽约不得而知，因弟

今春一面函询　尊处，一面函致吴君询其

意见，不料迄无回信，消息杳然，所以承　嘱俟

与吴君商酌后于该两办法中择一进行，势难

照办。故为今之计，惟有请

先生于年会中提出讨论，弟绝无意见，苟有议决

无不赞同。弟因此间研究正忙，十届时能否出席须

俟下星期方能决定，专先此草复，顺颂

公绥

弟　赵廷梅谨启

八月十二日

再弟前信所询并非别有意见，乞勿误会。又及

116

March 27, 1935

Dr. E. M. Patterson,
President,
American Academy of Political and Social Science,
3457 Walnut Street,
Philadelphia, Pa.

My dear Dr. Patterson:

In compliance with your letter of Dec, 12. 1934, which was recently referred to us by our Shanghai office, we feel greatly honored in appointing the following delegates to your annual Convention.

Mr. Harry Gaw, Osborn Zoological Lab.
Yale Univ., New Haven, Conn.
Mr. H. Y. Feng, 4509 Regent St., Phila.
Mr. S. C. Chen, Physics Lab., U. of P.

I trust that you will communicate with them directly and give them further information.

Wishing you a most successful Convention.

Very truly yours

(Secretary)

41

Secretary
S. C. Chen,
Physics Laboratory,
University of Penn.,
Philadelphia, Penn.

President
A. Kaiming Chiu,
13 Boylston Hall,
Harvard University,
Cambridge, Mass.

Treasurer
Harry Gaw,
Osborn Zoological Lab.,
Yale University,
New Haven, Connecticut

The American Branch of
THE SCIENCE SOCIETY OF CHINA

March 28, 1935

My dear Dr, Chiu:

Your letter of the twenty-sixth came to me at the same time when I heard from Mr. Gaw. He said that he wrote you again about a change in his plan. I wonder what the final arrangements are. I do hope that you could come to Philadelphia about the fifth of April. I understand that Mr. Gaw is planning to leave for Europe in the early part of May, and I think it would be necessary for us to get together to discuss our plans for the summer convention.

Hoping you could make that Phila. trip.

Sincerely yours,

Henry S. C. Chen

42

Secretary
S. C. Chen,
Physics Laboratory,
University of Penn.,
Philadelphia, Penn.

President
A. Kaiming Chiu,
13 Boylston Hall,
Harvard University,
Cambridge, Mass.

Treasurer
Harry Gaw,
Osborn Zoological Lab.,
Yale University,
New Haven, Connecticut

The American Branch of
THE SCIENCE SOCIETY OF CHINA

April 14, 1935.

Dear Dr. Chen:

Thank you very much for your letter of April 9. I think it is a good plan to write personal letters to persons whom we know well in addition to the official invitation. I have asked Mr. Gaw to write to Richard Kuo, Dr. Young and others. I have spoken to Palmer Sze asking him to write to Miss Sze.

If there are too many letters to write, perhaps you can prepare a mimeographed form letter first, and then fill in the name of committee on each copy. Please send out these invitation-appointments at your earliest convenience. Early returns will enable us to select other persons in case some shall decline our invitations.

With best wishes,

Very sincerely yours,

A. Kaiming Chiu

45

Secretary
S. C. CHEN,
Physics Laboratory,
University of Penn.,
Philadelphia, Penn.

President
A. KAIMING CHIU,
13 Boylston Hall,
Harvard University,
Cambridge, Mass.

Treasurer
HARRY GAW,
Osborn Zoological Lab.,
Yale University,
New Haven, Connecticut

The American Branch of
THE SCIENCE SOCIETY OF CHINA

April 15, 1935

Dr. A. Kaiming Chiu,
13 Boylston Hall,
Harvard University,
Cambridge, Mass.

My dear Dr. Chiu:

I am glad to inform you that at our last executive meeting, you have been elected as our representatives to serve on the General Committee for the Joint Convention of the Science Society and the Engineering Society, to be held in New York City in early September. Our representatives are Dr. P. T. Young, Dr. A. K. Chiu, and Mr. C. J. Luh. You and the representatives of the Engineering Society will form the compltet committee.

Thanking you for your cooperation, and wishing you every success.

Truly yours,

Henry S. C. Chen

(Secretary)

47

Secretary
S. C. Chen,
Physics Laboratory,
University of Penn.,
Philadelphia, Penn.

President
A. Kaiming Chiu,
13 Boylston Hall,
Harvard University,
Cambridge, Mass.

Treasurer
Harry Gaw,
Osborn Zoological Lab.,
Yale University,
New Haven, Connecticut

The American Branch of
THE SCIENCE SOCIETY OF CHINA

New Haven, Conn.
April 30, 1935

Dear Dr. Chiu:

So far I only received five new membership cards in response to our membership drive. I do hope that more will be sent in soon.

The annual session of the American Institute of Chemical Engineers is going to be held at Willmington, Del. from May 13-15. There is a Chinese student here at Yale who is a member of The Science Society of China and is studying chemical engineering. He is planning to attend the session and he wishes to know if he could apply some fund from the Society to cover part of his expenses and at the same time he hopes to be an official delegate from the society. What do you think of that? He asked me to write you about it.

I have sent the 60% of the dues and fees collected so far to the main office at Shanghai and the balance now is $18.78.

How are the convention affairs going. I am leaving with Dr. Chen on May 17th. for England. Before my departure, I shall send you the documents, etc. which are in my possession now.

Best wishes and let me hear from you.

Yours,
Harry Gaw

55

May 4, 1935

Mr. Harry Gaw, Secretary
Science Society of China
Yale University
New Haven, Connecticut

My dear Mr. Gaw:

Thank you very much for your letters of April 30 and May 2, enclosing a check for $1771 . I shall keep the money and the documents (not yet come to hand) in the library until the new officers of the Society have been elected. Please give me a detailed account of the past year's receipts and disbursements.

I am still waiting for Dr. Chen's information as to whether the persons, whom we have invited to serve on the various committees, have accepted our invitation. After their acceptance, I shall proceed speedily to the arrangement of the program for the coming convention. I am very sorry that you and Dr. Cheu could not stay for the convention. However, I appreciate very much your fine coöperation and service during the past year. It is a great pleasure for me to work with you and Dr. Cheu.

As to the question of sending a delegate to the annual session of the American Institute of Chemical Engineers, I don't think our finances could allow that . Moreover, we went to the Academy meeting in Philadelphia only on the instruction of our home office. It seems to me that the Chinese Chemical Society or the American Branch of the Engineering Society of China should send such a delegate.

With best wishes for a very pleasant voyage,

Very sincerely yours,

57

500 Riverside Drive,
New York City,
New York.
July 5, 1935.

My dear Mr. Chiu:

I take pleasure to inform you that I have satisfactorily completed my work at the Harvard Business School, and that I already commenced my work at the National City Bank of New York last monday. Everything has got along very smoothly. However, I regret, that, on account of the Bank's regulations, I am not allowed tot ake up any other activity other than the regular duty. I am sorry to inform you that I have to submit my resignation as the social committee of the Science Society for the coming convention.

Best regards to Mrs. Chiu and yourself as well, I am,

Yours truly,

Palmer C. Sze.

65

TEL. BEEKMAN 3-2555

CHINESE INSTITUTE OF ENGINEERS
AMERICAN SECTION
457 W. 123rd St.
~~84 WILLIAM STREET~~
NEW YORK, N. Y., U. S. A.

July 23, 1935

Dr. A. Kaiming Chiu
Harvard University
Cambridge, Mass.

Dear Dr. Chiu:

With time drawing close to the date of the 1935 Joint Annual Convention, I am quite anxious to know of the probable plans which the Science Society has made. It is unfortunate that the officers of both of our organizations are so widely scattered this year - thus making meetings almost impossible. But as the matter now stands, let us try and make the best of it.

First of all, let me ask you the following questions:

1. Do you wish to follow the general plans as set forth for last year's convention?
2. Do you wish to publish a convention pamphlet similar to that of last year? (It's rather late now)
3. What suggestions would you make to improve our method of conducting the convention this year?
4. Would it be possible for us to have at least one meeting between now and within the next two weeks? Can you or Mr. S. C. Chen, your Society secretary come to New York some week-end?

Mr. Paul Feng, who is secretary of the Joint Eastern Convention called on me this evening for information concerning our plans. I told him that I must first consult with your Society before giving him the answer. Under the circumstances, will you make definite decisions as to your plans? As far as we are concerned, I believe the general outlay of last year's program is quite satisfactory in view of the pressing time. However, there will be lots of room for improvement, and will be expecting some suggestions from you.

Thanking you in advance for your cooperation, and trusting that you will let me hear from you as soon as possible.

Very sincerely yours,

K. H. Chang

K. H. Chang, President C.I.E.

Please furnish us a tentative Program. Thanks!!

July 29, 1935.

Mr. K. H. Chang, President
American Section of the Chinese Institute of Engineers
457 West 123rd Street, New York City

My dear Mr. Chang:

In reply to your letter of July 23 I am enclosing herewith a copy of the Tentative Program of the Sixth Annual Convention of the American Branch of the Science Society of China. I agree with you that the general outline of last year's program is quite satisfactory. Will you please merge our program with that of your Society in its final form? I don't know whether we can afford to issue a separate convention pamphlet as we did last year, because Mr. Richard Kuo, whom we invited to be the Chairman of our Publication Committee, left for China and no one has been able to raise any fund or secure any advertisement. In order to save expenses, I think it is best to have the program of our Joint Convention published in the Conference notices or program of the Joint Eastern Chinese Students' Convention. That is the reason I have put down Mr. Paul Feng as being in charge of our publication affairs. Will you kindly urge Mr. Feng to do this for us? I am also enclosing a letter to him.

The affairs of our Society have been very much upset by the early departure for Europe in May of our Secretary Dr. S. C. Chen and our Treasurer, Mr. Kao. Everything is laid on my shoulder. I hope that we can straighten out the program without having another meeting as that involves so much expense.

Very sincerely yours,

73

月涵先生尊鑒：敬啟者，生擬介紹三人加入科學社，請將入社表格寄來三份，以便介紹。再者，生已於前日回霍布金校，下月月費請逕寄原有通信處九十五號信箱，相是為至荷。專此，順叩

鈞安

學生 彭光欽謹上

九月十六日

86

China Institute in America
119 WEST 57TH STREET
NEW YORK CITY

September 21, 1935.

My dear Dr. Chiu:

Replying to your kind letter of Sept. 18th, the Institute will be privileged to act as the permanent office of the Science Society, as well as custodian of its documents. As in the case of the Chinese Institute of Engineers, we will be able to place the name of your Society on the bulletin board of the building and also to take care of whatever telephone calls you may have from time to time.

You recall that I told you about our tentative plan of publishing a monthly bulletin. If the plan should materialize, we expect to publish in this bulletin news of all Chinese educational and cultural institutions in this country and China. We probably will be in a position to offer your Society some space in which you might publish the official news of the Society as well as some of the papers by its members (at least abstracts) that are of more or less general interest.

As soon as you make a formal request, I shall be glad to take the matter up with our Executive Committee. I am sure that all the officers will welcome such an arrangement.

Sincerely yours,

Chih Meng

Chih Meng,
Associate Director.

Dr. A. Kaiming Chiu,
23 Hammond St.,
Cambridge, Mass.

87

CHINA INSTITUTE IN AMERICA

Incorporated

119 West 57th Street, New York, N. Y.

Cable Address "Huamei" Telephone: CIrcle 7-3772

Oct. 30, 1935.

Dear Dr. Chiu:

This is to acknowledge with many thanks your kind letter of October 28th and your article on The Twentieth Anniversary of the Science Society of China and Its Future Program.

We will appreciate it if you will make known to the new President of the Society our desire to keep in close touch with the activities of the Society and whatever news or material the Society may have that may be of general interest for American readers who are seriously interested in China.

Sincerely yours,

Chih Meng,
Associate Director.

Dr. A. Kaiming Chiu,
23 Hammond Street,
Cambridge, Mass.

90

Secretary
S. C. Chen,
Physics Laboratory,
University of Penn.,
Philadelphia, Penn.

President
A. Kaiming Chiu,
13 Boylston Hall,
Harvard University,
Cambridge, Mass.

Treasurer
Harry Gaw,
Osborn Zoological Lab.,
Yale University,
New Haven, Connecticut

The American Branch of
THE SCIENCE SOCIETY OF CHINA

January 17, 1936.

Dr. Shen-wu Wan,
Box 104, S. D. O.
Yale University,
New Haven, Conn.

Dear Dr. Wan:

I have great pleasure to inform you that you have been elected the president of the American Section of the Chinese Science Society. The other officers elected are:- Secretary, Mr. Han-yee Feng (   ) c/o Chinese Library, Bolyston Hall, Harvard University, Cambridge, Mass. and Treasurer, Dr. Barn H. Chu 47 Mott Street, New York City. Since Mr. Feng is in Cambridge, I am going to hand over all the papers pertaining to his office to him. Will you please let me know where shall I send your papers?

Sincerely yours,

96

DEPARTMENT OF CHEMISTRY
CENTRAL CHINA COLLEGE
Wuchang, China.

March 1, 1936

Dr. A. Kaiming Chiu
13, Boylston Hall
Harvard University
Cambridge, Mass.

Dear Dr. Chiu,

Thank you very much for informing me of the great honor which has been bestowed on me in electing me as Preisdent of the American Branch of The Science Society of China. To my extreme regret it is impossible for me to serve in this capacity on account of my recent return to China. Will you please see that proper steps be taken to have the position filled by some other candidate. I am now on a government subsidy as professor of chemistry in Central China College, and will appreciate any news from our fellow members in America.

Your kind letter was forwarded to me from New Haven; hence my reply is unavoidably delayed. I am very sorry for this delay but hope that it has not caused too much inconvenience on the activities of the Society.

Very sincerely yours,

Shen-won Wan

30/3/36

100

CHINA INSTITUTE IN AMERICA
Incorporated
119 West 57th Street, New York, N. Y.
Cable Address "Huamei" Telephone: Circle 7-8772

April 15, 1936.

Dear Dr. Chiu:

We have just received an inquiry regarding a qualified teacher of physics. Knowing of your wide contacts of science students through the Science Society, we are wondering whether you would be good enough to furnish us a list of those who are specializing in physics and who may be ready to return to China this coming June.

I still recall with pleasure my enjoying your hospitality when I was in Cambridge the last time.

With warmest regards to you and Mrs. Chiu, I remain,

Very sincerely yours,

Chih Meng
Chih Zeng,
Associate Director.

Dr. A. Kaiming Chiu,
23 Hammond Street,
Cambridge, Mass.

Answered 29/4/36

103

社务文献

#1

List of Members of the Science Society of China, in U. S. A. (up to March 20, 1930)

No.	Name	Specialization	Address
	Chai, Nien Pu	Chemistry	830 E. Ontario St. 5548 Drexel Ave., Chicago, Ill.
	Chang, Hung Yuan	Chemical Eng.	Tech. Dorm., Cambridge, Mass.
4	Chao, Iping	Physiology	5738 Drexel Ave., Chicago, Ill.
5	Chao, Robert F. H.	Electrical Eng.	Tech. Dorm., Cambridge, Mass.
	Chou, Yung Tiao	Bio-chemistry	Box 6182 Univ. of Minn., Minneapolis, Minn.
11	Chow, Bacon Field	Chemistry	112 Trowbridge St., Cambridge, Mass. 351 Harvard St.
12	Chow, Tung Ching	Physics	Palmer Physical Laboratory, Princeton Univ., Princeton, N. J.
	Djang, Tse Gung	Chemistry	Box 298 Johns Hopkins Univ., Baltimore, Md.
	Hsiao, Ching Yun	Municipal Eng.	c/o Mr. Yenson Hu, Nanyang University, Shanghai, China
14	Hsiung, Sherchin C.	Chemistry	Box 1011 Johns Hopkins Univ., Baltimore, Md.
	Hsiung, Ta Shih	Zoology	Zoo. Dept., Iowa State College, Ames, Iowa.
19	Huang, Yu Hsien	Civil Eng.	74 Ellery St., Cambridge, Mass.
20	Jen, Chih Kung	Physics	67 Hammond St. 46 Carver St., Cambridge, Mass
	Kao, Chih	Chemistry	Box 1155 Johns Hopkins Univ., Baltimore, Md.
21	Kao, Tsi Yu	Organic Chemistry	Box 87 University Station, Urbana, Ill.
	Li, Keh Hung	Medicine	1804 W. Congress St., Chicago, Ill.
	Liang, Ssu Yung	Anthropology	46 Carver St., Cambridge, Mass.
	Lin, Hsun	Mathematics	5548 Drexel Ave., Chicago, Ill.
30	Liu, Chuan	Organic Chemistry	206 N. Gregory Avenue, Urbana, Ill.
31	Liu, Hu	Biochemistry	1300 5th St., S. E., Minneapolis, Minn.
	Loo, Y. T.	Neuroanatomy	c/o Mr. M. N. Loo, D. G. of Posts, Shanghai, China
	Ma, Chieh	Chemical Eng.	33 13th Ave., Columbus, Ohio
34	Mei, Y. C.	Physics	2645 Conn. Ave., Washington, D. C.
	Ou, Chia Wei	Chemistry	26 Clinton St., Cambridge, Mass.
	Pei, Chien	Botany	New York Botanical Garden, Bronx Park, New York City
38	Penn, Amos Benkov	Biology	Box 95 Johns Hopkins Univ., Baltimore, Md.
40	Tang, Pei Sung	Plant Physiology	Lab. of Plant Physiology, Johns Hopkins University, Baltimore, Md. M. B. L. Woods Hole, Mass.
43	Tsai, Liu Sheng	Physical Chemistry	5738 Drexel Avenue, Chicago, Ill.
	Wen, Chi C.	Medicine	1804 W. Congress St., Chicago, Ill.
	Wu, Lu Chiang	Chemistry	Research Lab. of Organic Chem., M. I. T., Cambridge, Mass.
	Yang, Wei	Chemical Eng.	172 W. Frambes Avenue, Columbus, Ohio
51	Yuan, Han Ching	Organic Chemistry	Box 94 University Station, Urbana, Ill.
	Tuan, Hsu Chuan	Botany & Biology	3711 Locust St., Phila., Pa.
16a	Hu, Ching Ming	Civil Eng.	c/o Mc Clintic Marshall Co., Penn. Building, Phila., Pa.
33	Mei, K. T.	Literature	85 Wendall St., Cambridge, Mass.
37	Pan, L. C.	Chemistry	419 W. 115 St., New York City
46	Wang, George T.C.	Chemistry	550 Riverside Drive, N. Y. C.
	Yang, S. T.	Chemistry	32 Lake St., New Haven, Conn.
50	Young, Timothy	Biology	Furnald Hall, Columbia Univ., New York City.
	Liu, Shao-kwang (M.D.)	Medicine & Med. Chem.	361 W. 119th. St., N.Y.C.

1

#2

THE SCIENCE SOCIETY OF CHINA - AMERICAN BRANCH

List of New Members

~~Tsai-Han Kiang~~	~~c/o Dept. of Mathematics, Princeton University, Princeton, N.J.~~
~~Shao-Kwang Liu~~	~~361 W. 119th. Street, New York City.~~
~~L. S. An~~	~~Y.M.C.A., San Antonio, Texas.~~
(2) N. F. Chang	208 Delaware Avenue, Ithaca, N. Y.
(6) W. Chen	Forest Home, Ithaca, N. Y.
7 Y. H. Chen	206 Delaware Avenue, Ithaca, N. Y.
10 C. Y. Chou 周承鑰	a/o Chinese Educational Mission, Washington, D.C.
15 T. Y. Hsu 徐振英	" " " "
18 H. Huang	212 N. Blackstone Avenue, Jackson, Mich.
23 F. C. Kuan	203 Linden Avenue, Ithaca, N. Y.
22 Y. T. Ku 顾毓琇	West Sibley College, Cornell University, Ithaca, N. Y.
24 C. C. Kwan	c/o Experimental Station, N. Y. State College/ of Agriculture, Geneva, N. Y.
25 P. M. Lee	311 Dryden Road, Ithaca, N. Y.
27 G. T. Lew	~~Robert Hall, Cornell University, Ithaca, N.Y.~~ ~~c/o Vine-Yard Laboratory, Fredonia, N. Y.~~
35 K. K. Moa	210 Linden Avenue, Ithaca, N. Y.
36 Kanyo Nieh	Cornell Cosmopolitan Club, Ithaca, N. Y.
39 T. Y. Tan	c/o G.B. Lim, 206 Delaware Ave., Ithaca, N. Y.
44 C. Y. Tsao	204 Stewart Avenue, Ithaca, N.Y.
~~S. C. Yang~~	~~c/o F. C. Kuan, 203 Linden Ave., Ithaca,~~ N. Y.
(31a) T. Liu*	c/o Chemistry Dept., Cornell University, Ithaca, N. Y.

* Old member newly located.

August 25, 1930

2

THE SCIENCE SOCIETY OF CHINA * AMERCIAN BRANCH

List of New Members #3

	~~C. P. Li (Dr.)~~	Rockefeller Institute, 66 Street and York Ave., New York City.
12a	H. J. Chu	57 Gorham Street, Cambridge, Mass.
46a	Heng-shou Wang	c/o Harvard Graduate School, Cambridge, Mass.
48a	Yu Chang Yin	941 N. Broadway, Baltimore, Md.
42a	Hsu Huai Ting	1352 Wilmot Street, Ann Arbor, Mich.

3

敬啓者本屆分社職員選舉提名投票計共收到票數二十六張茲將每職得票數最多之三人列為候選人即請投票決選最好請即日將票簽填寄下以便早日結束無任感荷之至此致

中國科學社留美分社社員諸君

司選委員 張洪沅 王德郅 梅貽琦 謹啓

十九年十月二十二日

中國科學社留美分社職員選舉票

分社長： 梅貽琦○ 張洪沅○ 湯佩松○

書　記 張洪沅○ 王德郅○ 徐之恭○

會　計 王德郅○ 周田○ 湯佩松○

選舉者　　　　簽名

請於每行被選人之○中作一✓號為誌

十九年十月　日

科學社社友諸君惠鑒：前者留美分社徵求社友，承

先生志願加入，無任歡迎。現新舊社友共有三十九人，旋於

三月間選舉職員，以便推行社務。截至目今，選舉票

計共收到三十張，茲將結果報告如后。至該票一束，除

轉寄新舉職員查閱外，將來即由書記吳君保存。

計被舉為理事長在二票以上者

梅貽琦 二十四票　張洪元 二票

被舉為書記在二票以上者

吳魯強 五票　張洪元 四票　湯佩松 四票

任之恭 四票　胡竟銘 二票　段續川 二票

周田 二票　彭光欽 二票

被舉為會計在二票以上者

黃育賢 七票　區家偉 三票　任之恭 二票

湯佩松 二票　趙訪熊 二票　趙以炳 二票

專此佈達，順頌

學祺不一

梅貽琦謹啟　十九年五月三十日

再啟者：琦謬承

社友諸君推任理事，自慚駑鈍，未敢言辭，惟望

諸君各本其愛護科學之心，共謀本社之發展，則凡有裨

可以襄助之處，無不盡力。至照前社中所應推行之事，約有

二端，謹為　諸君陳之，幸注意焉。

一、前聞「科學」經理部言，近來因留美同學投稿者不多，材料頗感缺乏，甚盼社友努力贊助。倘有撰著，希即投登；或友好中有科學稿件，亦請代為介紹，皆甚歡迎。

二、關于社務進行計畫，最好能在夏間得一聚集機會，以便大家面談一切。此事可與工程學會聯合進行。諸君對于開會地點、日期以及社中他事有何意見，務望函示，俾收集思廣益之效，幸甚幸甚。

琦又啟

敬啓者本屆分社職員選舉提名投票計共收到票數二十六張兹將每職得票數最多之三人列為候選人即請投票決選最好請多日將票簽填寄下以便早日結束無任感荷之至此致

中國科學社留美分社社員諸君

司選委員 張洪沅 王德郅 梅貽琦 謹啓

十九年十月二十二日

中國科學社留美分社職員選舉票

分社長：梅貽琦○ 張洪沅○ 湯佩松○

書記 張洪沅○ 王德郅○ 徐之恭○

會計 王德郅○ 周 田○ 湯佩松○

選舉者 簽名

請於每行被選人之○中作一✓號為誌

十九年十月 日

謹啓者：共收到分社職員選舉票四十張，其結果如左：

分社長　梅貽琦　39票　張洪沅　1票

書　記　張洪沅　26票　任之恭　10票

　　　　王德郅　4票

會　計　王德郅　18票　周田　11票

　　　　湯佩松　11票

除应通知新職員（最多數當選）就職並將各票案交書記保存外，謹此奉聞，順頌

公綏

司選委員

張洪沅
王德郅　謹啓
梅貽琦

十九年十一月三十日

26

科學社社友諸君惠鑒：前者留美分社徵求社友，承
先生志願加入，無任歡迎。現新舊社友共有三十九人，旋於
三月間選舉職員，以便推行社務。截至目今，選舉票
計共收到三十張，茲將結果報告如右。至該票一束，除
轉寄新舉職員查閱外，將來即由書記吳君保存。

計被舉為理事長在二票以上者
梅貽琦 二十四票　張洪元 三票

被舉為書記者在二票以上者
吳魯強 五票　張洪元 四票　湯佩松 四票
任之恭 四票　胡竟銘 二票　段續川 二票
周田 二票　彭光欽 二票

被舉為會計在二票以上者
黃育賢 七票　區家偉 三票　任之恭 二票
湯佩松 二票　趙訪熊 二票　趙以炳 二票

專此佈達，順頌
學祺不一

梅貽琦謹啟 十九年五月三十日

再啟者：琦謬承
社友諸君推任理事，鑽自慚鴑鈍，未敢言辭，惟望
諸君各本其愛護科學之心，共謀本社之發展，則凡有裨
可以襄助之處，無不盡力。至目前社中所應推行之事約有
二端，謹為
諸君陳之，幸注意焉：
一、前聞「科學」經理部言，近來因留美同學投稿者不多，材料頗感缺乏，甚盼社友努力贊助，備有撰著，希即投登，或友好中有科學稿件，亦請代為介紹，皆甚歡迎。
二、關于社務進行計畫，最好能在夏間得一聚集機會，以便大家面談一切。此事不比工程學会聯合進行，諸君對于開会地点日期，以及社中他事有何意見，務望賜示，俾收集思廣益之效，幸甚幸甚。

琦又啟

謹啓者：茲收到分社職員選舉票四十張，其結果如左：

分社長　梅貽琦 39票　張洪沅 1票

書　記　張洪沅 26票　任之恭 10票　王德郅 4票

會　計　王德郅 18票　周田 11票　湯佩松 11票

除應通知新職員（最多數當選）就職并將各票票交書記保存外，謹此奉聞，順頌

公綏

司選委員　王德郅　張洪沅　王德郅　梅貽琦　謹啓

十九年十一月三十日

中國科學社 美洲分會

The Science Society of China
American Branch

會長 梅貽琦

COMMITTEE ON ANNUAL CONVENTION

E. Y. H. CHANG	C. SHEN
Y. T. KU	E. C. STONE
K. S. LEE	T. C. WANG
T. S. SIH	

For the Chinese Engineering Society
American Section

C. M. HU	T. C. WANG
Y. S. HUANG	L. C. WU
C. PEI	

For the Science Society of China
American Branch

66

Convention Program

Day Light Saving Time
Saturday, August 30

7:15 P. M.—REGISTRATION

7:30 P. M.—OPENING SESSION
OPENING REMARK
By Mr. E. Y. H. Chang

ADDRESS
By Mr. Y. T. Ku, President of the Chinese Engineering Society—American Section

8:00 P. M.—ADDRESS
By Mr. Y. C. Mei, President of the Science Society of China—American Branch

8:30 P. M.—ADDRESS
By Dr. J. A. L. Waddell, Honorary Technical Advisor to the National Government of China

9:40 P. M.—SMOKER

67

DR. WADDELL'S LATEST TECHNICAL BOOKS

Bridge Engineering, 2 vols., 2,232 pages. Price $12.00, gold. Published by John Wiley & Sons, New York, N. Y.

Economics of Bridgework, 544 pages. Price $6.00, gold. Published by John Wiley & Sons, New York, N. Y.

Memoirs and Addresses of Two Decades, 1,184 pages. Price $5.00, gold. Published by Mack Printing Company, Easton, Pennsylvania.

Convention Program

Day Light Saving Time

Sunday, August 31

10:00 A. M.—TECHNICAL PAPER SESSION

12:00 A. M.—ANNUAL MEETING OF THE OFFICERS

✓ 2:00 P. M.—PRESENTATION OF PAPERS (for the Science Society only)

✓ 6:30 P. M.—CONVENTION BANQUET

✓ 8:30 P. M.—SOCIAL MEETING

Convention Program

Day Light Saving Time

Monday, September 1

10:00 A. M.—TECHNICAL PAPER SESSION

12:30 P. M.—ANNUAL LUNCHEON
Followed by Business Meeting

2:30 P. M.—EXCURSION

7:00 P. M.—FAREWELL DINNER

大學樓

中式食品 歡迎中西學界

COLLEGE INN

Best Chinese Food You Can Find in New York

3100 BROADWAY NEW YORK CITY

Telephone: UNIversity 2794

3160 BROADWAY GARAGE, Inc.

Good Service — Reasonable Rates
Capacity 300 Cars

3160-69 BROADWAY and MOYLAN PLACE
Two Blocks South of 125th Street
NEW YORK CITY

Telephone: MONument 9477-9478-9479
Nearest Garage from International House

THE NEW CHINA
CHINESE AND AMERICAN RESTAURANT

新中華

菜蔬新鮮 魚肉味美 餐室清潔 來必再

3140 BROADWAY
Near La Salle St.

Telephone:
UNIversity 8072

BOOKS For your needs now
For your needs at home
For all purposes and of all subjects

ENGINEERING
EDUCATIONAL
RECREATIONAL

BOOKS

The largest variety of Engineering Technical and Educational Books, both new and used at reduced prices, in America.

We ship books of all publishers to institutions and individuals all over the world.

Come in and make yourself known. We welcome guests from abroad and would like to serve you now and in the future.

BARNES & NOBLE

76 Fifth Avenue New York City

Near 14th St., Up one Flight

JOINT ANNUAL CONVENTION FOR 1931

By The Chinese Engineering Society, American Branch, &
The Science Society of China, American Branch.

PROGRAM

Sept. 11 - 7:00 P.M. Registration.
(Friday) 7:30 P.M. Opening Meeting.
Greetings by Chairmen of the TWo Societies.
8:30 P.M. Address (Speaker to be announced).
9:30 P.M. General Discussion.

Sept. 12 - 9:00 A.M. to 12 Noon. Presentation of Technical and
(Saturday) Scientific Papers.
2:00 P.M. to 5:00 P.M. Inspection Trip - to places of interest in New York, details to be announced later.
7:00 P.M. to Midnight. Dinner, Social & Dance - at Chin Lee Restaurant, 48th Street & Broadway.

Sept. 13 - 9:00 P.M. to 12 Noon. Presentation of Technical and
(Sunday) Scientific Papers.
2:00 P.M. to 5:00 P.M. Program to be announced.
6:30 P.M. Farewell Dinner at China Garden.

Time: September 11 - 13, 1931.
Place: The International House, 500 Riverside Drive, N. Y. C.

Important - A fee of $2.00 will be charged to each member to cover all expenses of the Convention including the cost for the dinner and dance party. Outside guests are welcome to the meetings, especially to the dinner and dance party. Members are expected to invite their lady friends; an additional fee of $1.25 will be charged to the member who invites a guest to the dinner and dance party.

Members are urged to prepare papers for presentation at the Convention. For scientific papers, please send the title and abstract of your paper to Dr. P. S. Tang, Marine Biological Laboratory, Woods Hole, Mass.

For room reservation please write to Mr. K. S. Lee, c/o Purdy and Henderson, 45 E. 17th Street, New York City

59

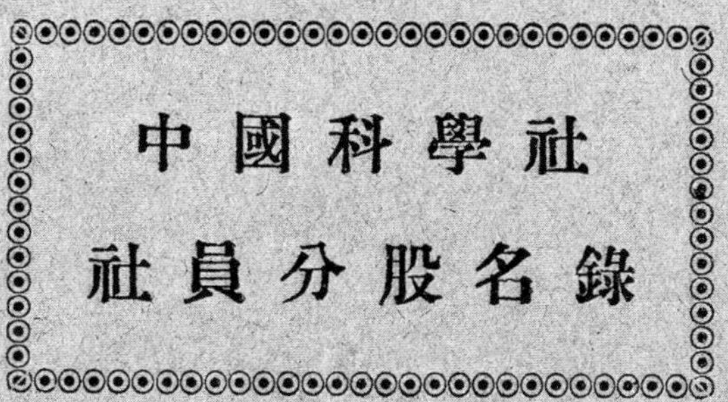

民國二十二年一月刊行

本社各部名稱地址表

上海社所	上海法租界亞爾培路五百三十三號
南京社所	南京成賢街
廣州社所	廣州九曜坊(廣東省政府指撥，未接管)
總辦事處	上海社所
明復圖書館	上海社所
生物研究所	南京社所
編輯部	上海社所
出版品總發行所	上海社所
印刷所	上海福煦路六百四十九號

電　話

上海社所	72551
南京社所	31407
印刷所	71046

有綫無綫電報掛號

上海南京二社所均爲 4430 (科)

118

緒 言

本社社員所專學科，門類繁多。故最初卽有分股委員會之設置，從事分類而便社員之聯絡研究。惟此項工作向未發表。年來蔡孑民先生在本社各種集會中亦屢經提及分股之重要，俾本社組織益見細密而有系統，凡遇科學上一種問題，卽可交有關係之一股或數股討論研究。在此組織之下，分之可爲各種科學之專會，合之卽爲中國科學社之全體。當此科學救國之重要時期中，本社之組織與地位實爲全國科學家分工合作所繫之唯一適當機關。本社有鑑於此，因先編印社員分股名錄，以資各分股組織時之參攷。此次編訂，係按照本社向來之科學分類。將全體社員分爲物質科學，生物科學，工程科學，及社會科學四大組。物質組下再分算學，物理，化學(化工合)，天文，地學（氣象附）五股。生物組下分生物，醫藥(體育附)，農林，心理，四股。工程組下分土木(建築附)，機工（造船附）電工，鑛冶，染織五股。社會組下分教育，經濟商業，法政，哲學，史學(社會附)，文藝六股。姓名之下仍附最近通訊處，故本編同時又爲最近社員通

119

訊錄。

各社員之學科，係參照其入社願書上所填者爲標準。惟其中或因時過境遷，或因學極專門，難免有未適當之歸類。社員通訊處亦多缺漏。爰于本編之末，特附社員學科住址調查表。希望同人擇其所知者報告本社，俾得於再版時修正，則幸甚矣。

民國二十一年十二月　　　　編者謹識

120

目　錄

附　　錄

122

社員分股名錄索引

(數字指面數)

二　畫

三　畫

四　畫

133

王瑞琳 89
王育瓚 78
王恭睦 27
王榮吉 84
王家楫 31
王逸之 89
王　度 53
王　謨 78
王　健 10
王　徵 89
王　華 89
王錫藩 78
王　璡 10
王鴻卓 71
王兼善 10
王毓祥 89
王魯新 71
王純燾 96
王義珏 10
王守競 6
王繩祖 100
王季眉 6
王舜成 45
王孝華 63
王德郅 10
王　敏 31
王化啓 6
王翰臣 71
王葆和 6
王翰辰 71
王輔世 6
王　賡 53
王以康 31
王耆亞 10
王愼名 71
水　梓 85
毛康山 10
戈定邦 31

五　畫

白敦庸 89
司徒錫 63
丘　畯 31
石心圃 78
田錫民 6
田世英 100
田和卿 11

六　畫

安立綏 46
安醫士 44
伊禮克 31
伍伯良 39
伍應垣 11
任　倬 39
任　誠 1
任嗣達 90
任鴻雋 11
任殿元 78
任之恭 6
朱少屏 85
朱文鑫 1
朱光燾 84
朱世明 63
朱世昀 103
朱其淸 71
朱亦松 90
朱家炘 63

124

七畫

金曾澄 85
金紹基 27
金 濤 55
金國寶 90
金劍清 72
金寶善 40
金鼎新 72
金賢藻 72
林文明 46
林文慶 40
林天驥 13
林士模 79
林可勝 40
林全誠 65
林和民 85
林祖光 65
林則衣 79
林景帆 90
林逸民 55
林喬年 32
林鳳歧 65
林繼庸 13
林 煖 73
林蔭梅 13
林襟宇 91
林 恂 65
周 仁 65
周文燮 79
周志宏 79
周 烈 79
周烈忠 2
周鼎培 85
周培源 7
周春臺 65
周延鼎 84
周 達 2
周明政 65
周明衡 55
周 威 40
周厚樞 13
周佛海 91
周 琦 72
周則岳 79
周開基 79
周 輪 55
周振禹 40
周 清 47
周 敏 79
周玆緒 72
周辨明 2
周 銘 13
周增奎 13
周德鴻 65
周連錫 84
周鍾歧 55
周榮條 47
周 田 13
周岸登 102
周同慶 7
周彥邦 55
周承鑰 46
周明牂 33
竺可楨 27
秉 志 32
邵元冲 90
邵家鱗 13

施宗嶽	96	唐之肅	80	高　志	15
施濟元	91	唐文悌	56	高濟宇	15
施仁培	2	唐在均	72	高崇德	7
保君建	91	唐啓宇	47	高　陽	86
柯成楙	14	唐昌治	47	高維魏	47
十　畫		唐恩良	56	高　華	72
郝坤巽	33	唐美森	15	高　銛	15
郝更生	41	唐仰虞	15	高振華	47
袁丕烈	66	唐鳴皋	72	韋以黻	66
袁同禮	86	唐慶貽	96	韋爾巽	15
袁祥和	72	唐燾源	15	韋憲章	84
袁復禮	27	唐　鉞	52	韋　慤	86
袁翰靑	15	唐嘉裝	14	孫天孫	91
馬玉銘	14	唐家珍	41	孫必昌	33
馬名海	2	高介淸	84	孫昌克	80
馬　和	14	黄　均	26	孫克基	41
馬　良	99	高長庚	15	孫宗彭	33
馬育騏	56	高崇熙	15	孫孝寬	41
馬愜蟲	80	高君珊	86	孫　洛	15
馬寅初	91	高　銶	15	孫雲鑄	28
馬磐基	28	高　魯	26	孫　科	97
馬　傑	14	高露德	15	孫　榮	26

128

129

陳文沛	84	陳家麒	80	陳煥鏞	34
陳中正	57	陳家麟	86	陳禮仁	57
陳方濟	16	陳宰均	48	陳翰笙	92
陳可忠	16	陳劍翛	52	陳納遜	34
陳良士	57	陳　器	16	陳鼎銘	17
陳宗賢	41	陳瑜叔	16	陳漢清	92
陳宗嶽	86	陳象岩	16	陳華甲	84
陳　容	86	陳清華	92	陳傳瑚	17
陳伯莊	17	陳　楨	34	陳　端	92
陳伯權	57	陳裕光	17	陳衡哲	100
陳明壽	66	陳裕華	57	陳寶年	91
陳炳基	73	陳德元	17	陳　羣	97
陳友琴	92	陳彰棋	17	陳　熹	92
陳去病	102	陳德芬	57	陳　嶸	48
陳烈勳	17	陳廣沅	66	陳　儁	48
陳長衡	92	陳兼善	34	陳　總	92
陳長源	73	陳蘭生	57	陳　維	17
陳克恢	42	陳福習	66	陳鶴琴	86
陳祖耀	57	陳燕山	47	陳懿祝	52
陳廷錫	91	陳　樸	92	陳思義	17
陳廷祥	47	陳慶堯	17	陳爲楨	48
陳延炆	73	陳　焜	17	陳可培	17

姓名	頁
梁引年	74
梁伯强	42
梁孟齊	18
梁　步	74
梁夢星	3
梁培穎	80
梁傳玲	18
梁思成	58
梁恩永	100
梁慶椿	91
莊長恭	18
莊秉權	58
莊　俊	58
莊　启	74
常宗會	48
常濟安	80
盛紹章	58
笪遠輪	67
淩　冰	86
淩　炎	57
凌其駿	16
凌道揚	48
凌鴻勛	57
崔宗塤	97
崔士傑	97
張一志	97
張士瀛	81
張乃燕	19
張乃鳳	48
張大斌	8
張天才	48
張文潛	84
張文湘	35
張元愷	87
張心一	48
張可治	67
張可光	81
張同亮	92
張本茂	67
張名藝	67
張巨伯	34
張宗成	48
張江樹	19
張廷翰	42
張廷玉	81
張宗文	100
張廷金	74
張　昇	58
張圩雯	42
張宗漢	34
張延祥	67
張其昀	28
張其濬	8
張承緒	74
張祖訓	92
張紹鎬	59
張紹聯	19
張紹忠	8
張東蓀	99
張自立	58
張　挺	34
張筱樓	3
張清漣	81
張爲儒	19
張　雲	26
張雲青	58

十二畫

姓名	股	姓名	股	姓名	股
黃金濤	81	黃國璋	28	馮漢驥	101
黃有書	81	黃實存	42	程干雲	67
黃美玉	20	黃漢河	104	程志頤	68
黃希聲	87	黃漢和	3	程孝剛	75
黃伯樵	67	黃漢樑	93	程宗陽	81
黃景康	67	黃際遇	3	程延慶	20
黃景新	35	黃育賢	59	程時煃	87
黃炳芳	20	黃　輝	75	程其保	87
黃俊英	20	黃　綬	97	程義法	81
黃家齊	59	黃寶球	93	程樹榛	104
黃振洪	20	黃均慶	20	程耀樞	21
黃　振	49	馮元勛	104	程耀椿	21
黃鈺生	87	馮　攸	93	程瀛章	21
黃　晃	49	馮家樂	20	程華燦	21
黃新彥	20	馮　稅	49	曾詒經	68
黃壽恆	59	馮祖荀	3	曾昭權	75
黃壽頤	59	馮景蘭	82	曾昭掄	21
黃壽仁	67	馮　偉	68	曾　省	35
黃篤修	75	馮樹銘	68	曾　義	21
黃　巽	8	馮肇傳	35	曾堿益	8
黃　植	49	馮斆棠	35	曾德鈺	75
黃國封	104	馮翰章	104	曾魯光	82

楊繼楨	104	葉桂馥	28	董　常	82
楊錫宗	60	葉建柏	75	董　時	87
楊鶴慶	42	葉建梅	75	董時進	50
楊　毅	59	葉善定	23	董榮清	22
楊肇燫	75	鄒邦元	42	董鴻詵	68
楊曾威	29	鄒秉文	36	褚民誼	43
楊允植	21	鄒　銘	101	褚鳳華	4
楊藎卿	8	鄒賡嶧	8	褚鳳章	76
楊善基	4	鄒應藼	36	雷沛鴻	98
楊蔭榆	87	鄒曾侯	93	雷海宗	101
楊鍾建	29	葛成慧	42	雷錫照	22
楊　偉	22	葛祖良	22	路敏行	22
楊樹勳	22	葛利普	28	齊清心	42
過養默	60	葛敬中	50	費德朗	8
葉元鼎	49	葛敬恩	98	費鴻年	36
葉元龍	93	葛敬應	50	萬兆芝	98
葉　志	4	葛德石	28	萬宗玲	36
葉企孫	8	葛綏成	28	賈念曾	22
葉雅各	49	裘維裕	76	經利彬	43
葉達前	98	裘翰興	4	虞振鏞	50
葉良玉	23	裘燮鈞	60	靳榮祿	4
葉良輔	28	裘開明	91	鄔保良	22

十四畫

十五畫

姓名	股	姓名	股	姓名	股
劉柏棠	94	劉劍秋	43	蔡鎦生	24
劉孝懃	76	劉　頤	60	蔡方蔭	60
劉季辰	29	劉體志	43	鄭肇經	61
劉崇樂	50	劉導誅	94	鄭允衷	69
劉紹禹	52	劉樹杞	23	鄭世夔	69
劉晉鈺	60	劉樹梅	94	鄭宗海	88
劉　復	102	劉樹墉	104	鄭　萊	94
劉學濬	60	劉　澗	82	鄭章成	43
劉承芳	69	劉寶濂	82	鄭恩聰	4
劉承霖	50	劉鞠可	68	鄭厚懷	29
劉惠民	104	劉寰偉	60	鄭祖穆	104
劉　銛	23	劉正經	5	鄭德柔	88
劉　勁	94	劉夢錫	60	鄭壽仁	94
劉榮基	50	劉仙洲	69	鄭　華	60
劉煒明	84	蔡元培	99	鄭禮明	76
劉朝陽	9	蔡　堡	37	鄭耀恭	24
劉　瑚	37	蔡增基	94	鄭法五	24
劉克定	94	蔡經賢	69	鄧胥功	98
劉　椽	23	蔡無忌	43	鄧福培	76
劉運籌	37	蔡　翔	82	鄧植儀	50
劉錫瑛	76	蔡　雄	82	鄧　傳	9
劉錫祺	76	蔡　翹	37	鄧鴻儀	23

戴　超　88
戴　晨　9
鍾心煊　37
鍾兆琳　77
鍾季襄　44
鍾榮光　88
鍾　利　95
鍾伯謙　83
鍾相青　95
應尚才　69
應尚德　38
應　時　98
謝玉鳴　9
謝作楷　77
謝恩增　44
謝恩隆　104
謝　惠　24
謝家榮　29
謝學瀛　61
謝寶善　9
謝汝鎮　5
龍裔禧　69

十八畫

薩本棟　77
薩本鐵　24
鄺培齡　104
鄺嵩齡　51
鄺壽堃　83
瞿祖輝　95
顏任光　9
聶光堉　62

十九畫

閻開元　104
閻道元　25
閻敦建　38
關漢光　69
關頌韜　44
關貴祿　9
關富權　61
關佰益　102
魏元光　61
魏嵒壽　25
魏樹勛　77
魏樹榮　25
魏　璧　5
魏菊峯　77
韓　安　88
韓　楷　104
韓組康　25
譚友岑　77
譚仲約　38
譚　眞　62
譚熙鴻　38
譚葆梧　95
譚葆壽　25
譚鐵肩　62
羅世嶷　25
羅　㐬　104
羅有節　95
羅　英　62
羅家倫　98
羅德民　51
羅萬年　83
羅慶蕃　69
羅　河　62

二十畫

二十一畫

中國科學社社員分股名錄

I. 物質科學組

1. 算學股

王世毅　剛森　江蘇吳縣　(1183)
(職)蘇州中學

任　誠　孟閑　江蘇　(1139)
(職)上海西門務本女子中學

朱文鑫　貢三　(421)
(職)鎮江江蘇省土地局

朱　籙　覺卿　江蘇無錫　(211)
(職)

宋立鈞　石齋　(837)
(通訊)

吳在淵　江蘇武進　(357)
(職)上海南市大同大學

吳定良　駿一　江蘇金壇(2.生物測量)　(1179)
(通訊)%Galton Lab., University College, Gower Street, London, W. C. I. England.

李　儼　樂知　(2.土木工程)　(147)
(職)河南靈寶隴海局

何衍璿　敬問　廣東　(999)
(職)廣州國立中山大學理科

何　魯　奎垣　(103)
(職)四川重慶大學理學院

1

143

呂子方　繼廉　四川(2.物理)　(846)
(通訊)四川重慶菜園壩重慶大學

余光烺　安徽　(1153)
(通訊)

周烈忠　(124)
(通訊)

周達　美權　安徽秋浦　(626)
(通訊)上海法租界馬斯南路八十八號

周辨明　(440)
(通訊)

武崇林　孟羣　安徽鳳陽　(1286)
(通訊)北平宣內前王公廠甲十一號

胡敦復　江蘇無錫　(300)
(通訊)上海呂班路萬宜坊十三號

段調元　子燮　四川江津　(138)
(職)南京國立中央大學

段育華　撫羣　江西南昌　(332)
(通訊)上海九江路一號中央銀行稽核處

施仁培　孔成　江蘇崇明　(1288)
(通訊)北平西城北溝沿四一號

馬名海　(212)
(職)廣西梧州廣西大學理學院

徐甘棠　(381)
(通訊)

夏峋　斧私　(688)
(通訊)四川成都省城窄巷子三六號

秦汾　景陽　江蘇無錫　(677)
(職)南京財政部

姜立夫 浙江 (35)
(職)天津南開大學
孫 鏞 光遠 浙江餘杭 (1116)
(職)北平清華大學
孫林翰 文青 河南 (1384)
(職)河南南陽縣教育局
陳 文 邃生 (349)
(通訊)
陳忠杰 子元 福建閩候 (1374)
(通訊)湖南長沙馬王街三十一號
梁夢星 兆庚 河北濮陽 (1191)
(通訊)
張筱樓 江蘇江寧 (1017)
(職)上海中華書局編譯所
張貽惠 少涵 安徽全椒 (732)
(職)北平北平大學師範院
張鴻基 山東平原 (1211)
(通訊)南京中央大學算學系
張崧年 申府 (259)
(通訊)
黃際遇 任初 廣東澄海 (442)
(職)青島大學理學院
黃漢和 福建思明 (1107)
(職)南京鐵道部
馮祖荀 漢叔 浙江 (1024)
(職)北平北京大學
華享平 江蘇無錫 (1018)
(職)上海中華書局編譯所

145

湯亨頤　樂甫　浙江紹興　(1300)
(通訊)上海辣斐德路一二五九B號

靳榮祿　宗岳　貴州貴陽　(784)
(通訊)

楊善基　安徽安慶　(1360)
(通訊)

楊克純　(1100)
(職)

楊卓新　華一　湖南新北　(436)
(職)湖南長沙湖南大學

楊武之　安徽合肥　(1174)
(職)北平清華大學

葉　志　靜遠　江蘇泰縣　(1023)
(職)武昌武漢大學

裘翰興　冲曼　浙江嵊縣　(645)
(職)杭州清波門花牌樓底雲居山莊二二號清波中學

褚鳳華　一飛　浙江嘉興　(1197)
(通訊)

趙九疇　廣東東莞　(762)
(通訊)

趙修乾　福建閩侯　(1287)
(通訊)

趙進義　希三　河北東鹿(2.天文)　(1189)
(職)北平師範大學

鄭思聰　達虞　(104)
(通訊)

熊慶來　迪之　江西　(771)
(職)赴法國

146

厲德寅 Li, Tehying浙江東陽 (1267)

(通訊) 823 W. Johnson St. Madison, Wisc.

蔣士彰 明甫 江蘇江都 (1081)

(通訊)

劉正經 乙閣 江西新建 (1285)

(通訊)

盧作孚 四川合川(2.心理3.社會) (1386)

(通訊)上海漢口路九號民生實業公司辦事處

薛光錡 仲華 (609)

(通訊)南京大紗帽巷四五號

謝汝鎮 安徽青陽 (1289)

(通訊)

魏 璧 湖南 (1012)

(通訊)

147

2. 物理股

丁佐成 浙江 (694)

(職)上海博物院路二十號大華儀器公司

丁緒寶 Ting Supao 安徽阜陽 (656)

(通訊) c/o The Institute of Applied Optics University of Rochester, Rochester, N. Y.,

丁燮林 巽甫 (695)

(職)上海霞飛路八九九中央研究院物理研究所

卞彭 江蘇 (670)

(職)赴美國

方光圻 千里 江蘇江都(2.數學) (614)

(職)

王葆和 聲山 河北深澤(無線電) (1354)

(通訊)河北省深澤縣濟和堂

王和 維克 江蘇金壇 (1097)

(通訊)金壇西橋巷七號

王守競 江蘇吳縣 (1306)

(職)北平北京大學理學院

王化啓 遼寧遼陽 (1301)

(通訊)

王季眉 浙江鎮海 (1307)

(職)上海棋盤街科學儀器館

王輔世 江蘇吳縣 (1379)

(通訊)同濟大學

田錫民 覺先 遼寧瀋陽 (1291)

(通訊)遼寧城內大北關火神廟胡同九八號

任之恭 Jen, Chih Kung 江西沁源(2.電工) (1249)

(通訊) 16 Wendell St. Cambridge, Mass

吳有訓　正之　江西高安　(892)
(職)北平清華大學
吳南薰　湖北沔陽　(1082)
(通訊)武昌龍神廟三五號
何育杰　吟苢　浙江慈谿　(814)
(通訊)上海新閘路福康里六二三A
李慶賢　浙江吳興　(1348)
(通訊)蘇州東吳大學
周培源　江蘇宜興　(1171)
(職)北平清華大學
周同慶　Chow, Tung Ching　江蘇崑山　(1225)
(通訊) Palmer Physical Lab., Princeton Univ. Princiton.
胡文耀　雪琴　浙江鄞縣　(823)
(職)上海市土地局
胡剛復　江蘇無錫　(60)
(職)上海霞飛路八九九號中央研究院物理研究所
胡範若　江蘇無錫　(1072)
(通訊)大同大學
查　謙　嘯仙　(833)
(職)南京中央大學
高崇德　宗山　(111)
(職)北平匯文大學
孫國封　(392)
(通訊)北平後門內蠟庫胡同四四號
夏建藩　桂初　(298)
(通訊)上海閔行鎮
徐仁銑　江蘇宜興(2.天文)　(1073)
(職)杭州浙江大學文理學院

149

徐景韓　　　　　　江蘇吳縣　　　　　　(1071)
　(職)蘇州東吳大學
桂質庭　　　　　　湖北　　　　　　(174)
　(職)武昌華中大學
許湞陽　濟羣　廣東翁源　　　　　　(1005)
　(通訊)美國張國藩轉
張國藩　　　　　　湖北安陸　　　　　　(1397)
　(通訊) 304 Ithaca Rd., Ithaca.
張大斌　新如　　　　　　(595)
　(通訊)四川成都少城桂花巷五號
張其濬　文淵　安徽太和　　　　　　(1098)
　(職)武昌武漢大學
張紹忠　藎謀　浙江嘉興　　　　　　(620)
　(職)杭州浙江大學文理學院
曾城益　　　　　　(755)
　(通訊)武昌武漢大學
温毓慶　　　　　　(251)
　(職)上海老北門國際無綫電管理局
黄　巽　繹言　廣東番禺(2電工)　　　　　　(1052)
　(職)廣州中山大學
楊藎卿　念忱　山東平度　　　　　　(1165)
　(職)北平海甸燕京大學
葉企孫　　　　　　江蘇上海　　　　　　(263)
　(職)北平清華大學
費德朗　繼孟　Miehel Vittrant, France　　　　　　(812)
　(職)上海震旦大學
鄒賡嶧　　　　　　遼寧瀋陽　　　　　　(1292)
　(通訊)北平東直門內小菊胡同二七號田宅轉

趙元任 Y. R.Chao, 江蘇武進 2.哲3.語4.樂 (5)

(通訊) Chinese Educational Mission 1360 Madison Street Northwest, Washiagton, D. C.,

趙修鴻 江蘇上海 (926)

(職)上海聖約翰大學

劉朝陽 浙江義烏 (1193)

(通訊)北平成府將家胡同二號或青島觀象台

鄧 傳 學魯 江蘇江寧 (952)

(職)鎮江江蘇教育廳

蔣德壽 迦安 江蘇江都 (1155)

(職)

戴 晨 晨風 江蘇吳縣 (1337)

(職)蘇州東吳大學

謝玉銘 Dr. Y. M. Hsich, 子瑜 福建晉江 (930)

(通訊) 167 S. Milson Avenue, Pasadena, Calrfon'a, U. S. A.

謝寶善 (551)

(通訊)

顏任光 廣東 (422)

(通訊)上海勞神父路六〇四號

關貴祿 爵五 遼寧復縣 (1290)

(通訊)吉林雙城縣南街路東烏宅

嚴濟慈 慕光 浙江東陽 (1143)

(職)北平東城根物理研究所

饒育泰 樹人 (55)

(通訊)上海廿世東路三德坊三號

顧靜徽 江蘇嘉定 (886)

(通訊)江蘇嘉定西大街

3. 化學股

丁嗣賢　　緒才　　安徽阜陽　　(619)
(職)

丁緒賢　　　　安徽阜陽　　(696)
(職)安慶安徽大學理學院

丁緒淮　　導之　　安徽　　(1399)
(通訊) 531 Forest Ave. Ann. Arbor, Mich,

王星拱　　撫五　　安徽懷寧　　(1058)
(職)武昌武漢大學

王德郅　　　　　　(1132)
(通訊)% Vulcan Detinning Co., Sewaren, N. J.,

王季茝女士 Dr. C. C. Wang　　(610)
(通訊) Chidren's Hospital. Elland and Bethesda Ave. Cincinnati, Ohio,

王　箴　　銘彝　　江蘇江陰　　(925)
(職)南京中央工業試驗所

王　璡　　季梁　　浙江黃巖　　(341)
(職)上海霞飛路八九九號化學研究所或本社

王　健　　晉生　　　　(98)
(通訊)

王義珏　　葮舲　　江蘇吳縣　　(1085)
(職)蘇州中學

王撘亞　　柱東　　四川三台　　(580)
(通訊)上海辛家花園十二甲

王兼善　　雲閣　　江蘇　　(645)
(通訊)

毛康山　　　　浙江奉化(2.工業管理)　　(1253)
(通訊)

田和卿 正本 浙江紹縣 (1329)
(職)上海小南門社會局

任鴻雋 叔永 四川 (11)
(職)北平南長街二二號中華教育文化基金董事會

伍應垣 所南 (529)
(通訊)四川重慶曾家岩工業中學校

朱成厚 安徽 (526)
(通訊)

朱耀芳 廣東新會 (1247)
(職)廣州市泰康路光華醫科大學

李運華 廣西貴縣 (915)
(職)北平清華大學化學系

李鉅元 浙江寧波 (1049)
(職)上海大西路底光華大學

李壽恆 江蘇宜興 (970)
(職)杭州浙江大學工學院

李大中 (277)
(通訊)

李善述 述初 浙江吳興 (756)
(通訊)

李敦化 意吾 (1126)
(通訊)廣東興寧縣西門聯合

李方琮 錦章 山東 (1372)
(通訊)青島金口一路新九號

李方訓 江蘇儀徵 (1350)
(通訊)南京金陵大學

李澄瀾 廣州 (497)
(通訊)

153

李　亮　亞明　江蘇江都　(1313)
(通訊)

汪元起　彥沈　安徽合肥　(1246)
(通訊)北平馬大人胡同十六號

汪　榕　冬生　(1293)
(職)湖南長沙明德中學

吳樹閣　麟葆　湖南醴陵　(1092)
(職)上海亞爾培路中法大學藥學專修科

吳文利　炳輝　廣東新會　(863)
(通訊)廣州東山龜崗大馬路二十八號二樓

吳欽烈　敬直　(193)
(通訊)南京軍政部兵工署

吳詩銘　Wü Shih Ming　安徽休寧　(1296)
(通訊)Dresden A. 24 Radetzkystr. 25 Germany.

吳魯强　廣東開平　(1216)
(通訊)廣州萬福路新廬

吳承洛　澗東　(204)
(職)南京下浮橋中央工業試驗所

吳　屏　伯藩　湖北廣濟　2地質　(1173)
(通訊)

沈熊慶　夢占　(840)
(職)上海霞飛路和合坊四號工業物品試驗所

沈燕謀　江蘇南通　(210)
(職)上海南京路保安坊大生紡織公司

沈　奎　星五　(444)
(通訊)

沈孟欽　(74)
(通訊)

沈溯明　浙江　(62)
(通訊)上海慕爾鳴路德慶里六三七號

宋文政 湖北當陽 (1108)

(通訊)

狄　憲 憲民 江蘇溧陽 (1376)

(通訊)上海亞爾培路中法大學藥科

余子明 廣東台山 (914)

(通訊)

余澤蘭 蘭園 福建古田 (646)

(通訊)北平大六部口三三號

林天驥 廣東汕頭 (940)

(職)上海四川路六號大中華火柴有限公司

林繼庸 廣東香山 (923)

(通訊)上海愛文義路872號温崇信先生轉

林蔭梅 一民 江西上饒 (851)

(職)天津西沽北洋大學工學院

周　田 Chow, Bacon Field 福建 (1126)

(通訊) 24 Chauncy. St, Cambridge, Mass.

周厚樞 星北 江蘇江都 (829)

(職)揚州中學

周　銘 江蘇泰興 (103)

(通訊)上海交通大學

周增奎 揆平 江蘇上海(2.工商管理) (379)

(通訊)

邵家麟 浙江湖州 (618)

(職)上海大夏大學

孟心如 江蘇武進 (936)

(職)杭州造幣廠

邱崇彥 宗岳 浙江諸暨 (50)

(職)天津南開大學

胡昭望　寧生　安徽績溪　(972)

(通訊)蕪湖西門内青石街二八號

胡　澤　國澤　四川璧山　(1310)

(通訊)四川重慶五福街何家花園胡宅

胡諤鈞　(269)

(通訊)

胡　讓　宸甫　四川　(533)

(通訊)

俞同奎　星樞　浙江德清　(963)

(通訊)北平西城都城隍廟街三〇號

洪　深　(陶業)　(432)

(通訊)

洪紹論　(152)

(通訊)

侯德榜　致本　(123)

(職)天津塘沽永利製鹼公司

紀育澧　星昀　浙江寧波　(623)

(職)杭州浙江大學理學院

柯成楙　箴心　浙江平湖　(218)

(職)上海交通大學

馬　傑　河南羅山　(1230)

(通訊)北平西鐵匠胡同21號馬秋圃先生轉

馬玉銘　爾遐　遼寧復縣　(860)

(通訊)

馬　和　君武　(831)

(職)廣西大學

唐家裝　廣東　(1283)

(通訊)

唐美森 J. C. Thomson, 美國 (1039)
(通訊)

唐仰虞 安徽含山 (558)
(通訊)河南焦作工學院化學系

唐燾源 凌閣 江蘇無錫(2.造紙) (1205)
(職)上海中央研究院理化研究所

袁翰青 Yuang, Han Ching 江蘇南通 (1219)
(通訊)Box 94 Univ. Station, Urbana, Ill.

高長庚 少白 山東 (909)
(通訊)濟南東關青龍街

高崇熙 仲明 山東 (1161)
(職)北平清華大學

高露德 廣東新會 (1187)
(通訊)廣州市大北直街西華二横巷五號

高 鈇 (521)
(通訊)

高 銛 (271)
(通訊)

高 志 廣東廣州 (1228)
(通訊)湖北武昌武漢大學

高濟宇 Kao Tse Yu 河內舞陽 (122)
(通訊)Box 82 Univ. Statiou, Urbana, Ill.

韋爾巽 S. D. Wilson 美國 (637)
(職)北平海甸燕京大學

孫 洛 洪芬 安徽 (49)
(職)北平南長街二二號中華教育文化基金董事會

孫學悟 穎川 (59)
(職)天津塘沽黃海化學工業研究社

徐名材　伯雋　(437)
(職)上海交通大學
徐作和　汝梅　江蘇吳江　(813)
(職)上海滬江大學
徐佩璜　君陶　江蘇　(109)
(通訊)上海霞飛路291號
徐善祥　鳳石　江蘇上海　(1061)
(通訊)上海靜安寺路一六九九衖三號
徐宗涑　天津　(1274)
(通訊)上海龍華上海水泥廠
姚醒黃　江蘇上海　(883)
(通訊)
時昭涵　湖北枝江　(449)
(職)上海徐家匯交通大學
柴冰梅　(143)
(通訊)
凌其峻　(陶瓷)　(241)
(通訊)
陳可忠　福建閩侯　(737)
(通訊)南京國立編譯館
陳瑜叔　湖南常德　(446)
(職)漢陽兵工廠理化課
陳　器　仲修　(243)
(職)上海博物院路八號建委會購料委員會材料課
陳象岩　(403)
(通訊)
陳方濟　禹成　(213)
(職)南京三牌樓中央大學農學院

陳裕光　景唐　浙江　(311)

(職)南京金陵大學

陳德元　調甫　江蘇吳縣　(453)

(職)天津塘沽永利製鹼總廠

陳彰琪　行可　四川宜賓　(1163)

(通訊)北平寮院胡同十六號

陳慶堯　慕唐　江蘇上海　(68)

(通訊)

陳　熀　Hwang Chen, 宗南　廣東　(1051)

(通訊) c/o Dr. Y. R. Chao. Chinese Educational Mission, 1360 Madison Street No.thwest, Washington, D.C.,

陳傳瑚　警庸　江蘇吳江　(954)

(通訊)北平西城兵馬司三八號

陳可培　浙江上虞　(1323)

(職)上海匯豐大夏馬爾康洋行

陳思義　誦宜　江蘇崇明(2.藥學)　(1305)

(通訊)上海愛文義路一六一三號

陳烈勳　浙江杭縣(造紙)　(540)

(通訊)杭州黃醋園

陳伯莊　廣東　(34)

(通訊)上海海格路159弄大勝胡同17號

陳鼎銘　湖北漢川　(1083)

(職)武昌武漢大學

陳　維　Chen, Wei 福建閩侯　(1266)

(通訊)317 College Ave., Ithaca N.Y.

陸啓先　廣西容縣　(921)

(通訊)廣西容縣南門街德祥交

陸志安　江蘇南通　(1295)

(通訊)天津南開大學教員宿舍五號

159

陶延橋　　安徽蕪湖　(1066)

(職)南京金陵大學

陶桐　嶧南　江蘇無錫　(1353)

(通訊)1414 E. 59th St., Chicago. Ill.

許植方　魯瞻　浙江黃岩　(1063)

(職)上海霞飛路八九九號化學研究所

許炳熙　希林　江蘇吳縣　(1311)

(通訊)上海廣東路三號恆信洋行

曹簡禹女士 Miss Tsao, Chien Yu 江蘇宜興(2.植物生理)　(1259)

(通訊)602 Busey St., Urbana, Ill.

曹任遠　四勿　四川富順　(495)

(通訊)

曹挺　銘先　廣東番禺　(560)

(職)常州戚墅堰電燈分廠

曹元宇　行素　江蘇吳縣　(1010)

(職)南京中央大學理學院

曹惠羣　梁廈　江蘇宜興　(355)

(職)上海南站大同大學

章元善　　江蘇吳縣　(950)

(通訊)北平東城榮廠胡同六號

梅冠豪　卓雄　廣東　(976)

(通訊)

梁傳玲　　　(376)

(通訊)

梁孟齊　　廣東新會　(1200)

(通訊)廣州市太平沙環珠里八號

莊長恭 C. K. Chuang 丕可　福建泉州　(382)

(通訊)Iui Frantz Friedlaenderweg 59/II. Göttingen, Germany,

張乃燕　君謀　浙江吳興　(809)
(通訊)上海大西路四九號
張江樹　雪帆　江蘇常熟　(932)
(職)南京中央大學
張爲儒　偉如　江蘇吳縣　(785)
(通訊)上海白克路老修德里底張一鵬律師事務所
張　準　子高　湖北枝江　(83)
(職)北平清華大學
張寶華　燦如　(662)
(職)天津啓新洋灰公司
張紹聯　(310)
(通訊)
張　拯　鴻年　江蘇吳縣　(849)
(通訊)蘇州吳縣橫街八三號
張澤堯　湘生　江西　(366)
(職)天津特二區華安街實業部天津商品檢驗局
張增佩　久香　浙江吳興　(752)
(通訊)
張貽志　(61)
(通訊)
張洪沅　(1221)
(通訊)南京中央大學
張資珙　廣東梅縣　(1227)
(職)武昌華中大學化學系
張　銓　克剛　浙江仙居(製革)　(1368)
(職)北平燕京大學
黃子卿　碧帆　廣東梅縣　(861)
(職)北平清華大學

黃友逢 廣東 (607)

(通訊)上海施高塔路恆盛里三十號

黃振洪 (65)

(通訊)

黃新彥 (163)

(通訊)香港九龍彌敦道七七八號

黃美玉 Miss Asta Ohu, (770)

(通訊) 1632 Le Roy Avenue, Berkeley, California

黃炳芳 廣東台山 (1160)

(通訊)廣州市惠福西路一三五號安園三樓

黃俊英 子碩 福建興化 (939)

(職)福建莆田省立莆田哲理中學

黃均慶 善餘 江蘇上海 (1369)

(通訊)上海南市青龍橋街八一號

區其偉 (769)

(通訊)

區嘉煒 廣東順德 (1218)

(通訊)廣州芳草街四八號

彭謙 同生 湖北 (1340)

(職)河南開封河南大學農學院

彭鴻章 用儀 四川巴縣 (1166)

(通訊)四川成都大學化學系

舒宏 (185)

(通訊)

馮家樂 康民 (593)

(通訊)四川成都大紅土地廟街里仁巷王希文君轉

程延慶 伯商 江蘇吳江 (99)

(職)杭州浙江大學文理學院

程耀樞　　　　　　　　　(286)

(通訊)

程耀椿　子茂　廣東香山　(546)

(通訊)上海虹口東有恆路五一號

[illegible]瀛章　寰西　江蘇吳江　(39)

(通訊)上海海格路三德里十七號

程華燦　　廣東中山　(1277)

(通訊)廣州河南聯鶴大街十七號

曾昭掄　叔偉　湖南湘鄉　(563)

(職)北平北京大學化學系

曾　義　　四川　(1157)

(通訊)四川重慶五福街何家花園胡宅

賀　闓　嘉伊　湖北北陵　(943)

(職)漢口揚子街九號實業部商品檢驗所

賀孝齊　　　　　　　　　(686)

(通訊)

湯騰漢　　福建龍溪(2.藥學)　(1330)

(職)青島大學

楊光弼　夢賚　　(283)

(通訊)北平東堂子胡同十六號

楊紹曾　石先　安徽懷寧　(674)

(通訊)北平宣內東太平街三三A或天津南開大學

楊道林　德參　山東膠州　(1070)

(通訊)

楊允植　絜夫　安徽懷寧　(1076)

(通訊)

楊子嘉　　　　　　　　　(597)

(通訊)

163

楊承訓 (406)

(通訊)南京小門口妙鄉十二號

楊守珍 Yang, Shou Chen 遼寧法庫 (1251)

(通訊)

楊 偉 陝西潼關 (1232)

(通訊)南京中央黨部楊天民先生轉

楊樹勳 建吾 廣東 (1394)

(通訊)Rockefeller Institute, 66th St. and N.Y. Ave. N. Y. C.

董榮清 浙江 (817)

(通訊)杭州新市場生長路二三號或上海廣東路十四號中孚化學製造股份有限公司

葛祖良 (244)

(通訊)

路敏行 季訥 江蘇宜興 (6)

(職)本社明復圖書館

賈念曾 季方 江蘇無錫 (605)

(通訊)無錫進士坊巷

鄔保良 廣東龍川 (1188)

(職)

雷錫照 廣東四會 (566)

(通訊)

趙廷炳 丹若 浙江嘉興 (964)

(通訊)杭州蒲場巷四二號

趙承嘏 石民 江蘇江陰 (798)

(職)北平東皇城根四十二號藥物研究所

趙學海 師軾 江蘇無錫 (872)

(通訊)北平崇內大羊毛胡同二一號

趙恩賜 廣東新會 (1210)

(職)廣州嶺南大學

趙　武　　江蘇崑山　(1343)

(通訊)上海郵箱第一二〇二號

熊正琍　　江西　(424)

(職)江西南昌心遠中學

熊祖同　　四川成都　(938)

(職)四川成都大學

熊學謙 Hsiung, Sherchin C. 湖北松滋　(1229)

(通訊)Box 1011 John's Hopkin's Univ., Baltimore, Md,

翟念甫　(1220)

(通訊)廣西桂林崇德街七七號徐念劬先生轉

榮達坊　　江蘇無錫　(848)

(通訊)上海華德路第四五五弄J G七三號

葉良玉　(144)

(通訊)

葉善定　　浙江鎮海　(1378)

(通訊)上海河南路20號大陸藥房轉

鄺恂立　心達　浙江嘉興　(1284)

(通訊)上海金神父路三〇六號

劉　拓　泛弛　湖北黃陂　(1162)

(職)北平師範大學

劉樹杞　楚青　湖北　(184)

(職)北平北平大學理學院

劉　銛　T. Liu　廣東梅縣　(657)

(通訊) Beker Lab. Cornell Univ. Ithaca.

劉　椽　　山東諸城　(1231)

(通訊)

鄧鴻儀　漸逵　(648)

(通訊)

鄭法五　　湖北　　(1299)
(職)四川萬縣市桐油檢驗局
鄭耀恭　　(287)
(通訊)
樂森璧　伯恆　　(178)
(通訊)
蔡鏐生 Tsai, Liu Sheng 福建泉州　　(1233)
(通訊)5738 Drexel Ave. Chicago, Ill. 或北平燕京大學收轉
潘祖馨　冠卿　江蘇青浦　　(154)
(通訊)上海法租界麥賽而蒂路四十號
潘愼明　　江蘇吳縣　　(931)
(通訊)蘇州東吳大學
潘履潔　L. C. Pan, 江蘇吳縣　　(870)
(通訊)
霍炎昌　　(425)
(通訊)
盧景肇　季始　廣東順德　　(937)
(通訊)
薛培元　燮之　河北臨城　　(1158)
(通訊)北平西城花園宮甲十號
戴增庠　育民　遼寧瀋陽　　(1294)
(通訊)
戴安邦　　江蘇鎮江　　(1275)
(職)南京金陵大學化學系
謝　惠　凝遠　浙江紹遠　　(538)
(通訊)
薩本鐵　必得　福建閩侯　　(1103)
(職)北平清華大學化學系

韓組康 湖南長沙(2.分析化學) (1370)

(通訊)上海薛華立路155弄三號

魏嵒壽 孟磊 浙江鄞縣 (1159)

(職)南京中央大學農學院

魏樹榮 岳東 (250)

(通訊)北平後門定府大街後大新路二號

譚葆壽 (275)

(通訊)

閻道元 (352)

(通訊)

羅世嶷 元叔 四川富順 (320)

(職)四川四川大學

嚴仁曾 曾符 河北天津 (417)

(通訊)天津文昌宮西

竇維廉W. H. Adolph美國 (427)

(職)北平海甸燕京大學

顧大榮 翼東 江蘇吳縣 (927)

(職)蘇州東吳大學

顧毓珍 敬異 江蘇無錫 (1400)

(通訊) M.I.T. Dorms. Cambridge, Mass.,

167

4. 天文股

王應偉　碩甫　江蘇吳縣(2.氣象)　(1182)
(職)青島觀象台或蘇州齊門路堵帶橋營門弄

余青松　福建同安　(1101)
(職)南京鼓樓天文研究所

高均　平子　江蘇　(877)
(職)南京鼓樓天文研究所

高魯　曙青　福建長樂　(827)
(通訊)南京監察院

孫榮　華亭　河北滄縣　(466)
(職)北平北京大學理學院或北平崇內東城根抽屜胡同一號

張雲　子春　廣東開平　(731)
(職)廣州中山大學天文台

5. 地學股(氣象附)

丁文江　在君　江蘇泰興(2.人類學)　(619)
(通訊)北平內務部街芳嘉園三二號
王恭睦　望楚　浙江黃岩(2.古生物)　(1080)
(職)南京山西路國立編譯館
朱庭祜　仲翔　江蘇川沙　(880)
(職)安徽省教育廳
李之常　愼吾　湖北沔陽(2.古生物)　(924)
(職)南京中央大學或焦狀元巷二七號
李四光　仲揆　(638)
(職)南京中央研究院地質研究所
李士林　文軒　綏遠清水河　(1119)
(通訊)
李殿臣　廷輪　河南葉縣　(1112)
(職)廣州兩廣地質調查所
李孤帆　浙江鄞縣　(1059)
(通訊)上海威海衛路中社轉
竺可楨　藕舫　浙江紹興(氣象)　(101)
(職)南京北極閣氣象研究所
金紹基　叔初　浙江吳興　(949)
(通訊)北平東四㚘㚘胡同十一號
孟憲民　應鰲　江蘇武進　(1115)
(職)南京中央研究院地質研究所
胡煥庸　江蘇宜興　(1093)
(職)蘇州中學
袁復禮　希淵　直隸徐水　(956)
(通訊)

169

馬磐基　Mar, Peter　廣東新甯　(395)
(通訊) Gordon Bell Res. Lab., Medical Coll., Winnipeg, Canada,
孫雲鑄　鐵仙　江蘇高郵(2.古生物)　(957)
(職)北平地質調查所
徐渊摩　厚孚　江蘇武進
(通訊)上海蒲石路九十六號
徐韋曼　寬甫　江蘇武進(2.採鑛)　(799)
(職)上海中央研究院出版品國際交換處
徐瑞麟　松石　湖南衡陽(2.生物)　(1087)
(通訊)
翁文灝　詠霓　浙江　(669)
(職)北平地質調查所
章鴻釗　演存　(691)
(職)北平地質調查所
黄國璋　海平　湖南湘鄉　(1094)
(職)北平清華大學
黄伯芹　廣東　(17)
(通訊)香港上環和昌金店
張鳴韶　賡虞　河南汝南　(1079)
(通訊)
張其昀　曉峯　浙江鄞縣　(1057)
(職)南京中央大學或南京蓁巷四號
葉良輔　左之　浙江杭縣　(876)
(職)南京中央研究院地質研究所
葉桂馥　廣東歸善　(514)
(通訊)
葛綏成　毅甫　浙江東陽　(1016)
(職)上海中華書局編譯所

葛利普 A. W. Grabau 美國 (862)
(職)北平地質調查所

葛德石 George B. Cressey 美國 (1025)
(通訊)

楊曾威 威伯 江蘇武進(2.古生物) (1110)
(職)北平清華大學

楊鍾健 克强 陝西華縣 (1382)
(職)北平西兵馬司九號地質調查所

劉季辰 寄人 江蘇上海 (805)
(通訊)

蔣丙然 右滄 福建閩侯(氣象) (821)
(職)青島青島市觀象臺

鄭厚懷 達才 安徽青陽 (887)
(職)南京中央大學

樂森璕 季純 貴州貴陽(2.古生物) (1078)
(通訊)

謝家榮 季驊 江蘇上海 (826)
(職)北平地質調查所

171

II. 生物科學組

1. 生物股

上官垚登　　　　婺西玉山(2.教育)　　　　(881)
(通訊)江西南昌花園角一號

王守成　　志稼　　江蘇吳縣　　(1048)
(通訊)蘇州呂印坊巷六五號

王彥祖　　　　(119)
(通訊)

王家楫　　仲濟　　江蘇奉賢　　(1131)
(職)南京本社生物研究所

王以康　　　　浙江　　(1388)
(通訊)南京中國科學社生物研究所

王　敏　　　　浙江杭縣　　(1322)
(通訊)南京閭奩營三號

戈定邦　　　　河北　　(1389)
(通訊)北平清華大學生物系

丘　晙　　寶疇　　廣東平遠　　(864)
(職)廣州市中山大學附屬中學

曲桂齡　　仲湘　　河南唐河　　(1324)
(通訊)河南輝縣百泉河南省立鄉村師範學校

伊禮克　J. T. Illick 美國　　(1036)
(職)南京金陵大學

朱庭茂　　　　(1133)
(通訊)

李良慶　　　　貴州貴陽　　(1356)
(通訊)北平西城東斜街昌堂門一號轉

李順卿　　幹臣　　山東　　(537)
(通訊)北平宣內回回營十號

31

李先聞　達聰　四川　(1186)
(職)

李　浚　濬庵　(2.地理)　(1123)
(通訊)雲南鄧川勸學所

李　琳　(161)
(通訊)

吳元滌　子修　江蘇江陰　(207)
(職)蘇州中學

吳家煦　和士　江蘇吳縣(2.理化)　(206)
(通訊)

吳貽芳　冬生　浙江杭縣　(917)
(職)南京金陵女子大學

吳韞珍　(666)
(職)北平清華大學

吳偉士 Woodworth U. S. A.美國　(820)
(通訊)University of California Berkeley, California.

沈宗瀚　浙江餘姚　(973)
(職)南京金陵大學

何文俊　四川　(1309)
(職)四川成都華西協合大學生物系

何畏冷　福建福清　(1053)
(通訊)南京鼓樓二條巷西口陰陽營二號

辛樹幟　湖南　(1152)
(職)南京國立編譯館

林喬年　展君　廣東遂溪　(980)
(通訊)廣東遂溪縣烏泥塘市求安堂

秉　志　農山　河南開封　(14)
(職)南京本社生物研究所

174

周明牂 Chao, M.T. 江蘇泰縣 (1359)

(通訊)Dept. of Entomology, Cornell University

祁天錫 N. Gist Gee 美國 (935)

(通訊)Yenching University,150 Fifth Avenue,New York City.

胡先驌 步曾 江西新建 (32)

(職)北平石駙馬大街靜生生物調查所

胡經甫 (447)

(職)北平海甸燕京大學生物系

胡梅基 廣州 (1358)

(通訊)

段續川 四川成都 (1244)

(通訊)天津大公報館段繼達先生轉

范贇 肖岩 江蘇武進 (1068)

(職)杭州筧橋浙江大學文理學院生物系

郝坤巽 象吾 河南武陟 (714)

(職)河南開封河南大學

涂治 湖北黃陂 (1044)

(通訊)河南開封大學農學院植物病理室

徐蔭祺 江蘇吳縣 (1363)

(通訊)

徐學楨 幹生 廣東番禺 (1077)

(通訊)廣州市太平沙庸常新街八號樓下成中山大學理工學院生物系

郜重魁 幼顯 雲南鶴慶 (977)

(通訊)

孫宗彭 稚孫 (1125)

(通訊)

孫必昌 東明 (2.地學) (828)

(通訊)

陳邦傑 逸塵 江蘇江都 (1373)
(通訊)

陳 楨 席山 江西鉛山 (736)
(職)北平清華大學

陳焕鏞 廣東新會 (810)
(職)廣州中山大學

陳兼善 達夫 浙江 (1109)
(通訊)

陳納遜 廣東中山 (1103)
(職)南京金陵大學

莫古禮 F. A. Mc Clure 美國 (1011)
(職)廣州嶺南大學

郭仁風 J. B. Griffing 美國(2.教育) (1041)
(通訊)

張念恃 作人 (789)
(通訊)Boite Posta'e No. 19217, Fontenay Aux Roses, Seine, France.

張春霖 震東 河南開封 (1333)
(職)北平静生生物調查所

張巨伯 歸農 廣東鶴山 (146)
(職)南京中央大學内江蘇省昆蟲局

張宗漢 眞衡 浙江嵊縣 (1154)
(通訊) 49 Snell Hall, Chicago University, U. S. A.

張 挺 鏡澄 安徽桐城 (505)
(職)武昌武漢大學

張 祿 L. Chang, 服眞 雲南(2.社會) (675)
(通訊)Box 62, College Sta., Pullman, Washington,

張景歐 海珊 江蘇 (852)
(通訊)

176

張景鉞 峴儕 江蘇武進 (663)
(通訊)
張和岑 浙江甯波 (1352)
(通訊)蘇州東吳大學
張 賢 浙江吳興 (1320)
(通訊)南京中央大學女生宿舍
張肇騫 冠超 浙江永嘉 (1313)
(通訊)南京中央大學生物系或大石橋海記里六號
張文湘 叔沅 四川永川 (1095)
(通訊)
黃易伯 四川巴縣 (1090)
(通訊)
黃景新 四川永川 (1096)
(通訊)
馮斅棠 Feng, H.T. 江蘇無錫 (1362)
(通訊) 208 Delware Ave. Ithea, N.Y.
馮肇傳 江蘇宜興 (542)
(職)南京中央大學農學院
彭光欽 Penn, Amos Benkow 四川 (1234)
(通訊)Box 95 Johns Hopkin's Univ, Baltimore Md.
曾廣澄 佐明 (501)
(通訊)
曾 愼 吉夫 四川 (1341)
(職)河南開封河南大學
曾 省 省之 浙江 (724)
(通訊)青島大學
喻兆琦 慕韓 江蘇 (751)
(通訊)

湯佩松 Tang, Pei Sung 湖北蘄水 (1235)
(通訊) Lab. of General Physiology, Harvard Univ.,
湯覺之 湖南長沙(2.生理) (1345)
(通訊)南京龍王廟堂子巷長治里一號
傅驌 有周 四川 (7)
(通訊)四川重慶城內小樑子逸公家祠
傅葆琛 (262)
(通訊)
楊保康 江蘇無錫(2.教育) (630)
(通訊)
楊風 Young, P. 浙江桐鄉 (933)
(通訊)
鄒秉文 江蘇吳縣 (52)
(通訊)上海薩坡賽路三一二號
鄒應藼 樹文 江蘇吳縣 (16)
(通訊)安慶忠孝街一號
費鴻年 浙江海甯 (801)
(通訊)
萬宗玲 四川永川 (1319)
(通訊)南京中央大學女生宿舍
裴鑑 季衡 四川成都 (1243)
(職)南京本社生物研究所
壽振黃 理初 浙江諸暨 (733)
(職)北平石駙馬大街靜生生物調查所
熊大仕 江西南昌 (1222)
(通訊)天津南開大學生物系
管家驥 Kwan Chia Chi 浙江上虞 (1258)
(通訊)Dept. of Plant Breeding, Cornell. U.

178

趙連芳　蘭屏　河南羅山(遺傳學)　(373)

(職)南京三牌樓中央大學農學院

劉　咸　仲熙　江西　(1030)

(通訊)青島大學

劉廷蔚　浙江温州　(1252)

(通訊)北平燕京大學劉廷芳先生收轉

劉　瑚　Liu, Hu　湖北嘉魚　(1217)

(通訊)Bio-Chem. Dept. St. Paul, Minneapolis, Minn.

劉運籌　伯量　四川巴縣　(1089)

(通訊)南京實業部或中央大學農學院

蔡　堡　作屏　浙江杭縣　(853)

(職)南京中央大學

蔡　翘　卓夫　廣東　(1065)

(職)上海中央大學醫學院

黎國昌　愼圖　廣東東莞　(981)

(通訊)廣州市惠愛西路粤華西街四號

潘光旦　江蘇寶山　(894)

(通訊)

鄧叔羣　福建　(1383)

(通訊)南京中國科學社生物研究所

歐陽翥　鐵翹　湖南長沙　(1043)

(通訊)

錢崇澍　雨農　浙江海甯　(18)

(職)南京本社生物研究所

薛德育　良叔　江蘇江陰　(1019)

(通訊)

鍾心煊　仲襄　江西南昌　(100)

(職)武昌武漢大學

盧于道　　　　浙江甯波(生理)　　　　(1237)
　　(職)北平東城芳嘉園一號心理研究所

應尙德　　　　　　　　　　　　(642)
　　(通訊)

閻敦建　　　　湖南長沙　　　　(1192)
　　(職)北平靜生生物調查所

譚熙鴻　仲逵　　　　　　　　　(557)
　　(通訊)南京實業部

譚仲約　　　　廣東新會　　　　(1257)
　　(通訊)

2. 醫藥股

丁求眞 任生 浙江天台(2.公共衞生) (698)

(職)杭州裏西湖葛嶺山脚一五號西湖療養院

方雪瓊女士 Miss S. S. Huong (1134)

(通訊)

王季茝 Dr. C. C. Wong (601)

(通訊)Children's Hospital, Elland and Bethsda Ave., Cincinnati, O, U. S. A.

王兆麒 江蘇無錫(獸醫) (554)

(職)上海市衞生局

伍伯良 廣東台山(2.公衆衞生) (1199)

(通訊)廣州舊倉巷伍漢特醫院

任 倬 維章 浙江杭縣 (918)

(通訊)杭州清泰門直街八八號

吉普思 Charles Shelby, Gibbs 美國 (1031)

(通訊)

江 鐵 (272)

(通訊)

李 岡 (307)

(通訊)上海靜安寺路1205號

李 定 愼徵 (690)

(通訊)

李賦京 陝西 (1113)

(職)河南開封河南大學

李克鴻 江蘇上海 (1240)

(通訊)

李振翩 湖南(2.細菌學) (1346)

(通訊)上海海格路國立上海醫院

181

吳克俊 (249)
(通訊)
吳興業 (285)
(通訊)
吳旭丹 (205)
(通訊)上海北京路73號三樓27號
吳 憲 陶民 (85)
(職)北平協和醫校
吳濟時 谷宜 江蘇 (397)
(通訊)蘇州公園對門
吳金聲 福建廈門 (452)
(通訊)
沈鴻翔 (256)
(通訊)天津海軍醫學校
宋杏邨 (270)
(通訊)上海蒲石路杜美新村十八號
宋梧生 浙江 (616)
(通訊)上海蒲石路杜美新村十八號
金寶善 楚珍 浙江紹興(2.公共衛生) (689)
(職)南京衛生署
林文慶 福建廈門 (885)
(職)廈門大學
林可勝 福建廈門 (968)
(職)北平協和醫學校
周 威 仲奇 江蘇江甯 (36)
(職)南京中央大學或南京韙家橋五號
周振禹 (299)
(通訊)

胡正祥 江蘇無錫 (220)
(職)北平協和醫學校
胡潤德 廣東佛山 (475)
(通訊)
胡宣明 (267)
(職)南京鐵道部衛生處
姚爾昌 (309)
(通訊)
郝更生 江蘇淮安(體育) (1332)
(通訊)
唐家珍 廣西 (1315)
(職)青島市立醫院
徐誦明 (535)
(通訊)
孫克基 庸皋 (219)
(職)上海紅十字會醫院
孫孝寬 (511)
(職)上海四川路靶子路寬民醫院
陰毓璋 山西太原 (1393)
(通訊)St. Lnke's Hospital, Bethlehem Pa.
翁文瀾 子營 浙江甯波 (843)
(通訊)
陸錦文 (175)
(通訊)
陳宗賢 (319)
(職)北平天壇中央防疫處
陳思義 誦誼 江蘇崇明 (1305)
(通訊)上海愛文義路一六一三號

陳克恢　子振　江蘇青浦　(564)
(通訊)
許陳琦　軹民　浙江天台　(984)
(通訊)
麥克樂　C. Mcloy, 美國(體育)　(882)
(通訊)
梁伯强　廣東梅縣　(1054)
(職)廣州百子路中山大學病理學研究院
湯兆豐　書年　(201)
(職)上海大馬路華英大藥房
張廷幹　子翔　廣東　(530)
(通訊)
張玗雯　心如　(706)
(通訊)
富文壽　彬侯　(745)
(通訊)上海靜安寺路一二〇五號
黃實存　(679)
(通訊)
楊俊階　少軒　山東諸城　(1268)
(通訊)
楊鶴慶　叔吉　(723)
(訊通)陝西西安開通巷六六號
齊清心　(380)
(通訊)
鄒邦元　叔慧　江西高安　(955)
(職)南京東南醫院
葛成慧　江蘇嘉定　(741)
(職)上海薩坡賽路一號尚賢堂婦孺醫院

褚民誼　　浙江吳興　　(969)

(職)上海辣斐德路中法工業學院

經利彬　　浙江上虞(2.生物)　　(260)

(職)北平北大學院生物系

趙燏黃　藥農　江蘇武進　　(1172)

(職)上海霞飛路八九九號化學研究所

趙楊步偉 Mrs. Chao, Y. R. 韻卿　安徽石埭　　(672)

(通訊)Chinese Educational Mission, 1360 Madison Street Northwest, Washington, D. C.,

趙以炳 Chao, eping 江西南昌　　(1241)

(通訊)5738 Drexel Ave., Chicags, Ill.

趙中天　罕言　　(1380)

(通訊)青島中山路一四三中和醫院

熊　佐　　廣東梅縣(2.細菌)　　(1021)

(通訊)

熊輔龍　省之　　(229)

(通訊)

聞亦齊　　湖北　　(1215)

(通訊)北平協和醫學校解剖科聞亦傅博士轉

劉劍秋　　江蘇下邳　　(919)

(職)上海莫利愛路一六號人和醫院

劉汝强　毅然　河北北平(2.體育)　　(469)

(通訊)

劉體志　　廣東番禺　　(451)

(通訊)

蔡無忌　　浙江紹縣(獸醫)　　(1047)

(職)上海博物院路商品檢驗局

鄭章成　　福建(2.公共衞生)　　(769)

(職)上海滬江大學

185

蔣育英 江蘇吳縣 (562)
(通訊)

魯德馨 進修 湖北天門 (765)
(職)山東濟南齊魯大學

樂文照 浙江鎮海 (1020)
(通訊)

鍾季襄 江西南昌 (167)
(職)南昌射步亭三二號季襄醫院

謝恩增 雋甫 河北天津 (257)
(通訊)北平崇文門內九四號

關頌韜 亦强 廣東番禺 (508)
(通訊)

嚴康倈 壽慈 江蘇上海 (534)
(通訊)上海

嚴智鍾 季約 (685)
(通訊)天津文昌宮西

龐斌 敦敏 (獸醫) (236)
(通訊)北平南長街北口路東

Dr. Mary N. Andrews, 安醫生 English (1387)
(通訊)Henry Lester Institute of Medical Research, Shanghai.

186

3. 農林股

丁 穎 君穎 廣東茂名(2.作物) (978)
(職)廣州中山大學農林科

卜 凱 J. Cossing Buck. 美國(2.農經濟) (1034)
(職)南京金陵大學農科

尤志邁 懷皋 江蘇吳縣(2.畜牧) (21)
(通訊)上海康腦脫路一六八號自由農場

王金吾 直卿 河南安陽(2.棉作) (368)
(職)杭州筧橋浙江大學農學院

王舜成 契華 (569)
(通訊)江蘇太倉王宅前街

王善佺 (242)
(職)北平北京大學農學院

江書祥 子荃 (587)
(職)四川成都東門外農業大學院

朱學鋤 新予 浙江蕭山(蠶絲) (1164)
(職)江蘇鎮江中國合衆蠶桑改良會蠶業講習所

吳 球 庶晨 (林) (577)
(職)浙江餘杭北鄉杭北林牧有限公司

李永振 鷺賓 江蘇南匯 (494)
(職)南通學院農科

李允彬 (128)
(通訊)

李汝祺 叉新 河北天津(畜牧傳種) (850)
(職)北平海甸燕京大學

李迪華 (327)
(通訊)

李沛文 質生 廣西蒼梧(果樹學) (1260)
(通訊) Cornell University, Ithaca, N. Y.

(87)

李寅恭 勰丞 安徽 (森林) (173)
(職)南京中央大學農學院
李繼侗 (林) (1121)
(職)南京金陵大學
李國楨 陝西渭南 (1391)
(職)陝西省建設廳
安立綏 甘肅 (1264)
(通訊)
沈鵬飛 卓寰 廣東番禺(森林) (761)
(職)南京教育部高等教育司
佘耀彤 季可 (森林) (547)
(通訊)四川成都刁子巷二一號
余森 森郎 (26)
(通訊)
余嵘 天御 (217)
(通訊)
何尚平 伊渠 福建閩侯(蠶桑) (824)
(職)上海亞爾培路蠶桑改良會
汪呈因 安徽桐城(2.農細菌學) (1347)
(通訊)
金邦正 仲藩 安徽 (森林) (12)
(職)北平上海銀行北平分行經理室
林文明 郁齋 福建興化(森林園藝) (556)
(職)福建興化聖路加醫院
邱培涵 養吾 浙江 (1298)
(通訊)上海霞飛路七四二號
周承鑰 Chou, Cheng Yao 江蘇(育種) (1262)
(通訊)104 Harvard Place, Ithaca, N. Y.

188

周榮條 Chou, Yung Tiao 湖南長沙 (1239)

(通訊)Box 6182 Univ. of Minn., Minneapolis Minn.

周 清 友山 (575)

(通訊)

胡憲生 江蘇無錫 (301)

(職)上海南車站大同大學

范師軾 (126)

(通訊)

唐啓宇 御仲 江蘇江都(2.鄉村教育) (610)

(職)南京紅紙廊中央政治學校

唐昌治 荎生 江蘇吳江(2.園藝) (214)

(通訊)

高維魏 孟徵 (573)

(通訊)杭州雙陳衕一號

高振華 京亞 河南洛陽(森林 2.氣象) (1336)

(職)南京交通部技術室

孫恩麐 (384)

(職)南通南門三元橋西南通學院農科

孫豫方 (410)

(通訊)

姚傳法 心齋 浙江 (森林 2.造紙) (606)

(通訊)

原頌周 廣東 (343)

(通訊)南京太平橋

陳燕山 江蘇上海(棉) (974)

(職)南京金陵大學

陳延翔 鳳文 江蘇 (347)

(通訊)鎮江城內水陸寺巷

189

陳嶸　宗一　浙江　(森林)　(215)
(職)南京金陵大學
陳儁　雋人　江蘇上海(2.植物病害)　(572)
(通訊)上海大東門外沙場街正興坊五號
陳鴦楨　家麟　江蘇江陰　(1321)
(通訊)南京中央大學農學院
陳宰均　孺平　浙江杭縣(家禽學)　(552)
(通訊)
陸費執　叔辰　浙江嘉興(園藝植物)　(386)
(職)江蘇省農鑛廳農業推廣委員會
郭守純　廣東　(224)
(職)上海膠州路九一號貧兒教養院
許振英　山東　(畜牧)　(1261)
(通訊)山東泰安福全街五號
淩道揚　廣東　(森林)　(142)
(職)南京東窪市陰陽營十一號
常宗會　安徽全椒　(1037)
(職)南京太平門外合衆蠶桑改良會製種場
張宗成　(787)
(通訊)上海跑馬廳張家浜八二號
張天才　範村　廣東　(135)
(職)杭州將軍路浙江省建設廳第四科
張通武　子旂　(608)
(職)南通大學農科
張心一　甘肅　(664)
(通訊)南京金陵大學或南京乾河沿陶園
張乃鳳　浙江吳興　(1263)
(通訊)

190

張世杓 葆靈 浙江覲縣 (1318)
(通訊)甯波江東東湖濟

黃 振 (56)
(通訊)

黃 晃 廣東台山 (900)
(通訊)

黃 植 枯桐 廣東梅縣(林) (979)
(通訊)廣州舊倉巷伍漢特醫院轉

區紹安 (林) (29)
(通訊)

馮 稅 梯霞 廣東番禺 (780)
(職)河北定縣城內中華平民教育促進會農業教育部

傅煥光 志章 江蘇太倉(森林) (1050)
(職)南京中山陵園辦公處

董金耀 浙江山陰 (792)
(通訊)

曾濟寬 (216)
(通訊)

溫文光 瀚周 廣東台山 (441)
(通訊)

賀 康 亞賓 江蘇無錫(蠶桑) (726)
(通訊)

楊炳勛 浙江 (743)
(職)上海海甯路南高壽里二九三三號速記學校

葉元鼎 安徽 (668)
(職)上海博物院路十五號上海商品檢驗局

葉雅各 雅谷 廣東番禺(森林) (1033)
(職)南京金陵大學

葛敬中　運成　　(蠶桑)　(567)
(職)鎮江中國合衆蠶桑改良會蠶桑製種場

葛敬應　夢魚　浙江嘉興(園藝2.製茶)　(1212)
(職)青島市農林事務所

董時進　　四川墊江(經濟)　(750)
(職)北平大學農學院

虞振鏞　謹庸　浙江　(157)
(通訊)

熊正瑾　洛生　江西南昌　(590)
(通訊)江西南昌岡上街

趙琴風　仿琴　四川巴縣　(1091)
(通訊)

趙　武　　江蘇崑山　(1343)
(通訊)上海郵局信箱一二〇二號

廖崇眞　　　(594)
(職)廣州廣東建設廳農林局

魯佩璋　白純　　(701)
(通訊)

劉榮基　　　(903)
(通訊)

劉承霖　慰農　　(78)
(通訊)

劉崇樂　覺民　福建閩侯(2.昆蟲)　(857)
(通訊)北平西觀音寺三三號施宅

鄧植儀　槐庭　廣東東莞(土壤)　(650)
(職)廣州廣東建設廳農林局土壤調查所

錢天鶴　安濤　浙江杭縣(蠶桑)　(27)
(職)南京中央研究院自然歷史博物館

192

戴芳瀾　觀亭　(48)

(職)南京金陵大學農科

鄺嵩齡　廣東香山　(901)

(職)廣州中山大學

羅德民 Waetter C. Lowdermilk 美國(森林2.人文地理)　(1032)

(通訊)

顧　鍙　青虹　江蘇無錫(蠶桑)　(1035)

(職)南京金陵大學

顧　復　震吉　(林)　(165)

(通訊)

193

4. 心理股

王長平　鴻猷　山東　(1271)
(通訊)北平西直門後桃園二五號
艾 偉　險舟　湖北　(2.統計)　(1029)
(職)出國
何運暄　潄石　湖北　(896)
(通訊)
唐 鉞　擘黃　福建福州　(28)
(通訊)北平大方家胡同五七號
孫國華　小孟　山東濰縣(2.動物學)　(1156)
(職)北平清華大學心理學系
陳劍脩　江西　(1062)
(職)
陳懿祝　福建海澄　(1104)
(通訊)
陸志韋　(794)
(職)北平海甸燕京大學
郭任遠　廣東潮陽(2.教育)　(496)
(職)
張耀翔　湖北漢口(2.教育)　(528)
(通訊)
楊希東　(370)
(通訊)
趙 畸　太侔　山東　(2.文學)　(985)
(職)青島大學或北平宣外潘家河沿七一號
劉紹禹　四川　(893)
(職)四川成都大學
劉廷芳　亶生　(317)
(職)北平燕京大學

194

III. 工程科學組

1. 土木股(附建築)

丁人錕　西崙　江蘇吳縣(2.水力學)　(548)
(職)杭州浙江大學工學院

丁燮和　江蘇泰興　(1270)
(通訊)北平芳嘉園三五號

尤乙照　芸閣　江蘇無錫　(114)
(通訊)北平西城南太常寺街七號

尤寅照　敬清　江蘇無錫　(782)
(通訊)天津義界六馬路八號

方頤樸　(582)
(通訊)北平宣武門外米市胡同三四號

王志遠　(1127)
(通訊)

王元康　江蘇泰縣　(945)
(通訊)

王　度　(1130)
(通訊)

王之翰　君幹　直隸豐潤　(916)
(通訊)

王　賡　受慶　浙江　(軍事)　(280)
(通訊)

朱　復　啓明　(413)
(職)天津英租界菜市對面維多利亞大院十三號福中總公司

朱　彬　　　　　廣東南海(建築)　　(500)
(通訊)

朱漢年　　　　　　(290)
(通訊)

朱德和　漢儔　江蘇上海　　(1371)
(通訊)上海大南門內喬家柵二七號

江元仁　　　　　福建閩侯　　(904)
(通訊)

李　卓　兆焯　廣東開平　　(667)
(職)廣州清海路西三巷裕泰建築公司

李　育　涵三　江西上饒　　(910)
(職)杭州方谷園浙江省公路局

李屋身　孟博　浙江餘姚　　(4)
(通訊)上海福煦路成和邨六〇五號

李書田　耕硯　河北昌黎(2.水利工程)　　(890)
(通訊)天津英租界三三號永和里一四號

李　協　儀祉　陝西　(水利工程)　　(133)
(職)陝西省水利局

李　昶　倜夫　湖南長沙　　(458)
(職)天津法租界大陸大樓中國大陸商業公司

李　儼　樂知　　(2.算學)　　(147)
(職)廣東韶州弓翦街粵漢鉄路株韶段韶樂總段工程處

李兆卓　　　　　　(362)
(通訊)

沈在善　百先　浙江吳興(2.水利工程)　　(905)
(通訊)南京導淮委員會或蘇州盛家帶二號

沈　怡　君怡　浙江　　(1178)
(職)上海市工務局或上海亞爾培路亞爾培坊二六號

沈 劭 福建 (855)
(通訊)
沈慕曾 賓顏 江蘇 (369)
(通訊)
沈家楨 纘周 江蘇南通(建築) (727)
(通訊)
宋希尙 達庵 浙江嵊縣 (1118)
(職)南京沈舉人巷揚子江水道整理委員會
汪胡楨 幹夫 浙江嘉興(2.水利工程) (776)
(職)南京復成橋導淮委員會
汪禧成 意成 江蘇無錫 (498)
(職)
汪卓然 (247)
(通訊)
杜鎮遠 四川江北 (591)
(職)杭州杭江鐵路籌備處
金 濤 旬卿 江蘇 (561)
(通訊)江蘇蘇州燕家巷
林逸民 廣東新會 (1013)
(通訊)
周明衡 (252)
(通訊)
周彥邦 河南南陽 (1338)
(職)福建漳州漳龍區公路分局
周 輪 愼餘 (555)
(通訊)蘇州平橋直街七六號
周鍾岐 (305)
(通訊)

胡竟銘 安徽滁縣 (1245)
(通訊)安徽滁縣東門
胡光燾 寄羣 四川廣安 (889)
(通訊)北平西城北溝沿四一號
胡步川 竹銘 浙江臨海(水利工程) (1060)
(職)浙江黃岩西江閘工程處
胡品元 香泉 江蘇江陰(水利工程) (1342)
(職)南京鐵湯池全國經濟委員會工程司
茅以昇 唐臣 江蘇鎮江 (202)
(通訊)天津英租界十號路福兆里五號
洪紳 福建 (874)
(職)
柳克準 叔平 湖南長沙 (720)
(職)長沙湖南大學
范永增 藹春 江蘇上海 (208)
(通訊)上海徐家匯孝友里四衖八八號
查德利 Herbert Chatley, England (825)
(職)上海浚浦工程局
馬育騏 (132)
(通訊)南京乾河沿三六號
唐文悌 瑞庭 江蘇崑山 (599)
(通訊)上海廣東路一號公和洋行轉交
唐恩良 蜀眉 山東益都 (1181)
(通訊)青島觀象一路一號
孫寶墀 頌丹 江蘇江陰 (448)
(職)青島膠濟鐵路管理局
孫煜方 伯羣 安徽壽縣 (137)
(通訊)上海海格路六三二號

徐乃仁 南騶 江蘇震澤 (199)
(職)杭州浙江大學工學院
徐世大 行健 浙江紹興 (460)
(職)天津義租界華北水利委員會
涂羽卿 湖北 (617)
(職)上海滬江大學
陳蘭生 (鐵道管理) (195)
(通訊)
陳中正 思謙 河南商城 (504)
(通訊)
陳裕華 浙江鄞縣 (1265)
(通訊)
陳體仁 (302)
(職)
陳良士 廣東東莞 (585)
(通訊)
陳祖耀 日如 (360)
(通訊)
陳伯權 廣東台山 (481)
(通訊)
陳德芬 (356)
(通訊)
淩 炎 劍存 廣東番禺(建築) (1201)
(職)廣州市錦榮街廣東測地學會
淩鴻勛 竹銘 廣東 (304)
(職)廣東韶州粵漢路韶樂段總工程處
陸元昌 沅卿 江蘇武進 (155)
(通訊)

陸鳳書 漱芳 江蘇無錫 (71)
(職)武昌武漢大學
許心武 介忱 江蘇儀鎮(水利工程) (975)
(職)河南大學
許守忠 文蓀 浙江嘉興 (992)
(職)青島市工務局
郭美瀛 (791)
(職)上海濬浦總局
莊秉權 江蘇上海 (941)
(通訊)
莊 俊 達卿 江蘇上海(建築) (1067)
(通訊)
盛紹章 允丞 (129)
(職)哈爾濱東省鐵路阿什河站
梁思成 廣東新會(1.建築2.市政) (1281)
(通訊)
張丙昌 午中 陝西富平 (1390)
(通訊)陝西西安西倉內五十五號
張雲青 謨實 浙江甯波 (777)
(職)杭州浙江大學工學院
張潤田 倬甫 河北灤縣 (888)
(通訊)
張澤熙 豫生 江西鄱陽 (710)
(通訊)北平清華大學土木工程系
張 昇 以旭 廣東汕頭 (473)
(通訊)
張自立 若猷 湖南安化(鐵路建築) (465)
(通訊)

張紹鎬 (434)

(通訊)

張善琛 獻之 湖北武昌(鐵路管理) (576)

(通訊)

張海平 江蘇高郵 (622)

(通訊)

彭祿炳 (592)

(通訊)雲南省城華洋義賑會轉

彭濟羣 志雲 遼甯鐵嶺(1.建築2.數學) (680)

(通訊)

黄家齊 定余 廣東惠陽 (327)

(職)汕頭潮汕鐵路局

黄育賢 江西崇仁(1.水利2.道路) (1223)

(通訊)

黄壽恆 (290)

(職)唐山大學

黄壽頤 復憲 (431)

(通訊)

項志達 葵璋 浙江杭縣 (1327)

(職)鎮江京滬鐵路工務處

童 雋 遼甯瀋陽 (1279)

(通訊)

湯震龍 悟庵 湖北蘄水 (636)

(通訊)上海福履理路一四八號

須 愷 君悌 江蘇 (753)

(職)南京復成橋導淮委員會

楊 毅 莘臣 浙江吳興(鐵路工程) (120)

(職)南京鐵道部技術標準委員會

楊錫宗 （建築） (315)
（通訊）
過養默 江蘇無錫 (358)
（職）上海江西路六十號東南建築公司
趙世暄 幼梅 (409)
（職）南京揚子江水道整理委員會
裘燮鈞 星遠 (328)
（職）上海市工務局
翟鶴程 H. C. Chai, 河北永淸 (1351)
（通訊）135 Blair Street, Ithaca, N. Y., U, S. A.
裴益祥 季浩 安徽壽縣 (491)
（職）
劉敦楨 士能 湖南新寧（建築） (1169)
（職）北平中央公園內中國營造學社
劉晉鈺 祖棨 福建閩侯（建築） (811)
（通訊）上海薛華立路一〇三弄內二一號
劉學灤 熙泉 (740)
（通訊）
劉頤 利川 河北天津（2.鐵路工程） (508)
（通訊）
劉寰偉 廣東 (10)
（通訊）眞茹車站對面四才閣十五號
劉夢錫 陝西 (228)
（通訊）南京中山陵園郵局轉陣亡將士公墓會
蔡方蔭 孟劬 江西南昌 (1278)
（職）北平淸華大學
鄭華 輔華 福建 (77)
（職）南京下關首都輪渡工程處

鄭肇經　權伯　江蘇泰興　(1203)
(通訊)上海廿世東路三德坊五號

廖慰慈　復生　福建閩侯　(23)
(通訊)福建福州城內吉庇巷二一號

錢宗賢　海如　浙江(理工科)　(1064)
(通訊)浙江平湖荷花池頭

錢寶琮　琢如　浙江嘉興(2.算學)　(948)
(職)杭州浙江大學文理學院

盧樹森　奉璋　浙江桐鄉(建築)　(1168)
(職)南京中央大學工學院建築科

盧思緒　孝侯　江蘇江寧　(1326)
(職)南京中央大學工學院

盧景泰　(70)
(通訊)

薛卓斌　(344)
(職)上海濬浦總局

薛次莘　惺仲　(建築)　(247)
(職)上海市工務局

薛繩祖　爾宜　浙江杭縣(建築)　(292)
(通訊)上海同孚路三一五弄二九號

謝學瀛　吉士　江蘇無錫　(1276)
(職)青島膠濟路局工務局

魏元光　(549)
(職)天津河北工業學院

關富權　杭州　(1256)
(通訊)

蕭慶雲　江西泰和(市政工程)　(1214)
(職)上海市工務局

聶光堉Nieh, Kanyo 湖南衡山(1.鐵路工程)(2.實業工程) (1254)

(通訊)301 Bryang Ave. Ithaca, N. Y.

譚　眞 (346)

(通訊)

譚鐵肩 (178)

(通訊)

羅　英　懷伯　江西 (38)

(職)

羅　河　潤九　江蘇溧水 (1314)

(職)鎮江京滬鐵路駐鎮工程處

蘇紀忍　伯安　山西 (532)

(通訊)山西猗氏嵋陽鎮

蘇　鑑　廣西 (122)

(通訊)

嚴宏淮　仲絜　安徽含山 (493)

(職)青島市工程事務所

顧世楫　濟之　江蘇吳縣 (296)

(職)杭州閘口之江大學

顧宜孫　晴洲　江蘇南匯 (730)

(職)河北唐山交通大學

2. 機工股(附造船)

方培壽　蔭孫　江西南昌　(393)

(通訊)北平南灣子官豆腐坊一號

王　助　禹朋　河北南宮(飛機)　(965)

(通訊)上海亞爾培路逸安里一號

王成志　學農　(203)

(通訊)

王孝華　安徽歙縣　(1316)

(通訊)

王孝豐　穀男　(1.飛機2.海軍)　(200)

(通訊)

王國樹　叔培　(586)

(通訊)四川成都少城順河街

司徒錫　震東　廣東　(471)

(通訊)

朱樹馨　木君　(673)

(通訊)湖北孝感宋河高洪泰轉

朱世明　季煌　湖南湘鄉　(869)

(通訊)

朱起蟄　浙江杭縣(造船)　(390)

(職)南京鐵道部建設司

朱家炘　季明　(91)

(通訊)

江超西　其恭　(108)

(通訊)上海新閘路鴻慶里B一三二號

汪泰基　養餘　安徽旌德(造紙)　(550)

(通訊)北平護國街蔴花胡同五號

李得庸 (329)

(職)漢口法租界德託美領事街二十三號得庸公司

李世瓊 拔峩 (1122)

(通訊)上海福履理路一三〇弄三號

李祥亭 以卜 河北寧晉 (866)

(通訊)河北寧晉縣東汪鎮

李家驥 安徽合肥 (906)

(通訊)上海愛而近路三五號

李右人 幼誠 江蘇無錫 (898)

(通訊)

李維國 憤泉 湖南彬縣 (180)

(通訊)

李蔭芬 雪初 浙江慈溪 (474)

(職)青島工務局自來水廠

李蔚芬 炳英 (722)

(通訊)

沈宜甲 安徽 (2.採鑛) (1088)

(通訊)

沈艾 保艾 福建 (9)

(通訊)

沈祖衞 遽士 (飛機) (707)

(通訊)

何壽田 季威 廣東大埔 (839)

(通訊)

何孝沅 筱秋 (115)

(通訊)

阮尙介 介藩 江蘇奉賢 (423)

(通訊)

杜光祖 江蘇無錫 (455)
(通訊)上海西蒲石路平安里一三號

余謙六 騫陸 江蘇丹徒 (786)
(通訊)北平南長街頭條錢寓轉

余靜安 靜盦 (623)
(通訊)

邢契莘 (造船) (84)
(通訊)

邱秉剛 健中 (697)
(通訊)

金秉時 潤農 浙江海寧(造船) (416)
(職)南京中央大學工學院

林鳳歧 江蘇無錫 (418)
(職)青島四方機廠

林祖光 廣東 (478)
(通訊)

林全誠 (517)
(職)福建廈門自來水公司

林 恂 四川富順(2.數學) (1236)
(通訊)四川成都橫通順街十六號

周春台 (鐵路管理) (402)
(通訊)

周 仁 子競 江蘇南京 (13)
(職)上海霞飛路八九九號工程研究所

周明政 浙江甯波 (479)
(通訊)

周德鴻 伯彬 (405)
(通訊)四川重慶玉帶街馬家巷

宓 齊 遊存 (684)

(通訊)

茅以新 江蘇 (1056)

(職)杭州裏西湖三號杭江鐵路局機務股

袁丕烈 江蘇吳興 (946)

(職)上海九江路二二號新通公司

徐燕謀 祖善 (造船) (107)

(通訊)

韋以黻 作民 浙江 (51)

(職)南京交通部

姚律白 江蘇鹽城 (796)

(通訊)

夏彥儒 四川 (907)

(通訊)

時照澤 湖北 (602)

(通訊)

殷源之 (58)

(職)上海霞飛路八九九號工程研究所

陳明壽 受明 江蘇吳縣 (689)

(通訊)

陳福習 麥孫 福建 (54)

(通訊)

陳廣沅 贊清 江蘇江都 (868)

(職)濟南大槐樹津浦鐵路局機廠

郭承恩 伯良 廣東潮州 (401)

(職)上海中央造幣廠

郭 霖 澤五 湖北當陽(2.造船) (1176)

(職)武昌武漢大學

郭承志 叔良 廣東潮州(2.攝影) (989)
(職)上海南京路中華照相館
筲遠輪 經甫 江蘇鎮江 (859)
(職)北平清華大學土木工程系
許 坤 (235)
(通訊)
張名藝 (112)
(職)青島四方機廠
張可治 (240)
(職)南京實業部
張延祥 (775)
(職)南京首都電燈廠
張本茂 健鶴 (313)
(通訊)
張瑞書 (飛機) (268)
(通訊)
曹勵恆 廉恩 江蘇寶山(2.人類學) (1349)
(通訊)上海郵箱四一九號
黃伯樵 江蘇太倉(2.工業管理) (1177)
(職)上海市工用局或上海環龍路九八號
黃景康 廣東順德 (912)
(通訊)
黃元熾 (367)
(通訊)江西南昌甲種工業學校
黃壽仁 (766)
(通訊)
程干雲 松生 (588)
(通訊)

程志頤　覺民　浙江紹興(1.鋼鐵2.工廠管理)　(503)
(通訊)上海海格路大勝胡同129弄四十號

馮樹銘　浙江海鹽　(947)
(通訊)

馮　偉　(24)
(通訊)

曾詒經　稔畬　福建閩侯(專航空發動機)　(254)
(通訊)上海亞爾培路五百號逸安里十號

傅德同　濟宏　江蘇江甯(1.海軍輪機2.無線電)　(960)
(通訊)

傅爾攽　冰芝　(造船)　(294)
(職)天津塘沽永利製鹼公司

華鳳翔　毅如　河北天津(造船)　(942)
(職)河北唐山交通大學

賀懋慶　勉吾　江蘇丹徒(造船)　(333)
(通訊)

鈕因祥　瑞人　(400)
(通訊)哈爾濱南岡龍子胡同四號

董鴻謙　(643)
(通訊)

楊雨生　安徽石埭　(1149)
(職)青島膠濟鐵路管理局庶務課

楊　銓　杏佛　江西　(2.經濟)　(15)
(職)南京中央研究院總辦事處或上海中央研究院

趙國棟　松生　(92)
(通訊)

劉鞠可　(25)
(通訊)

劉仙洲　　河北定縣　(1331)
(通訊)北平西長安街大六部口三二號啓明眼科醫院轉

劉承芳　仲芬　(725)
(通訊)

蔡經賢　諒友　浙江德淸(機織)　(818)
(職)杭州蒲場巷虎林絲織公司

鄭允衷　叔懷　(596)
(職)廣西南甯建設廳

鄭世夔　虞生　安徽　(920)
(通訊)

鮑國寶　　廣東香山　(457)
(職)南京建設委員會或首都電燈廠

錢昌祚　莘覺　浙江　(飛機)　(742
(通訊)

應尙才　　浙江奉化　(470)
(通訊)

關漢光　　(308)
(通訊)上海仁記路25號六樓509號兆福公司

嚴迪恂　　(194)
(通訊)

龍裔禧　融笙　廣東連縣　(763)
(通訊)

羅慶蕃　椒衍　浙江餘姚　(884)
(通訊)

顧毓瑔　　(2.工業管理)　(1250)
(職)南京實業部技術廳

顧　振　湛然　江蘇　(76)
(通訊)上海外灘十二號開灤煤礦公司

顧穀成 (通訊) 職西 江蘇無錫 (544)

3. 電工股

文澄 藻青 (531)
(通訊)四川成都東桂街22號或四川省教育廳

方子衞 浙江寧波 (779)
(通訊)上海法租界萬宜坊七一號

王魯新 江蘇松江 (589)
(通訊)上海九江路二二號新通公司

王翰辰 董豪 河北定縣 (1026)
(通訊)

王翰臣 (350)
(通訊)

王崇植 受培 江蘇常熟(無線電) (1213)
(通訊)南京市政府社會局

王鴻卓 (73)
(職)北平電燈廠

王愼名 Sherman R. Wang. 餘齋 河北北平 (1395)
(通訊) 1360 Madison St. N. W. Washington, D. C.

朱其清 江蘇上海(無線電學) (844)
(通訊)上海尙文門外學潔里內三號

朱物華 江蘇江都 (1075)
(職)

沈良驊 志開 (354)
(職)上海勞勃生路一四零號安迪生電器公司或上海福煦路模範村七號

李英標 俠成 四川巴中 (1105)
(通訊)

李熙謀 振吾 浙江嘉善(電力工程) (326)
(職)杭州浙江大學工學院

吳維嶽　　湖南平江　(459)
(職)上海霞飛路八九九號物理研究所
吳毓讓　君立　福建閩侯　(865)
(通訊)上海海防路六一〇號
金劍清　　浙江餘姚　(1190)
(職)
金鼎新　大剑　吉林　(653)
(通訊)北平王府井大街甜水井二號
金賢藻　圖南　浙江嘉興　(1392)
(通訊)南京綱巾市 62 號
周　琦　季舫　江蘇宜興　(524)
(職)上海漢口路七號益中機器公司
周茲緒　在文　貴州安順　(612)
(通訊)
易鼎新　修吟　(445)
(職)杭州浙江大學工學院
林　煖　樹春　(391)
(職)上海勞勃生路安迪生公司
胡光麃　叔潛　四川廣安　(192)
(職)天津法租界馬家口中國無線電業有限公司
袁祥和　　河北唐山(綿織)　(873)
(職)天津英租界敦橋道華蔭西里三百號華光貿易公司或河北唐山南稻地大昌恆
唐鳴皋　建章　四川重慶　(153)
(通訊)四川重慶江北洗布塘
唐在均　孟平　(744)
(通訊)
高　華　君實　江蘇吳縣　(454)
(通訊)

孫繼丁　丙炎　(102)

(職)鄭州隴海鐵路局機務處

徐尙　志鄉　江蘇　(131)

(通訊)南京鼓樓二條巷二三號

徐恩曾　可均　浙江吳興　(994)

(職)南京中央黨部

徐繼文　叉連　(176)

(通訊)

徐學禹　浙江紹興　(1381)

(職)上海江西路西門子電廠

(通訊)上海金神父路金谷村五八號

翁爲　存齋　江蘇武進　(804)

(職)江蘇浦口津浦鐵路電汽廠

倪尙達　江蘇上海(無線電)　(858)

(職)南京中央大學物理系

陳延炆　笛孫　(795)

(通訊)廣州市都府街十號或青島膠濟鐵路局

陳茂康　四川　(735)

(通訊)上海愚園路一八四衖一號

陳炳基　一公　(196)

(通訊)

陳長源　(179)

(通訊)

陸法曾　富如　江蘇吳縣　(284)

(通訊)南京沈舉人巷六號

郭克悌　河南洛陽　(961)

(職)瀋陽大西邊門外大昌實業公司經理室

許厚鈺　式度　安徽蕪湖　(854)

(通訊)上海呂班路萬宜坊五五號

許應期 (1167)
(職)國立中央大學工學院
許先甲 肇南 貴州 (237)
(通訊)
曹仲淵 浙江温嶺(無線電) (995)
(通訊)上海金神父路金谷村二八號
曹鳳山 江蘇江都 (944)
(職)杭州浙江大學工學院
梅貽琦 月涵 (509)
(職)北平清華大學
梁乃鑑 希甫 廣東南海 (477)
(通訊)
梁 步 (202)
(通訊)
梁引年 廣西桂林 (456)
(通訊)
莊 启 (363)
(職)常州建設局
張廷金 貢九 江蘇無錫(無線電) (660)
(通訊)上海徐家匯路孝友里十八號
張蘭閣 河北鉅鹿 (520)
(通訊)
張承緒 (774)
(通訊)上海南翔毛家灣大街張和記
張寶桐 問渠 江蘇吳縣 (682)
(職)蘇州觀前街電氣廠事務所
張維正 瀋陽 (電磁學) (1366)
(通訊)

康清桂 湖南衡山 (1335)

(職)南京山西路國立編譯館

彭鍾琯 虞笛 (527)

(職)四川成都學道街工科大學院

黃篤修 Huang T. S. 廣東嘉應 (450)

(通訊)509 Huntington Ave., Boston, Mass;

黃 煇 Huang, Hui 福建 (2.水力工程) (1255)

(通訊)c/o Mr. Y. T. Ku, Sibley College, Cornell Univ. Ithaca, N. Y.

程孝剛 叔時 江西 (81)

(通訊)

温嗣康 少鶴 (371)

(通訊)四川重慶城內柑子壩金陵温寓

曾德鈺 金璧 (539)

(職)四川重慶曾家岩工業中學校

曾昭權 湖南 (151)

(通訊)長沙湖南大學

單毓斌 允工 江蘇泰縣 (713)

(通訊)泰縣蕭家巷或上海靜安寺路靜安別墅109號

楊培芳 芷芬 (407)

(通訊)天津英租界五八號路三二號

楊孝述 允中 江蘇松江(2.物理) (1)

(職)上海亞爾培五三三號中國科學社

楊肇燫 季璠 四川潼南(2.物理) (476)

(職)上海霞飛路八九九號物理研究所

葉建柏 新甫 (172)

(通訊)

葉建梅 和軒 (389)

(通訊)

裘維裕　次豐　江蘇無錫 2.物理)　(248)
(職)上海徐家匯交通大學
褚鳳章　漢雛　(295)
(通訊)
趙訪熊 Chao, Robert F. H. (江蘇常州)(數學)　(1242)
(通訊) Tech. Do me. Cambridge, Mass,
趙　訒　壽岡　(197)
(通訊)
熊正理　雨生　江西南昌(2.物理)　(79)
(職)長沙湖南大學
歐陽祖綬　穀貽　(415)
(通訊)江西南昌干家後巷
劉其淑　(398)
(職)上海江西路二二號中國電氣公司
劉錫祺　(348)
(職)上海漢口路七號益中機器公司
劉崇佺　福建福州　(822)
(通訊)
劉孝懃　(652)
(通訊)
劉錫瑛　(342)
(通訊)
鄭禮明　朗昭　福建閩侯　(1084)
(職)河南豐樂鎮六河溝煤礦
鄧福培　栽岑　江蘇無錫　(658)
(通訊)上海靜安寺滄洲別墅四號
黎智長　長卿　河南正陽　(959)
(通訊)

218

潘先正 覺粹 (396)

(通訊)

潘銘新 (325)

(職)杭州浙江省電氣局

樓兆緜 浙江 (1361)

(通訊)

錢國鈕 (148)

(通訊)

盧文湘 (472)

(通訊)

薛紹清 守澄 江蘇 (353)

(職)杭州浙江大學工學院

蕭冠英 菊魂 (624)

(通訊)

鍾兆琳 琅書 浙江德清 (849)

(職)上海徐家匯交通大學

謝作楷 廣東新會(2.礦務工程) (1015)

(職)Kwangtung Electric Suppy Co. Ltd. Canton.

魏樹勛 岳東 (351)

(通訊)北平後門定府大街後大新開路二號魏寓

魏菊峯 江蘇上海(2.機械) (1367)

(通訊)青島廣西路十九號

薩本棟 亞棟 福建閩侯 (913)

(職)北平清華大學

譚友岑 質維 浙江麗水 (1003)

(通訊)常州城內磨盤橋新屋二樓

顧維精 心一 江蘇無錫 (105)

(通訊)無錫石塘灣久徵堂內

4. 鑛冶股

王正黼　子文　浙江　(345)
(職)

王　謨　求定　(97)
(職)上海郵政匯業總局

王錫藩　(231)
(通訊)

王育瓚　(414)
(通訊)

石心圃　集齋　河南濟源　(463)
(通訊)河南濟源添漿鎮

任殿元　式三　河南南陽(採鑛)　(484)
(職)河南焦作福中鑛務學校

朱翽聲　弼成　廣東興寧(採鑛)　(717)
(通訊)廣州市上西關高第坊內福綸西街十四號

李待琛　白芹　(1125)
(職)南京軍政部兵工廠

李國欽　炳麟　(278)
(通訊)

李葆和　河聲　河南濟源　(483)
(通訊)

李輝光　璧文　(181)
(通訊)

李餘慶　善堂　河南襄城(2.應用地質)　(488)
(通訊)

李　珠　子明　(583)
(通訊)天津鄉大畢莊

阮寶江 (46)
(通訊)

吳 鑛 靄宸 (288)
(通訊)

吳維基 (139)
(通訊)

宋國祥 福建興化 (598)
(通訊)

林則衣 (121)
(通訊)

林士模 (334)
(通訊)

周志宏 偉民 江蘇江都 (928)
(通訊)揚州大佛庵巷

周則岳 (338)
(通訊)湖南益陽三里橋周正泰轉交

周 烈 繼武 (525)
(通訊)四川成都少城東門街一〇三號

周 敏 (513)
(通訊)

周文燮 仲理 江蘇上海 (490)
(通訊)

周開基 子建 (158)
(通訊)

胡汝麟 石靑 河南 (783)
(通訊)

胡庶華 春藻 湖南攸縣 (1185)
(職)湖南大學

胡博淵　維傾　江蘇武進　(639)
(職)南京實業部鑛業司
胡嗣鴻　濟平　(232)
(通訊)
洪彥亮　瞿士　浙江瑞安　(692)
(訊通)浙江温州瑞安林宅巷
姜榮光　藜輝　(113)
(通訊)
馬恆矗　戴之　河南安陽　(464)
(職)河南焦作福中鑛務大學
唐之蕭　敬亭　山西平定　(581)
(職)山西太原民生煉鋼機器廠
孫昌克　劭勤　(44)
(通訊)
孫延中　景稚　河南商邱　(485)
(通訊)河南焦作工學院採鑛冶金科
常濟安　露庵　(117)
(通訊)
梁培穎　(186)
(通訊)
陳家騏　康六　(360)
(通訊)
陶文端　子琛　(435)
(職)四川重慶川東聯合會縣立甲種工業學校
陶鳴燾　繼魯　(317)
(通訊)
許本純　粹士　安徽歙縣(2.地質)　(1280)
(通訊)

曹誠克　勝之　安徽績溪　(361)
(通訊)北平鑛冶學會
張廷玉　連成　(579)
(通訊)
張可光　正平　江蘇江寧(2.地質)　(967)
(通訊)
張廣輿　仲魯　河南鞏縣　(462)
(職)河南焦作福中鑛務大學
張軼歐　翼後　江蘇無錫　(758)
(職)南京實業部
張清漣　文濤　河南南陽　(487)
(通訊)
張士瀛　海樵　(264)
(通訊)
陸志鴻　筱海　浙江嘉興　(1072)
(職)南京中央大學工學院
黄有書　仲通　(336)
(通訊)
黄漢和　(1107)
(職)南京鐵道部
黄昌穀　詒孫　(291)
(通訊)
黄金濤　(439)
(通訊)
程宗陽　(198)
(職)蚌埠淮南煤鑛局
程義法　(110)
(通訊)

馮景蘭　懷西　河南沘縣(2.地質)　(486)
(職)天津西沽北洋大學
曾應聯　(786)
(通訊)
曾魯光　漁生　(127)
(通訊)
勞兆丁　(168)
(通訊)
董　常　次平　(651)
(職)山東坊子魯大公司煉炭所
熊說岩　築雲　(681)
(通訊)
趙元貞　(253)
(職)甘肅教育廳
劉　澗　(164)
(通訊)
劉寶濂　楚材　陝西西安　(116)
(職)南京兵工署內兵工研究委員會
黎鴻業　(246)
(通訊)
蔣尊鄴　(276)
(通訊)杭州東坡路三二號
蔡　翔　怡亭　(95)
(通訊)青島黃縣路新五號
蔡　雄　聲白　(88)
(職)上海美亞織綢廠
盧　伯　平長　江蘇泰縣　(875)
(通訊)浙江溫州道司前省立第十中學

盧其駿　　捷之　(238)
　　(職)

錢家翰　　浩如　(67)
　　(通訊)

諶　立　　湛溪　　貴州織金　(66)
　　(通訊)北平拴馬樁苦水井

薛桂輪　　志伊　(40)
　　(通訊)

鍾伯謙　　奚若　(82)
　　(通訊)

鄺壽堃　　　　廣東　(899)
　　(職)北平門頭溝煤鑛公司

羅萬年　　祝民　(721)
　　(通訊)

嚴　莊　　敬齋　(57)
　　(職)南京實業部

嚴恩棫　　治之　(429)
　　(通訊)

5. 染織股

王榮吉 浙江杭縣 (510)
(職)上海兆豐路錦雲綢廠
朱光燾 謀先 浙江杭縣 (819)
(通訊)杭州板橋路十一號
周連錫 百朋 (223)
(通訊)
周延鼎 君謀 浙江吳興 (377)
(通訊)杭州西大街四九號
韋憲章 (189)
(通訊)
高介清 惜冰 (746)
(通訊)
陳華甲 孟孚 (647)
(通訊)蘇州城北顏家巷二六號
陳文沛 浙江 (584)
(通訊)
張文潛 濬思 (754)
(職)南通南門外大生副廠
張 佶 枀山 河北昌黎 (1282)
(通訊)
許炳堃 潛夫 浙江德清 (430)
(通訊)南京綢巾市十號世界學會
劉北禾 (365)
(職)南京江蘇教育經費管理處
劉煒明 耀辰 河北文安 (570)
(通訊)天津西勝芳鎮南榮祥轉交安屯里積善堂

IV 社會科學組

1. 教育股

王文培　仲達　(193)
　(通訊)
水　梓　楚琴　(659)
　(通訊)
朱　經　經農　江蘇寶山(2.歷史)　(306)
　(職)湖南省教育廳
朱斌魁　君毅　浙江江山　(800)
　(職)南京立法院編譯處
朱少屏　江蘇上海　(37)
　(職)上海卡德路寰球中國學生會
汪懋祖　典存　江蘇吳縣(2.心理)　(412)
　(通訊)蘇州中學
李應南　次薰　(1124)
　(職)廣州中山大學附屬中學
李紹昌　景周　(2.社會)　(92)
　(通訊)
林和民　有任　(90)
　(通訊)
金曾澄　湘帆　廣東番禺　(729)
　(通訊)廣州高第街叉六十四號之六
周鼎培　舉鈞　廣東高要　(1196)
　(職)廣州中山大學
孟憲承　江蘇武進　(578)
　(職)浙江大學文理學院教育系

85

俞慶棠　鳳岐　江蘇無錫　(1325)

(通訊)無錫江蘇省立教育學院

袁同禮　守和　河北　(目錄學)　(891)

(職)北平中海北平圖書館

高君珊　福建　(1086)

(通訊)上海膠州路合豐里1027號

高　陽　踐四　江蘇無錫　(130)

(職)江蘇無錫中央大學民衆教育院

韋　愨　捧丹　廣東　(141)

(通訊)上海愚園路九八三衖十七號

凌　冰　濟東　(314)

(職)古巴公使

孫貴定　江蘇無錫　(1099)

(職)福建廈門大學

陳家麟　紱卿　(702)

(通訊)

陳宗嶽　(433)

(通訊)

陳　容　主素　江蘇松江　(331)

(通訊)

陳鶴琴　浙江上虞　(632)

(通訊)上海匯山路四八號

陸士寅　敬夫　江蘇武進　(408)

(職)南京外交部

推　士　G. R. Twiss　美國　(物理)　(728)

(通訊)2595 Summiel St., Columbus, Ohis,

陶知行　江蘇　(339)

(通訊)

許壽棠　　浙江　(519)

(職)南京成賢街中央研究院

許崇清　(790)

(通訊)廣州市文德東路五號

郭秉文　鴻聲　江蘇上海　(337)

(通訊)

張元愷　舜舉　山西　(895)

(職)山西汾陽銘義中學校

張昭漢　默君　湖南　(649)

(通訊)南京立法院

程其保　稚秋　(1207)

(通訊)南京成賢街安樂里二號赴歐洲

程時煃　柏廬　江西　(655)

(職)福建教育廳

姬振鐸　金聲　遼寧開原　(1304)

(通訊)北平後門內蜡庫胡同四四號孫宅轉

黄鈺生　子堅　湖北沔陽(2.心理)　(781)

(職)天津南開大學

黄希聲　　廣東台山(2.心理)　(1195)

(職)廣州廣東教育廳

楊蔭榆　　江蘇無錫(2.數理化)　(518)

(通訊)無錫北門外長安橋

楊蔭慶　子餘　(143)

(通訊)

楊若堃　伯欽　(541)

(通訊)

董　時　任堅　浙江杭縣(2.心理)　(568)

(通訊)上海愚園路新邨十二號

廖世承　茂如　江蘇嘉定　(708)
(職)上海大西路底光華大學
熊元鍌　季貞　(222)
(通訊)
熊夢賓　禮民　山東陽穀　(816)
(通訊)
鄭德柔　初年　(712)
(職)上海西門西林路西區小學
鄭宗海　曉滄　浙江　(125)
(職)杭州浙江教育廳
蔣夢麟　浙江　(387)
(職)北平北京大學
歐陽祖經　先詒　(2.理化)　(415)
(通訊)江西南昌干家巷後
戴超　志騫　江蘇青浦(圖書館學)　(482)
(通訊)
鍾榮光　廣東中山　(136)
(職)廣州嶺南大學校董會
韓安　竹坪　(335)
(通訊)

2. 經濟商業股

刁培然　　四川江津(財政)　　(1357)
(通訊)

尹寰樞　任先　　(財政)　　(258)
(職)天津法界六路一一四號西北實業公司

卞肇新　淑成　　(商科)　　(385)
(通訊)天津英租界電燈房後

王敬禮　毅侯　浙江黃巖　　(375)
(職)南京中央研究院

王　徽　文伯　　(商)　　(233)
(通訊)

王　華　　(商)　　(378)
(通訊)

王毓祥　祉偉　　(商科)　　(171)
(職)上海大夏大學

王禹偁　　廣東香山(商業管理)　　(922)
(通訊)

王瑞林　　安徽蕪湖(銀行會計)　　(987)
(通訊)

王逸之　　安徽蕪湖　　(998)
(通訊)

白敦庸　　四川西充(2.市政管理)　　(951)
(通訊)北平西四南小院胡同二九號

江啓泰　　福建德化　　(1364)
(通訊)

江之泳　　(商)　　(719)
(通訊)

任嗣達 (商科) (170)
(通訊)
朱亦松 江蘇江寧 (929)
(通訊)
沈元鼎 籟清 (商) (340)
(通訊)上海法租界陶爾斐司路四合里三四號
李思廣 (銀行) (303)
(通訊)
宋子文 廣東香山 (1001)
(職)南京財政部
吳永珊 玉章 (399)
(通訊)四川榮縣蔡家堰
何思源 仙槎 山東荷澤 (1204)
(職)山東教育廳
何德奎 中流 浙江金華(商) (983)
(通訊)上海江西路英工部局華總辦事處
何廉 醉甯 湖南 (1.財政2.統計) (1045)
(職)天津南開大學
祁暄 (商) (94)
(通訊)
邵元冲 翼如 浙江紹縣(2.社會) (962)
(職)南京立法院
邱正倫 宇清 四川井研(銀行) (512)
(職)上海復旦大學
金國寶 侶琴 江蘇吳江 (984)
(通訊)
林景帆 (財政) (835)
(通訊)

林襟宇　　　　浙江永嘉(會計)　　　　(281)
(職)南京審計部
周佛海　　　　湖南沅陵　　　　(988)
(職)鎮江江蘇教育廳
保君建　既星　　　　(生計)　　　　(600)
(通訊)
胡紀常　　　　江蘇無錫　　　　(1272)
(職)南京鷄鳴寺路社會研究所
施濟元　　　　(324)
(通訊)
俞寶濟　　　　(銀行)　　　　(166)
(職)上海河南路道一銀行
孫天孫　謌高　　　　(商)　　　　(411)
(通訊)
裘開明A.Kaiming Chiu,闇輝　浙江鎮海(2.統計3.圖書館學)(1396)
(通訊)Oriental Library,Harvard Univ.Camb.,Mass.
馬寅初　　　　浙江　　　　(879)
(通訊)
徐新六　振飛　浙江杭縣(2.冶金)　　　　(678)
(職)上海浙江興業銀行
徐調均　　　　江蘇青浦(商科)　　　　(1308)
(職)上海科學儀器館
梁慶椿　　　　廣東中山(財政)　　　　(1365)
(通訊)
陳廷錫　淮鍾　　　　(商)　　　　(93)
(通訊)
陳寶年　蔚青　　　　(商)　　　　(149)
(通訊)上海愛文義路聯珠里一五四三號

陳友琴 廣東三山 (1170)
(通訊)廣州市文德西路七號光廬
陳長衡 伯修 (188)
(通訊)南京第一公園北門東廠街二號
陳清華 澄中 (商) (468)
(職)上海黃浦灘中央銀行祕書處
陳翰笙 江蘇無錫(2.外交史) (545)
(職)南京鷄鳴寺路一號中央研究院社會研究所
陳漢清 浙江定海(商法) (902)
(職)南京下關二馬路七七號律師事務所
陳 總 岱孫 福建閩侯 (1114)
(職)北平清華大學
陳 端 心銘 (330)
(職)南京市政府首都建設委員會或南京三茅宮一號
陳 樸 友古 (80)
(通訊)
陳 熹 紹平 福建閩侯(銀行學) (502)
(通訊)
郭泰楨 湖北廣濟(商業) (997)
(通訊)
陶履恭 孟和 (793)
(通訊)北平北新橋小三條十五號
張同亮 梅孫 浙江 (757)
(通訊)
張福運 景吾 (700)
(職)南京財政部
張祖訓 慰慈 (559)
(通訊)

張　釗　彥三　甘肅　(492)
(通訊)
張　度　納川　江蘇　(2.商業)　(1206)
(通訊)上海辣斐德路益餘坊二一號
童啓顏　冠賢　河北　(2.社會)　(991)
(職)南京中央大學法學院
馮　攸　次行　浙江慈谿(2.商業)　(990)
(通訊)
黃漢樑　廣東　(2.政治)　(89)
(通訊)
黃寶球　(商)　(42)
(通訊)
區兆慶　詠篤　(銀行)　(773)
(通訊)
湯　松　(商)　(75)
(通訊)
傅　霖　(2.政治)　(428)
(通訊)
楊端六　湖南長沙(2.政治)　(1008)
(職)湖北武昌武漢大學商學系
楊　銓　杏佛　江西(1.工商管理 2.機械工程)　(15)
(職)中央研究院
楊津生　福建　(2.商業管理)　(1209)
(通訊)青島觀海一路五號
鄒曾侯　魯如　江西南昌(2.政治)　(1355)
(通訊)江西南昌進外慧園街四四號
葉元龍　安徽　(739)
(職)安慶安徽省財政廳

趙興昌　炳生　　(商)　(383)
(職)上海四川路二九號漢冶萍鑛務公司
黎照寰　曜生　廣東　(生計)　(322)
(職)上海交通大學
劉大鈞　君謨　　(621)
(通訊)上海霞飛路興業里六號
劉樹梅　　湖南沅陵(1.統計2.社會3.工業管理)　(489)
(職)福州福建鹽務稽核所
劉克定　鴻生　江蘇　(1248)
(通訊)上海四川路六號中國企業公司
劉乃宇　宜芬　　(商)　(159)
(職)上海郵政儲金總局
劉柏棠　　　(商)　(279)
(通訊)
劉　勁　　　(銀行)　(145)
(通訊)
劉導誅　　　(2.生計)　(797)
(通訊)
鄭壽仁　鐵如　　(商)　(230)
(職)香港中國銀行
鄭　萊　蓬仙　廣東香山(銀行)　(1009)
(職)上海九江路一號C字財政顧問辦事處
蔡增基　　　(709)
(職)上海市政府財政局
衞挺生　琛父　湖北棗陽(財政金融)　(190)
(職)南京立法院
蕭純錦　叔絅　江西永新　(759)
(通訊)北平黃化門大街四號

鍾　利　　義甫　　廣東新會(商科)　　(929)
　　(通訊)
鍾相青　　幼誠　　湖北漢川(1.保險2.統計)　　(867)
　　(通訊)北平新華門前花園大院六號
瞿祖輝　　季剛　　　　(商)　　(273)
　　(職)上海國華銀行
羅有節　　　　　　　　(42)
　　(通訊)
譚葆梧　　秀蒼　　廣東新會(2.政治)　　(764)
　　(通訊)
顧宗林　　　　　　(會計)　　(460)
　　(通訊)
顧翊羣　　季高　　江蘇淮安(商業管理)　　(953)
　　(職)上海中孚銀行

3. 法政股

王世杰　雪艇　(1111)
(通訊)
王純燾　伯秋　(266)
(通訊)南京王府園
吳之椿　湖北江陵　(996)
(職)北平清華大學
吳敬恆　稚暉　江蘇無錫　(1007)
(通訊)上海環龍路志豐里十號
宋春舫　浙江吳興(2.經濟3.海洋學)　(1180)
(通訊)青島福山路新一號
汪英賓　安徽婺源(2.新聞)　(871)
(通訊)
汪兆銘　精衞　(767)
(職)南京國民政府行政院
汪大燧　炎武　安徽　(市政)　(1339)
(通訊)
金岳霖　(293)
(職)北平清華大學
孟森　心史　江蘇常州　(1006)
(通訊)
季警洲　惕凡　江蘇崇明　(911)
(職)南京外交部
施宗嶽　廣東　(萬國公法)　(1014)
(通訊)廣東廣州寶源大街三九號
唐慶貽　江蘇無錫　(374)
(職)上海徐家滙交通大學

孫　科　　哲生　　廣東中山(2.經濟)　　(359)
　(職)

孫紹康　　(394)
　(通訊)

孫浩煊　　守剛　　江蘇崇明　　(1036)
　(職)上海大夏大學

徐淑希　　廣東汕頭　　(480)
　(職)北平燕京大學

徐公肅　　江蘇吳縣(1.國際法2.外交史)　　(1273)
　(通訊)上海西愛咸斯路恆愛里五號

陳　峯　　人鶴　　(715)
　(通訊)

郭泰祺　　復初　　湖北廣濟　　(997)
　(職)南京外交部

章　壽　　浙江杭縣　　(815)
　(通訊)

崔宗塤　　河南南陽　　(1042)
　(職)安慶安徽大學或南京高樓門傅厚崗一號

崔士傑　　景三　　山東臨淄　　(1377)
　(通訊)青島平原路五號或青島膠濟鐵路局

張一志　　江蘇儀徵(2.社會)　　(1069)
　(通訊)鎮江萬全樓旅社二號

張海澄　　江蘇鎮江(2.經濟)　　(1344)
　(職)南通江蘇省南通中學

張　耘　　奚若　　(150)
　(職)北平清華大學

黃　綬　　元資　　四川西克　　(1312)
　(職)四川富榮縣富榮西鹽場

楊汝梅 河北磁縣(2.經濟) (903)
(通訊)
萬兆芝 元甫 (57)
(通訊)
葉達前 上之 江蘇松江 (419)
(通訊)上海法租界平濟利路紹安里五號
葛敬恩 (1208)
(職)南京航空署
雷沛鴻 賓南 廣西南寧(2.經濟) (1000)
(通訊)上海金神父路三五四號
翟俊千 覺羣 廣東東莞 (1074)
(通訊)
壽天章 松江 (1385)
(通訊)陝西西安大湘子廟街四八號陝西省水利局
鄧胥功 只純 四川巴縣(2.經濟) (671)
(通訊)四川成都少城吉祥街十七號
應 時 溥泉 浙江吳興 (808)
(職)上海薛華立路第二特區法院
羅家倫 志希 (716)
(通訊)南京中央大學

4. 哲學股

吳 康　致覺　江蘇吳縣　(239)
(通訊)

胡 適　適之　安徽　(8)
(職)北平南長街二二號中華教育文化基金董事會

馬 良　相伯　江蘇丹徒　(830)
(通訊)上海徐家匯土山灣貧兒院內

張 頤　眞如　四川敘永　(1106)
(職)北平馬神廟北大學院

張東蓀　浙江　(802)
(通訊)

喬萬選　子靑　(2.法律)　(749)
(職)南京航空署

趙元任　江蘇武進(2.數3.理4.語5.樂)　(5)
(職)美國留學生監督

蔡元培　孑民　浙江　(2.民族學)　(261)
(職)上海中央研究院

5. 史學股(附社會)

王繩祖　成祖　江蘇　(2.地理)　(1184)
(職)
王玉章　江蘇江陰　(1028)
(通訊)
田世英　安徽阜陽　(1302)
(通訊)江陰大司馬坊沈宅轉
李濟　濟之　湖北　(1.人種學2.心理學)　(803)
(通訊)北平後門外方磚廠二一號
何炳松　柏丞　浙江金華(2.政治)　(807)
(通訊)上海極司非而路中振坊十四號
武同舉　霞峯　江蘇灌雲　(1328)
(通訊)
柳詒徵　翼謀　江蘇丹徒　(734)
(職)河南大學
胡卓　江蘇無錫　(573)
(職)上海南站大同大學
陳衡哲　湖南　(87)
(通訊)北平大羊儀賓胡同九號
梁思永　廣東新會(人類學)　(1238)
(通訊)北平北海蠶壇
張宗文　浙江　(1.社會學2.人類學)　(1175)
(通訊)
黃人望　百新　浙江金華(2.政治)　(806)
(通訊)
傅斯年　孟眞　(1198)
(職)北平北海公園歷史研究所

馮漢驥　　伯良　　湖北宜昌(人類學)　　(1398)

(通訊)351 Harvard St., Cambridg, Mass.

鄒　銘　　(社會)　　(182)

(通訊)

雷海宗　　伯倫　　北平永清　　(817)

(通訊)

錢端升　　江蘇上海　　(971)

(通訊)北平府右街餑餑房八號

6. 文藝股

周岸登　癸叔　四川 (1317)
(職)四川重慶大學文學院
徐崇欽 (1133)
(通訊)
陳去病 (788)
(通訊)
張孝若　江蘇南通 (22)
(通訊)江蘇南通濠南別業
張道藩　貴州盤縣 (1269)
(職)南京交通部
梅光迪　迪生　安徽 (19)
(通訊)
曾峻岡　孝同 (551)
(通訊)四川重慶沙井灣
楊振聲　今甫　山東蓬萊(2.心理學) (1202)
(通訊)山東蓬萊縣水城楊宅
趙志道　江蘇 (420)
(通訊)上海霞飛路霞飛坊五號
劉　復　半農　江蘇江陰(語音學) (1117)
(通訊)北平大元寶胡同三〇號
蕭友梅　(音樂) (644)
(職)上海辣非德路國立音樂院
關伯益　伯益　河南開封(考古) (1375)
(通訊)河南開封博物館
顧燮光　鼎梅　浙江紹興(金石學) (1297)
(職)上海河南路六二號科學儀器館

學科不明待查者

王心一 (1129)
（通訊）
王希閔　子蕎 (523)
（通訊）
朱世昀 (245)
（通訊）
李志仁 (704)
（通訊）
李保白 (1128)
（通訊）
李　衷 (438)
（通訊）
李　駿　顯章 (318)
（通訊）
李　鐸 (234)
（通訊）
吳祖耀　覺生 (665)
（通訊）
沈祖榮　紹期 (842)
（通訊）　武昌巡道嶺一三號
金宗鼎　定九 (705)
（通訊）
胡　珍　儒誠 (834)
（通訊）
區公沛 (69)
（通訊）
黃漢河 (62)
（通訊）
黃國封 (772)
（通訊）
馮元勛 (631)

103

（通訊） 四川成都建設廳

馮翰章 (1122)

（通訊）

程樹榛 慕頤 (683)

（通訊）

稅紹聖 西恆 (747)

（通訊）

楊繼楨 (1055)

（通訊） 四川成都少城東勝街建設廳

趙正平 厚生 (913)

（通訊） 上海陶爾非司路二五號

趙 昱 (20)

（通訊）

劉惠民 (841)

（通訊）

劉樹墉 (748)

（通訊）

鄭祖穆 (718)

（通訊）

鮑 鍈 遠聲 (702)

（通訊）

閻開元 (553)

（通訊）

韓 楷 子揆 (1136)

（通訊） 四川成都少城四二道街二六號

羅 流 (633)

（通訊）

酈培齡 (289)

（通訊）

管際安 江蘇吳縣 (1334)

（通訊）

謝恩隆 孟博 (595)

（通訊）

補　錄

（下列新社員，係在本刊印刷後通過，不及列入各股名單中，玆補錄于后）

陳思誠　復初　廣東中山　土木工程　(1401)

（職）上海京滬滬杭甬兩路工務處

鄺西谷　安徽廬江　教育　(1402)

（職）上海南市陸家浜上海中學

嚴瑞章　浙江鎮海　化學　(1403)

（通訊）上海麥特赫斯脫路五十六弄張園舊址十一號

劉淦芝　河南商城　昆蟲　(1404)

（通訊）北平清華大學吳宓先生轉

胡金昌　廣東順德　數學，天文　(1405)

（職）廣州中山大學數學天文系或廣州粵華東二街十一號三樓

羅端先　陝西高陵　數學，教育　(1406)

（通訊）陝西西安九府街六二號

石解人　陝西華陰　醫藥　(1407)

（職）陝西省立醫院

方際運　龍丁　江蘇金山　電機　(1408)

（職）上海百老滙路二六九號亞洲電器公司

魯　波　澤普　河北獻縣　化學工程　(1409)

（通訊）614 Riverview Dr, Parchment, Kalamazoo, Mich.

吳　光　國光　浙江　動物學　(1410)

（通訊）Zoology Depart. Univ. of Michigan, Ann Arbor Mich.

翁元慶　Y.C.Owng　琴孫　江蘇常熟　電機工程　(1411)

（通訊）411 Hamilton Place, Ann Arbor, Mich., U.S.A.

吳大猷　Ta-You Wu, 廣東高要　物理，數學　(1412)

（通訊）Department of Physics, Univ. of Michigan, Ann Arbor.

105

袁丕濟 Pae-Tsi Yuan, 雲南昆明 數理統計學 (1413)

(通訊)336 E. Washington St. Ann Arbor. Mich., U.S.A.

李 達 Ta Li 湖北羅田 化學工程 (1414)

(通訊)411 Hamilton. Place, Ann Arbor, Michigan.

高文源 味根 Men-Yuan Kao 陝西西安 心理，生理 (1415)

(通訊)609 Monroe St. Ann Arbor, Mich.

饒欽止 Chin-Chih Jao, 考祥 四川巴縣 生物 (1416)

(通訊)713 Church St, Ann Arbor. Michigan.

何增祿 Tseng-Loh Ho, 浙江諸暨 物理 (1417)

(通訊) Calif. Institute of Tech, Pasadena, Calif. U.S.A.

周北屏 P. P. Cheo, 安徽無為 物理，工程 (1418)

(通訊)℅Mr. S. P. Cheo 1430 Cambridge Rd, Ann Arbor, Mich.

陳建宜 Frank Laingi Chan, 來義 廣東汕頭 化學工程 (1419)

(通訊)Chemistry Depart. Univ. of Michigan, Ann Arbor, Mich.

林文彪 Wen-Piao Lin, 廣東 化學工程 (1420)

(通訊)226 So. 38th St, Philadelphia, Pa., U.S.A.

廖温義 T. W. Liao, 東美 福建彰州 化學工程 (1421)

(通訊)713 Church St., Ann Arbor, Mich., U.S.A.

沈鴻烈 成章 湖北天門 海軍 1422)

(通訊) 青島觀海一路二十九號

張孝庭 浙江鎮海 工業化學 (1423)

(職)上海愛文義路平喬里六號東方化學廠

王海波 安徽懷遠 經濟 (1424)

(通訊)南京新街口忠林坊十三號

安漢 傑三 陝西南鄭 農業 (1425)

(職)南京實業部

248

職員表

董事會

馬　良　孟　森　蔡元培　吳敬恆　熊希齡

汪兆銘　宋漢章　胡敦復　孫　科　（書記）任鴻雋

理事會

王　璡（社長）　楊孝述（總幹事）　周　仁（會計）　翁文灝　胡先驌

竺可楨　任鴻雋　楊　銓　趙元任　胡剛復　秉　志　丁文江

李　協　孫洪芬　胡庶華

美國分社

社　長　湯佩松　書　記　任之恭　會　計　周　田

社友會

南京　理事長　蔡元培　書記　王　璡　會計　葉元龍

北京　理事長　丁文江　書記　楊光弼　會計　白敦庸

上海　理事長　曹惠羣　書記　何尚平　會計　朱少屏

廣州　理事長　陳宗南　書記　張　雲　會計　黃炳芳

蘇州　理事長　汪懋祖　書記　王義珏　會計　王剛森

青島　理事長　蔣丙然　書記兼會計　嚴宏淮

杭州　理事長　李熙謀　書記　張紹忠　會計　錢寶琮

生物研究所

所長 秉志 祕書 錢崇澍

動物部主任教授 秉志 教授 王家楫

植物部主任教授 錢崇澍 教授 裴鑑 鄧叔羣

圖書館

主任 路敏行

委員會 竺可楨 周仁 秉志 楊孝述 楊銓

編輯部

編輯主任 王璡 專任編輯 路敏行

編輯 李協 李儼 沈良驊 竺可楨 葛綏成 楊鶴慶

趙修鴻 蕭純錦 趙燏黃 尤志邁 吳在淵 董時 楊肇燫

科學教育委員會

委員長 張子高

委員 丁緒寶 王璡 姜立夫 錢崇澍 周厚樞

名譽社員

*張　謇　　Mitlon J. Greenman

贊助社員

王雲五　王敏芳　王　岑　江恆源　宋漢章　宋子文　吳毓麟

*范源廉　姚永淸　徐世昌　唐紹儀　許　沅　*袁希濤　黃炎培

*梁啓超　張載陽　張靜江　張乃驥　張　謇　陳陶遺　傅增湘

蔣中正　齊燮元　葉恭綽　楊庶堪　趙鳳昌　熊克武　*黎元洪

熊希齡　盧永祥　閻錫山　謝蘅牕　韓國鈞　*譚延闓　*嚴　修

嚴家熾

特社員

汪兆銘　吳偉士　吳敬恆　周　達　胡敦復　馬　良　馬　和

孫　科　張軼歐　蔡元培　葛拉布

（以上社員均以筆畫多少爲序）　*已故

永久社員

胡敦復　任鴻雋　竺可楨　温嗣康　孫　洛　許先甲　徐乃仁

孫昌克　朱文鑫　劉柏棠　陳寶年　黃昌穀　黎照寰　關漢光

金邦正　趙志道　程時煃　陳衡哲　李垕身　侯德榜　朱　籙

胡　適　周　仁　鍾心煊　曹惠羣　謝家榮　秉　志　譚熙鴻

張軼歐　李　協　程耀椿　姜立夫　王　璡　胡先驌　熊慶來

張乃燕　胡剛復　楊孝述　楊　銓　楊端六　程瀛章　劉夢錫

王　徵　何　魯　丁文江　翁文灝　稅紹聖　劉惠民　朱經農

李孤帆　盧　伯　嚴　莊　廖慰慈　張昭漢　葉元龍　王伯秋

段子燮　鄒秉文　萬兆芝　莊　俊　高君珊　李　儼　程志頤

黃伯樵　胡庶華　孫國封　楊振聲　顧燮光　田世英　徐宗涑

楊光弼　吳承洛　劉樹梅　陳　端　王　賡　吳　憲　盛紹章

姬振鐸　郝更生　劉仙洲　周厚樞　蔡　堡　涂　治　湯雲龍

葉善定　盧于道

歐美籍社員

W. H. Adolph　(竇維廉)

Mary N. Andrews　(安權露)

J. C. Buck　(卜　凱)

H. Chatley　(查得利)

G. B. Cressey　(葛石德)

C. S. Gibbs　(吉普思)

Gee Nathaniel Gist　(祁天錫)

A. W. Grabau　(葛利普)

J. B. Griffing　(郭仁風)

J. T. Illick　(伊利克)

W. C. Lowdermilk　(羅德民)

F. A. McClue　(莫古禮)

C. M. Mcloy　(麥克樂)

J. C, Thomson　(唐美森)

G. R. Twiss　(推　士)

M. Vittrant　(費德朗)

C. W. Woodworth　(吳偉士)

已故社員錄

楊永言	酈昺眞	計大雄	錢天任	陳 藩
朱 正	葉承豫	孫潤江	藍兆乾	陳鎮海
何運煌	徐 昌	曹麗明	汪夔龍	吳家高
吳大昌	顧珊臣	衞錫鈞	劉經庶	徐允中
羅富生	夏重民	史 逸	胡明復	梁杜蘅
金紹城	李 昂	凌善昭	朱 璡	過探先
呂彥直	宋繼瀛	巴玉藻	劉述員	顧 璐
劉潤生	劉濟生	金 湯	孫多蕙	孔繁祁
楊克念	汪元超	王子苓	黃海平	陶 烈
唐腴廬	江逢治	鄭 泗	王錫恩	阮志明
程振鈞	胡鴻基	沈祖偉	黃敏才	

1360 Madison St., N.W.
Washington, D C.
September 27, 1932.

Dear Fellow Members:

Since notifying you about the final list of candidates, there has been no additional nominees from members, but Mr. Ting Supao has declined his nomination, and so the final list appears as on the Ballot. Kindly vote by checking one name for each officer and return to reach above address by October 12.

Faithfully yours,

Election Committee
Y. R. Chao
P. S. Tang
C. Y. Hui

BALLOT FOR ELECTION OF OFFICERS OF THE SCIENCE SOCIETY OF CHINA, AMERICAN BRANCH.

Chairman:	Tang, Dr. Pei Sung	湯佩松
	Chow, Dr. Bacon Field	周　田
	Jen, Dr. Chih Kung	任之恭
Secretary:	Jen, Dr. Chih Kung	任之恭
	Wang, Sherman R.	王慎名
	Chao, Ting Ping	趙廷炳
Treasurer:	Chow, Dr. Bacon Field	周　田
	Hsiung, Sherchin C.	熊學謙
	Wang, Pao Ho	王葆和

Signature: ____________________

UNITED STATES POSTAGE
3 CENTS 3
WASHINGTON, D.C. 13
SEP 28
1932
Stephen M.K. Hu
615 N. Wolfe St
Baltimore, Md.
RETURNED TO SENDER
AFTER 5 DAYS RETURN TO
1360 MADISON STREET N. W.
WASHINGTON, D. C.
Soc, of China

BALTIMORE MD
OCT 1
1932

UNITED STATES POSTAGE
3 CENTS
AIR-MAIL
SAVES TIME
WASHINGTON, D.C. 3
SEP 28
9-PM
1932
MISDIRECTED
RETURNED TO SENDER
AFTER 5 DAYS RETURN TO
1360 MADISON STREET N.W.
WASHINGTON, D. C.

NEW YORK, N.Y.
SEP 30
5 30 PM
1932

1360 Madison St., N.W.
Washington, D C.
September 27, 1932.

Dear Fellow Members:

Since notifying you about the final list of candidates, there has been no additional nominees from members, but Mr. Ting Supao has declined his nomination, and so the final list appears as on the ballot. Kindly vote by checking one name for each officer and return to reach above address by October 12.

Faithfully yours,

Election Committee
Y. R. Chao
P. S. Tang
C. Y. Hui

BALLOT FOR ELECTION OF OFFICERS OF THE SCIENCE SOCIETY OF CHINA, AMERICAN BRANCH.

Chairman:	Tang, Dr. Pei Sung	湯佩松
	Chow, Dr. Bacon Field	周田
	Jen, Dr. Chih Kung	任之恭
Secretary:	Jen, Dr. Chih Kung	任之恭
	Wang, Sherman R.	王慎名
	Chao, Ting Ping	趙廷炳
Treasurer:	Chow, Dr. Bacon Field	周田
	Hsiung, Sherchin C.	熊學謙
	Wang, Pao Ho	王葆和

Signature: ________________

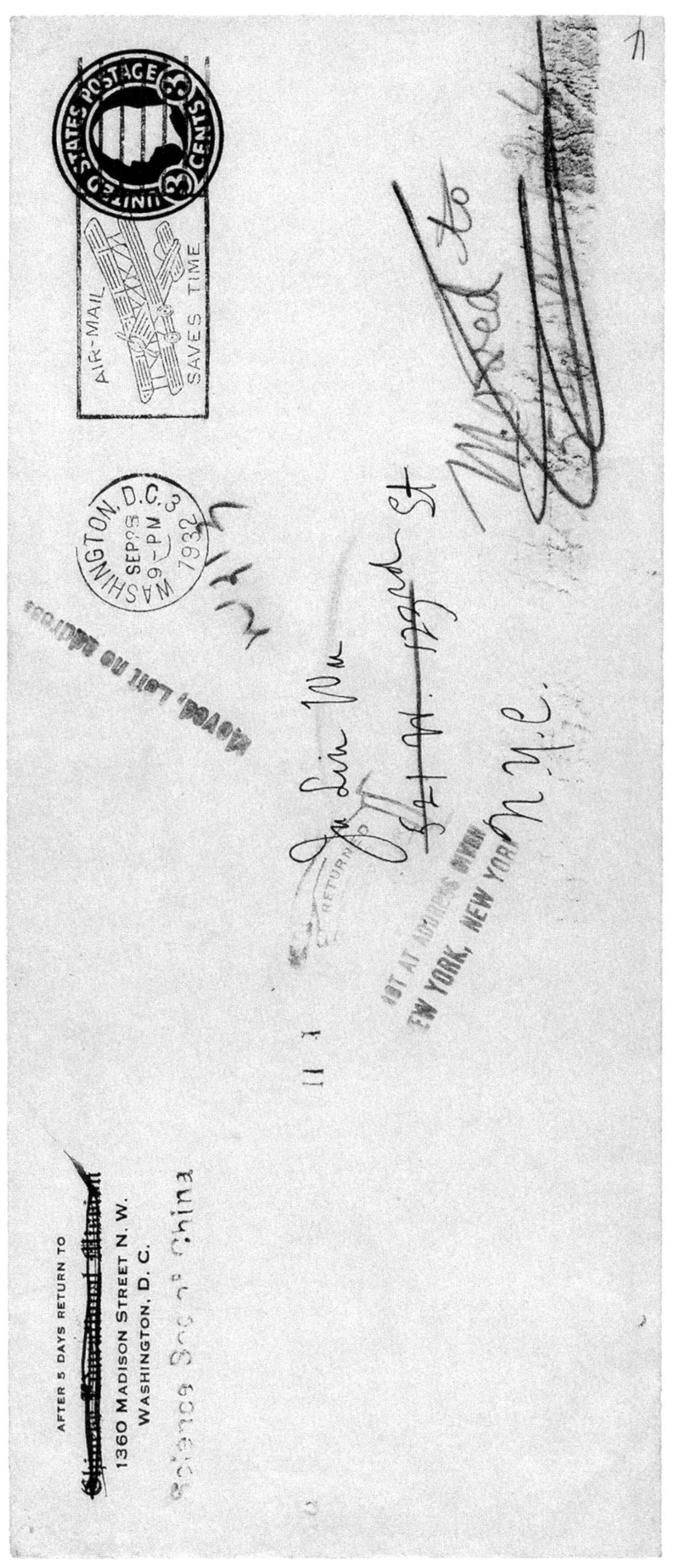
UNITED STATES POSTAGE
3 CENTS
AIR-MAIL
SAVES TIME
WASHINGTON, D.C. 3
SEP 28
9-PM
1932
Moved, Left no address
NEW YORK, NEW YORK
AFTER 5 DAYS RETURN TO
1360 MADISON STREET N. W.
WASHINGTON, D. C.

NEW YORK, N.Y.
SEP 30
2-PM
STA. J

UNITED STATES POSTAGE 3 CENTS 3
NOTIFY YOUR CORRESPONDENTS OF CHANGE OF ADDRESS
WASHINGTON, D.C. 13
SEP 28
9:30 PM
1932
MINNEAPOLIS
OCT 15
AM
1932
MINN.
AFTER 5 DAYS RETURN TO
1360 MADISON STREET N. W.
WASHINGTON, D. C.
Science Soc of China
RETURN TO WRITER
UNCLAIMED

UNITED STATES POSTAGE
3 CENTS
AIR-MAIL
SAVES TIME
WASHINGTON, D.C. 3
SEP 29
9-PM
1932
ITHACA
SEP 30
930 AM
N.Y.
1932
Wei C. Chang
208 Delaware Ave
Ithaca, N.Y.
MINNEAPOLIS
OCT 5
9 AM
1932
MINN.
AFTER 5 DAYS RETURN TO
1360 MADISON STREET N. W.
WASHINGTON, D. C.
Science Soc. of China
RETURN
TO WRITER
UNCLAIMED

DIRECTORY OF THE MEMBERS OF SCIENCE SOCIETY OF CHINA
AMERICAN BRANCH

Name	Province	Field	Address
Chai, Ho Cheng	Hopei	C. E.	105 Oxford Pl., Ithaca, N. Y.
Chang, Ho Tseng		Bot.	Dept. of Plant Physio., Cornell U.
~~Chang, N. F.~~			~~834 Delaware Ave., Ithaca, N. Y.~~
~~Chang, Tsung Han~~		~~Physio.~~	~~49 Snell Hall, U. of Chicago.~~
Chang, Wei C.			208 Delaware Ave., Ithaca, N. Y.
Chao, Bu Wei Yang	Anhwei	Med. Sc.	1360 Madison St.N.W., Washington, D.C.
Chao, Iping	Kiangsu	Physio.	5738 Drexel Ave., Chicago, Ill.
Chao, Robert F. H.	Kiangsu	E. E.	10 Trowbridge St., Cambridge, Mass.
Chao, Ting Ping			~~233~~ Linden Ave., Ithaca, N. Y.
Chao, Yuen Ren	Kiangsu	Philo.	1360 Madison St.N.W., Washington, D.C.
Chen, Wei	Fukien	Chem.	~~Baker Chemical Lab., Cornell Univ.~~
Cheo, MingTsung		Entom.	Dept. of Entomology, Cornell Univ.
Chou, Cheng Yao	Kiangsu	Plant Brd.	104 Harvard Pl., Ithaca, N. Y.
Chou, Yung Tiao	Hunan	Bio-Chem.	Box 6182 Univ. of Minn.
Chow, Bacon F.	Fukien	Chem.	24 Chauncy St., Cambridge, Mass.
Chow, Tung Ching	Kiangsu	Physics	Palmer Physical Lab., Princeton Univ.
Feng, H. Tang		Entom.	208 Delaware Ave., Ithaca, N. Y.
Hou, T. P.		Chem.	c/o Box 582, W.Lafayette, Ind.
Hsiang, C. C.			1752 17th St.N.W., Washington, D. C.
Hsiung, Sherchin C.	Hupei	Chem.	Box 1011, Johns Hopkins Univ.
~~Hsu, Tseng Ying~~	~~Shangtung An.Hue.~~		~~c/o Wyoming Hereford Ranch, Cheyenne Wyoming~~
Hsu, Yin Chi		Entom.	Dept of Entom., Cornell Univ.
Hu, Stephen M. K.		Entom.	615 N. Wolfe St., Baltimore, Md.
Huang, T. S.	Kwangtung	E. E.	509 Huntington Ave., Boston, Mass.
Huong, Miss S. S.			Sch. of Medicine, Boston Univ.
Jen, Chih Kung	Shansi	Physics	16 Wendell St., Cambridge, Mass.
Kuan, F. C.	Kiangsu	C. E.	Sch. of C. E., Cornell Univ.
Kwan, Chia Chi	Chekiang	Plant Brd.	Dept of Plant Breeding, Cornell U
Lee, Pui Man	Kiangsu	Pomol.	Cornell Univ.
Lee, T. Y.			923 W. Johnson St., Madison, Wis.
Li, Liang Ching		Plant Morph.	157 W. 8th Ave., Columbus, Ohio
Li, Tehying	Chekiang	Statis.	~~823 W. Johnson St.~~, Madison, Wis.
Liang, Ching Chun		Econ.	10 Trowbridge St., Cambridge, Mass.
Liu, Hu	Hupei	Bio-Chem.	Bio-Chem. Dept., St. Paul, Minn.
Liu, T.	Kwangtung	Chem.	~~21 Fall Creek Dr.~~, Ithaca, N. Y.
Lou, Chao Mien	Chekiang	E. E.	Purdue Univ, Lafayette, Ind.
Mar, Peter	Kwangtung	Geo.	~~296 Ellen St.~~, Winnipeg,
Ohn, Miss Asta			1632 Le Roy Ave., Berkeley, Calif.
Pan, L. C.	Kiangsu	Ch. Eng.	419 W. 115th St., N. Y. C.
Penn, Amos B.	Szechuen	Bio.	Box 95, Johns Hopkins Univ.
Tai, An Pang		Chem.	John Jay Hall, Columbia Univ.
Tang, Pei Sung	Hupei	Plant Physio.	Lab. of General Physio., Harvard
Tao, Philip T.	Kiangsu	Chem.	~~5711 Maryland Ave.~~, Chicago, Ill.
Ting, Supao	Anhwei	Physics	~~c/o H. H. Ting~~
Ting, Hsu Huai	Anhwei	Ch. Eng.	531 Forest Ave., Ann Arbor, Mich.
Tsai, Liu Sheng	Fukien	Chem.	5738 Drexel Ave., Chicago, Ill.
Tsao, Miss Cien Yu		Bio-Chem.	~~803 S. Coler St.~~, Urbana Ill.
Tsou, Tseng Hou		Econ.	823 W. Johnson St., Madison, Wis.
Twiss, G. R.	U. S. A.	Physics	2595 Summit St., Columbus, Ohio
Wang, George T. C.	(correct add. below)		550 Riverside Dr., N. Y. C.
Wang, Pao Ho	Hopei	E. E.	c/o Dr. C. K. Jen
Wang, Sherman R.	Hupei	E. E.	1360 Madison St.N.W., Washington, D.C
Woodworth, C. W.	U.S.A.		Univ. of Calif., Berbeley, Calif.
Wu, Ju Lin	—	—	521 W. 123rd St., N. Y. C.
Yang, S. C.	Anhwei	Math.	~~84 Ellery St., Cambridge, Mass.~~
Yang, Shou Chen	Liaonien	Chem.	~~Cornell Univ.~~
Yin, Yu Chang	Shansi	Med.	St. Luke's Hospital, Bethlehem, Pa.
Young, C. C.	Shangtung	Bio-Chem.	307 N. Orchard St., Madison, Wis.
Yuan, Han Ching	Kiangsu	Chem.	Box 94 Univ. Station, Urbaha, Ill.
Yang, P. S.			66th and N. Y. Ave., N. Y. C.
Tsai, L. S.		Chem.	Jones Chemical Lab., Univ. of Chicago
Li, C. C.			Box 641 Station A., Champaign, Ill.
Wang, George T. C.			c/o Vulcan Detinning Co., Sewaren, N. J.

7

BALLOT FOR ELECTION OF OFFICERS OF THE SCIENCE SOCIETY OF CHINA, AMERICAN BRANCH.

Chairman:	Tang, Dr. Pei Sung	湯佩松	✓
	Chow, Dr. Bacon Field	周田	
	Jen, Dr. Chih Kung	任之恭	
Secretary:	Jen, Dr. Chih Kung	任之恭	✓
	Wang, Sherman R.	王慎名	
	Chao, Ting Ping	趙廷炳	
Treasurer:	Chow, Dr. Bacon Field	周田	✓
	Hsiung, Sherchin C.	熊學謙	
	Wang, Pao Ho	王葆和	

Signature: 周同慶

Chow Tung Ching

8

BALLOT FOR ELECTION OF OFFICERS OF THE SCIENCE SOCIETY OF CHINA, AMERICAN BRANCH.

Chairman: Tang, Dr. Pei Sung ✓湯佩松
Chow, Dr. Bacon Field 周田
Jen, Dr. Chih Kung 任之恭

Secretary: Jen, Dr. Chih Kung ✓任之恭
Wang, Sherman R. 王慎名
Chao, Ting Ping 趙廷炳

Treasurer: Chow, Dr. Bacon Field ✓周田
Hsiung, Sherchin C. 熊學謙
Wang, Pao Ho 王葆和

Signature: 丁绪宝

廿,九,廿

MR. TING SUPAO
INSTITUTE OF APPLIED OPTICS
UNIVERSITY OF ROCHESTER
ROCHESTER, N. Y., U. S. A.

~~MR. TING SUPAO~~
~~ANN ARBOR, MICH., U. S. A.~~

请注意

9

BALLOT FOR ELECTION OF OFFICERS OF THE SCIENCE SOCIETY OF CHINA, AMERICAN BRANCH.

Chairman:	Tang, Dr. Pei Sung	湯佩松 (circled)
	Chow, Dr. Bacon Field	周田
	Jen, Dr. Chih Kung	任之恭
Secretary:	Jen, Dr. Chih Kung	任之恭 (circled)
	Wang, Sherman R.	王慎名
	Chao, Ting Ping	趙廷炳
Treasurer:	Chow, Dr. Bacon Field	周田 (circled)
	Hsiung, Sherchin C.	熊學謙
	Wang, Pao Ho	王葆和

Signature: 熊學謙

10

C. Y. Hui

BALLOT FOR ELECTION OF OFFICERS OF THE SCIENCE SOCIETY OF CHINA, AMERICAN BRANCH.

Chairman:	Tang, Dr. Pei Sung ✓	湯佩松
	Chow, Dr. Bacon Field	周田
	Jen, Dr. Chih Kung	任之恭
Secretary:	Jen, Dr. Chih Kung ✓	任之恭
	Wang, Sherman R.	王慎名
	Chao, Ting Ping	趙廷炳
Treasurer:	Chow, Dr. Bacon Field ✓	周田
	Hsiung, Sherchin C.	熊學謙
	Wang, Pao Ho	王葆和

Signature: I. Chao.

11

BALLOT FOR ELECTION OF OFFICERS OF THE SCIENCE SOCIETY OF CHINA, AMERICAN BRANCH.

Chairman: ✓Tang, Dr. Pei Sung 湯佩松
Chow, Dr. Bacon Field 周田
Jen, Dr. Chih Kung 任之恭

Secretary: ✓Jen, Dr. Chih Kung 任之恭
Wang, Sherman R. 王慎名
Chao, Ting Ping 趙廷炳

Treasurer: ✓Chow, Dr. Bacon Field 周田
Hsiung, Sherchin C. 熊學謙
Wang, Pao Ho 王葆和

Signature: C. C. Kwan

12

1360 Madison St., N.W.
Washington, D C.
September 27, 1932.

Dear Fellow Members:

Since notifying you about the final list of candidates, there has been no additional nominees from members, but Mr. Ting Supao has declined his nomination, and so the final list appears as on the ballot. Kindly vote by checking one name for each officer and return to reach above address by October 12.

Faithfully yours,

Election Committee
Y. R. Chao
P. S. Tang
C. Y. Hui

BALLOT FOR ELECTION OF OFFICERS OF THE SCIENCE SOCIETY OF CHINA, AMERICAN BRANCH.

Chairman:	Tang, Dr. Pei Sung	湯佩松	X
	Chow, Dr. Bacon Field	周田	
	Jen, Dr. Chih Kung	任之恭	
Secretary:	Jen, Dr. Chih Kung	任之恭	X
	Wang, Sherman R.	王慎名	
	Chao, Ting Ping	趙廷炳	
Treasurer:	Chow, Dr. Bacon Field	周田	X
	Hsiung, Sherchin C.	熊學謙	
	Wang, Pao Ho	王葆和	

Signature: 丁绪淮

13

1360 Madison St., N.W.
Washington, D. C.
September 27, 1932.

Dear Fellow Members:

Since notifying you about the final list of candidates, there has been no additional nominees from members, but Mr. Ting Supao has declined his nomination, and so the final list appears as on the ballot. Kindly vote by checking one name for each officer and return to reach above address by October 12.

Faithfully yours,

Election Committee
Y. R. Chao
P. S. Tang
C. Y. Hui

BALLOT FOR ELECTION OF OFFICERS OF THE SCIENCE SOCIETY OF CHINA, AMERICAN BRANCH.

Chairman:	Tang, Dr. Pei Sung	湯佩松	✓
	Chow, Dr. Bacon Field	周田	
	Jen, Dr. Chih Kung	任之恭	
Secretary:	Jen, Dr. Chih Kung	任之恭	✓
	Wang, Sherman R.	王慎名	
	Chao, Ting Ping	趙廷炳	
Treasurer:	Chow, Dr. Bacon Field	周田	✓
	Hsiung, Sherchin C.	熊學謙	
	Wang, Pao Ho	王葆和	

Signature: 彭光欽

14

BALLOT FOR ELECTION OF OFFICERS OF THE SCIENCE SOCIETY OF CHINA, AMERICAN BRANCH.

Chairman:	Tang, Dr. Pei Sung	湯佩松
	Chow, Dr. Bacon Field	周田
	Jen, Dr. Chih Kung	任之恭 ✓
Secretary:	Jen, Dr. Chih Kung	任之恭
	Wang, Sherman R.	王慎名 ✓
	Chao, Ting Ping	趙廷炳
Treasurer:	Chow, Dr. Bacon Field	周田
	Hsiung, Sherchin C.	熊學謙 ✓
	Wang, Pao Ho	王葆和

Signature: 湯佩松

15

BALLOT FOR ELECTION OF OFFICERS OF THE SCIENCE SOCIETY OF CHINA, AMERICAN BRANCH.

Chairman:	Tang, Dr. Pei Sung	湯佩松
	✓ Chow, Dr. Bacon Field	周　田
	Jen, Dr. Chih Kung	任之恭
Secretary:	✓ Jen, Dr. Chih Kung	任之恭
	Wang, Sherman R.	王慎名
	Chao, Ting Ping	趙廷炳
Treasurer:	Chow, Dr. Bacon Field	周　田
	✓ Hsiung, Sherchin C.	熊學謙
	Wang, Pao Ho	王葆和

Signature: C. Y. Tsao

602 S. Busey St.,
Urbana, Ill.

16

1360 Madison St., N.W.
Washington, D C.
September 27, 1932.

Dear Fellow Members:

Since notifying you about the final list of candidates, there has been no additional nominees from members, but Mr. Ting Supao has declined his nomination, and so the final list appears as on the ballot. Kindly vote by checking one name for each officer and return to reach above address by October 12.

Faithfully yours,

Election Committee
Y. R. Chao
P. S. Tang
C. Y. Hui

BALLOT FOR ELECTION OF OFFICERS OF THE SCIENCE SOCIETY OF CHINA, AMERICAN BRANCH.

Chairman:	Tang, Dr. Pei Sung	湯佩松
	Chow, Dr. Bacon Field	周田
	√ Jen, Dr. Chih Kung	任之恭
Secretary:	Jen, Dr. Chih Kung	任之恭
	Wang, Sherman R.	王慎名
	√ Chao, Ting Ping	趙廷炳
Treasurer:	Chow, Dr. Bacon Field	周田
	√ Hsiung, Sherchin C.	熊學謙
	Wang, Pao Ho	王葆和

Signature: H. T. Tieng

17

BALLOT FOR ELECTION OF OFFICERS OF THE SCIENCE SOCIETY OF CHINA, AMERICAN BRANCH.

Chairman:	Tang, Dr. Pei Sung	湯佩松	✓
	Chow, Dr. Bacon Field	周田	
	Jen, Dr. Chih Kung	任之恭	
Secretary:	Jen, Dr. Chih Kung	任之恭	✓
	Wang, Sherman R.	王慎名	
	Chao, Ting Ping	趙廷炳	
Treasurer:	Chow, Dr. Bacon Field	周田	
	Hsiung, Sherchin C.	熊學謙	
	Wang, Pao Ho	王葆和	✓

Signature: 厲德寅

Tehying Li

18

BALLOT FOR ELECTION OF OFFICERS OF THE SCIENCE SOCIETY OF CHINA, AMERICAN BRANCH.

Chairman:	Tang, Dr. Pei Sung	湯佩松
	Chow, Dr. Bacon Field	周田
	Jen, Dr. Chih Kung	任之恭✓
Secretary:	Jen, Dr. Chih Kung	任之恭
	Wang, Sherman R.	王慎名✓
	Chao, Ting Ping	趙廷炳
Treasurer:	Chow, Dr. Bacon Field	周田
	Hsiung, Sherchin C.	熊學謙
	Wang, Pao Ho	王葆和✓

Signature: Robert 宋 H. Chao
趙訪熊

19

BALLOT FOR ELECTION OF OFFICERS OF THE SCIENCE SOCIETY OF CHINA, AMERICAN BRANCH.

Chairman:	Tang, Dr. Pei Sung	湯佩松
	Chow, Dr. Bacon Field	周田
	Jen, Dr. Chih Kung	任之恭 ✓
Secretary:	Jen, Dr. Chih Kung	任之恭
	Wang, Sherman R.	王慎名 ✓
	Chao, Ting Ping	趙廷炳
Treasurer:	Chow, Dr. Bacon Field	周田 ✓
	Hsiung, Sherchin C.	熊學謙
	Wang, Pao Ho	王葆和

Signature: Philip T. Tao

20

BALLOT FOR ELECTION OF OFFICERS OF THE SCIENCE SOCIETY OF CHINA, AMERICAN BRANCH.

Chairman:	Tang, Dr. Pei Sung	湯佩松	
	Chow, Dr. Bacon Field	周田	
	Jen, Dr. Chih Kung	任之恭	✓
Secretary:	Jen, Dr. Chih Kung	任之恭	
	Wang, Sherman R.	王慎名	✓
	Chao, Ting Ping	趙廷炳	
Treasurer:	Chow, Dr. Bacon Field	周田	
	Hsiung, Sherchin C.	熊學謙	✓
	Wang, Pao Ho	王葆和	

Signature: Bacon F. Chow
周田

21

BALLOT FOR ELECTION OF OFFICERS OF THE SCIENCE SOCIETY OF CHINA, AMERICAN BRANCH.

Chairman: Tang, Dr. Pei Sung 湯佩松 X
Chow, Dr. Bacon Field 周田
Jen, Dr. Chih Kung 任之恭

Secretary: Jen, Dr. Chih Kung 任之恭 X
Wang, Sherman R. 王慎名
Chao, Ting Ping 趙廷炳

Treasurer: Chow, Dr. Bacon Field 周田 X
Hsiung, Sherchin C. 熊學謙
Wang, Pao Ho 王葆和

Signature: T. C. Hou

22

BALLOT FOR ELECTION OF OFFICERS OF THE SCIENCE SOCIETY OF CHINA, AMERICAN BRANCH.

Chairman:	Tang, Dr. Pei Sung	湯佩松
	Chow, Dr. Bacon Field	周田
	✓Jen, Dr. Chih Kung	任之恭
Secretary:	Jen, Dr. Chih Kung	任之恭
	✓Wang, Sherman R.	王慎名
	Chao, Ting Ping	趙廷炳
Treasurer:	Chow, Dr. Bacon Field	周田
	Hsiung, Sherchin C.	熊學謙
	✓Wang, Pao Ho	王葆和

Signature: M. T. Chao

23

1360 Madison St., N.W.
Washington, D C.
September 27, 1932.

Dear Fellow Members:

Since notifying you about the final list of candidates, there has been no additional nominees from members, but Mr. Ting Supao has declined his nomination, and so the final list appears as on the ballot. Kindly vote by checking one name for each officer and return to reach above address by October 12.

Faithfully yours,

Election Committee
Y. R. Chao
P. S. Tang
C. Y. Hui

BALLOT FOR ELECTION OF OFFICERS OF THE SCIENCE SOCIETY OF CHINA, AMERICAN BRANCH.

Chairman:	Tang, Dr. Pei Sung	湯佩松	✓
	Chow, Dr. Bacon Field	周田	
	Jen, Dr. Chih Kung	任之恭	
Secretary:	Jen, Dr. Chih Kung	任之恭	
	Wang, Sherman R.	王慎名	✓
	Chao, Ting Ping	趙廷炳	
Treasurer:	Chow, Dr. Bacon Field	周田	
	Hsiung, Sherchin C.	熊學謙	✓
	Wang, Pao Ho	王葆和	

Signature: C. K. Jen 任之恭

24

1360 Madison St., N.W.
Washington, D. C.
September 27, 1932.

Dear Fellow Members:

Since notifying you about the final list of candidates, there has been no additional nominees from members, but Mr. Ting Supao has declined his nomination, and so the final list appears as on the Ballot. Kindly vote by checking one name for each officer and return to reach above address by October 12.

Faithfully yours,

Election Committee
Y. R. Chao
P. S. Tang
C. Y. Hui

BALLOT FOR ELECTION OF OFFICERS OF THE SCIENCE SOCIETY OF CHINA, AMERICAN BRANCH.

Chairman:	Tang, Dr. Pei Sung	湯佩松	
	Chow, Dr. Bacon Field	周田	
	Jen, Dr. Chih Kung	任之恭	✓
Secretary:	Jen, Dr. Chih Kung	任之恭	
	Wang, Sherman R.	王慎名	
	Chao, Ting Ping	趙廷炳	✓
Treasurer:	Chow, Dr. Bacon Field	周田	
	Hsiung, Sherchin C.	熊學謙	
	Wang, Pao Ho	王葆和	✓

Signature: S. C. Yang

63 Charles Field St.
Providence
R. I.

25

BALLOT FOR ELECTION OF OFFICERS OF THE SCIENCE SOCIETY OF CHINA, AMERICAN BRANCH.

Chairman: X Tang, Dr. Pei Sung 湯佩松
Chow, Dr. Bacon Field 周田
Jen, Dr. Chih Kung 任之恭

Secretary: Jen, Dr. Chih Kung 任之恭
Wang, Sherman R. 王慎名
X Chao, Ting Ping 趙廷炳

Treasurer: Chow, Dr. Bacon Field 周田
Hsiung, Sherchin C. 熊學謙
X Wang, Pao Ho 王葆和

Signature: W. Chen
317 College ave
Ithaca, N.Y.

26

1360 Madison St., N.W.
Washington, D C.
September 27, 1932.

Dear Fellow Members:

Since notifying you about the final list of candidates, there has been no additional nominees from members, but Mr. Ting Supao has declined his nomination, and so the final list appears as on the **ballot**. Kindly vote by checking one name for each officer and return to reach above address by October 12.

Faithfully yours,

Election Committee
Y. R. Chao
P. S. Tang
C. Y. Hui

BALLOT FOR ELECTION OF OFFICERS OF THE SCIENCE SOCIETY OF CHINA, AMERICAN BRANCH.

Chairman:	✓ Tang, Dr. Pei Sung	湯佩松
	Chow, Dr. Bacon Field	周田
	Jen, Dr. Chih Kung	任之恭
Secretary:	✓ Jen, Dr. Chih Kung	任之恭
	Wang, Sherman R.	王慎名
	Chao, Ting Ping	趙廷炳
Treasurer:	✓ Chow, Dr. Bacon Field	周田
	Hsiung, Sherchin C.	熊學謙
	Wang, Pao Ho	王葆和

Signature: George T. C. Wang 王绳[illegible]

27

1360 Madison St., N.W.
Washington, D C.
September 27, 1932.

Dear Fellow Members:

Since notifying you about the final list of candidates, there has been no additional nominees from members, but Mr. Ting Supao has declined his nomination, and so the final list appears as on the ballot. Kindly vote by checking one name for each officer and return to reach above address by October 12.

Faithfully yours,

Election Committee
Y. R. Chao
P. S. Tang
C. Y. Hui

BALLOT FOR ELECTION OF OFFICERS OF THE SCIENCE SOCIETY OF CHINA, AMERICAN BRANCH.

Chairman:	Tang, Dr. Pei Sung	湯佩松
	Chow, Dr. Bacon Field	周田 X
	Jen, Dr. Chih Kung	任之恭
Secretary:	Jen, Dr. Chih Kung	任之恭 X
	Wang, Sherman R.	王慎名
	Chao, Ting Ping	趙廷炳
Treasurer:	Chow, Dr. Bacon Field	周田
	Hsiung, Sherchin C.	熊學謙
	Wang, Pao Ho	王葆和 X

Signature: Peter G. Mao

28

Mr. C. Y. Hui

1360 Madison St., N.W.
Washington, D C.
September 27, 1932.

Dear Fellow Members:

Since notifying you about the final list of candidates, there has been no additional nominees from members, but Mr. Ting Supao has declined his nomination, and so the final list appears as on the ballot. Kindly vote by checking one name for each officer and return to reach above address by October ~~12~~. 14

Faithfully yours,

Election Committee
Y. R. Chao
P. S. Tang
C. Y. Hui

BALLOT FOR ELECTION OF OFFICERS OF THE SCIENCE SOCIETY OF CHINA, AMERICAN BRANCH.

Chairman:	Tang, Dr. Pei Sung	✓	湯佩松
	Chow, Dr. Bacon Field		周田
	Jen, Dr. Chih Kung		任之恭
Secretary:	Jen, Dr. Chih Kung	✓	任之恭
	Wang, Sherman R.		王慎名
	Chao, Ting Ping		趙廷炳
Treasurer:	Chow, Dr. Bacon Field	✓	周田
	Hsiung, Sherchin C.		熊學謙
	Wang, Pao Ho		王葆和

Signature: C.Y. Hui

29

Mr. G. F. Djang

1360 Madison St., N.W.
Washington, D C.
September 27, 1932.

Dear Fellow Members:

Since notifying you about the final list of candidates, there has been no additional nominees from members, but Mr. Ting Supao has declined his nomination, and so the final list appears as on the ballot. Kindly vote by checking one name for each officer and return to reach above address by October ~~12~~ 14.

Faithfully yours,

Election Committee
Y. R. Chao
P. S. Tang
C. Y. Hui

BALLOT FOR ELECTION OF OFFICERS OF THE SCIENCE SOCIETY OF CHINA, AMERICAN BRANCH.

Chairman:	Tang, Dr. Pei Sung	湯佩松	
	Chow, Dr. Bacon Field	周田	
	Jen, Dr. Chih Kung	任之恭	✓
Secretary:	Jen, Dr. Chih Kung	任之恭	
	Wang, Sherman R.	王慎名	✓
	Chao, Ting Ping	趙廷炳	
Treasurer:	Chow, Dr. Bacon Field	周田	✓
	Hsiung, Sherchin C.	熊學謙	
	Wang, Pao Ho	王葆和	

Signature: G. F. Djang

30

BALLOT FOR ELECTION OF OFFICERS OF THE SCIENCE SOCIETY OF CHINA, AMERICAN BRANCH.

Chairman:	Tang, Dr. Pei Sung	湯佩松 ✓
	Chow, Dr. Bacon Field	周田
	Jen, Dr. Chih Kung	任之恭
Secretary:	Jen, Dr. Chih Kung	任之恭 ✓
	Wang, Sherman R.	王慎名
	Chao, Ting Ping	趙廷炳
Treasurer:	Chow, Dr. Bacon Field	周田 ✓
	Hsiung, Sherchin C.	熊學謙
	Wang, Pao Ho	王葆和

Signature: Pao Ho Wang

31

1360 Madison St., N.W.
Washington, D C.
September 27, 1932.

Dear Fellow Members:

Since notifying you about the final list of candidates, there has been no additional nominees from members, but Mr. Ting Supao has declined his nomination, and so the final list appears as on the ballot. Kindly vote by checking one name for each officer and return to reach above address by October 12.

Faithfully yours,

Election Committee
Y. R. Chao
P. S. Tang
C. Y. Hui

BALLOT FOR ELECTION OF OFFICERS OF THE SCIENCE SOCIETY OF CHINA, AMERICAN BRANCH.

Chairman:	Tang, Dr. Pei Sung	湯佩松 ✓
	Chow, Dr. Bacon Field	周田
	Jen, Dr. Chih Kung	任之恭
Secretary:	Jen, Dr. Chih Kung	任之恭 ✓
	Wang, Sherman R.	王慎名
	Chao, Ting Ping	趙廷炳
Treasurer:	Chow, Dr. Bacon Field	周田 ✓
	Hsiung, Sherchin C.	熊學謙
	Wang, Pao Ho	王葆和

Signature: 王慎名

32

1360 Madison St., N.W.
Washington, D C.
September 27, 1932.

Dear Fellow Members:

Since notifying you about the final list of candidates, there has been no additional nominees from members, but Mr. Ting Supao has declined his nomination, and so the final list appears as on the Ballot. Kindly vote by checking one name for each officer and return to reach above address by October 12.

Faithfully yours,

Election Committee
Y. R. Chao
P. S. Tang
C. Y. Hui

BALLOT FOR ELECTION OF OFFICERS OF THE SCIENCE SOCIETY OF CHINA, AMERICAN BRANCH.

Chairman:	Tang, Dr. Pei Sung	湯佩松	主
	Chow, Dr. Bacon Field	周田	
	Jen, Dr. Chih Kung	任之恭	
Secretary:	Jen, Dr. Chih Kung	任之恭	书
	Wang, Sherman R.	王慎名	
	Chao, Ting Ping	趙廷炳	
Treasurer:	Chow, Dr. Bacon Field	周田	会
	Hsiung, Sherchin C.	熊學謙	
	Wang, Pao Ho	王葆和	

Signature: Buwei Yang Chao

33

1360 Madison St., N.W.
Washington, D. C.
September 27, 1932.

Dear Fellow Members:

Since notifying you about the final list of candidates, there has been no additional nominees from members, but Mr. Ting Supao has declined his nomination, and so the final list appears as on the ballot. Kindly vote by checking one name for each officer and return to reach above address by October 12.

Faithfully yours,

Election Committee
Y. R. Chao
P. S. Tang
C. Y. Hui

BALLOT FOR ELECTION OF OFFICERS OF THE SCIENCE SOCIETY OF CHINA, AMERICAN BRANCH.

Chairman:	Tang, Dr. Pei Sung	湯佩松	✓
	Chow, Dr. Bacon Field	周田	
	Jen, Dr. Chih Kung	任之恭	
Secretary:	Jen, Dr. Chih Kung	任之恭	✓
	Wang, Sherman R.	王慎名	
	Chao, Ting Ping	趙廷炳	
Treasurer:	Chow, Dr. Bacon Field	周田	✓
	Hsiung, Sherchin C.	熊學謙	
	Wang, Pao Ho	王葆和	

Signature: [illegible]

34

1360 Madison St., N.W.
Washington, D. C.
September 27, 1932.

Dear Fellow Members:

Since notifying you about the final list of candidates, there has been no additional nominees from members, but Mr. Ting Supao has declined his nomination, and so the final list appears as on the ballot. Kindly vote by checking one name for each officer and return to reach above address by October 12.

Faithfully yours,

Election Committee
Y. R. Chao
P. S. Tang
C. Y. Hui

BALLOT FOR ELECTION OF OFFICERS OF THE SCIENCE SOCIETY OF CHINA, AMERICAN BRANCH.

Chairman:	Tang, Dr. Pei Sung	湯佩松正正正丁	17
	Chow, Dr. Bacon Field	周田丁	2
	Jen, Dr. Chih Kung	任之恭正下	8
			27
Secretary:	Jen, Dr. Chih Kung	任之恭正正正丁	17
	Wang, Sherman R.	王慎名正丁	7
	Chao, Ting Ping	趙廷炳下	3
			27
Treasurer:	Chow, Dr. Bacon Field	周田正正正一	16
	Hsiung, Sherchin C.	熊學謙正	5
	Wang, Pao Ho	王葆和正一	6
			27

Signature: ____________________

35

1360 Madison Street, N.W.
Washington, D. C.
October 14, 1932.

Dear Fellow Members:

We beg to announce the results of the election of 1932-33 officers as follows:

Chairman:	Dr. Pei Sung Tang	17 votes
	Dr. Bacon Field Chow	2 "
	Dr. Chih Kung Jen	8 "
Secretary:	Dr. Chih Kung Jen	17 votes
	Sherman R. Wang	7 "
	Ting Ping Chao	3 "
Treasurer:	Dr. Bacon Field Chow	16 votes
	Sherchin C. Hsiung	5 "
	Pao Ho Wang	6 "

Dr. Tang is therefore elected Chairman; Dr. Jen is therefore elected Secretary; and Dr. Chow is therefore elected Treasurer.

Faithfully yours,
Election Committee
Y. R. Chao, P. S. Tang, C. Y. Hui

For your convenience, we are adding some corrections and supplements to the recently distributed directory, as follows:

Chai, Mien Pu	left country
Chen, Huang	c/o M.K. Kan Box 104 Univ. Sta., Urbana, Ill.
Chao, Ting Ping	129 Linden Ave, Ithaca, N.Y.
Chen, Wei	317 College Ave. Ithaca. N.Y.
Chiu, A.Kaiming	Oriental Library, Harvard Univ. Camb., Mass.
Djang, G.F.	304 Ithaca Road, Ithaca, N.Y.
Hui. C.Y.	c/o G.F.Djang 304 Ithaca Rd, Ithaca N.Y.
Koo, Eugene C	M.I.T Dorms, Cambridge, Mass
Kwan, Chia Chi	misprint Kwau
Li, Tehying	436 Frances St, Madison. Wis
Mar, Peter	Gordon Bell Research Lab., Medical College, Winnipeg, Man., Canada.
Tao, Philip T.	1414 E. 59th St, Chicago, Ill.
Ting. Supao	Institute of Applied Optics. University of Rochester., Rochester, N.Y.
Tsao, Chien Yu	602 Busey St., Urbana, Ill.
Yang, S.C.	63 Charles Field St., Providence, R.I.

Members who know the addresses of the following members, whose ballots were returned undelivered by the Post Office, will kindly inform Secretary Jen, Research Lab of Physics, Harvard Univ., Cambridge, Mass.: Chang, Wei C., Hu, Stephen M.K., and Wu, Ju Lin.

36

Corrected Directory according to the list compiled by Dr. Y. R. Chao, Oct. 14, 1932.

DIRECTORY OF THE MEMBERS OF SCIENCE SOCIETY OF CHINA
AMERICAN BRANCH

Name	Province	Field	Address
Chai, Ho Cheng	Hopei	C. E.	105 Oxford Pl., Ithaca, N. Y.
Chang, Ho Tseng		Bot.	Dept. of Plant Physio., Cornell U.
Chang, N. F.			208 Delaware Ave., Ithaca, N. Y.
Chang, Tsung Han		Physio.	49 Snell Hall, U. of Chicago.
? Chang, Wei C.			208 Delaware Ave., Ithaca, N. Y.
Chao, Bu Wei Yang	Anhwei	Med. Sc.	1360 Madison St. N. W., Washington, D.C.
Chao, Iping	Kiangsi	Physio.	5738 Drexel Ave., Chicago, Ill.
Chao, Robert F. H.	Kiangsu	~~E. E.~~ Math.	10 Trowbridge St., Cambridge, Mass.
Chao, Ting Ping			~~203~~ 139 Linden Ave., Ithaca, N. Y.
Chao, Yuen Ren	Kiangsu	Philo.	1360 Madison St. N. W., Washington, D.C.
Chen, Wei	Fukien	Chem.	~~Baker Chemical Lab., Cornell Univ.~~ 317 College Avenue Ithaca, N. Y.
Cheo, MingTsung		Entom.	Dept. of Entomology, Cornell Univ.
? Chou (Chiu), Cheng (K.) Yao	Kiangsu	Plant Brd.	~~104 Harvard Pl., Ithaca, N. Y.~~ Oriental Library, Harvard Univ. Camb.
Chou, Yung Tiao	Human	Bio-Chem.	Box 6182 Univ. of Minn.
Chow, Bacon F.	Fukien	Chem.	24 Chauncy St., Cambridge, Mass.
Chow, Tung Ching	Kiangsu	Physics	Palmer Physical Lab., Princeton Univ.
~~Feng~~ Djang, H. C. T. Tang		Entom.	~~208 Delaware Ave., Ithaca,~~ 304 Ithaca Road Ithaca N. Y.
Hou, ~~Y~~ T. P.		Chem.	c/o Box 522, W. Lafayette, Ind.
Hsiang, C. C.			1752 17th St. N. W., Washington, D. C.
Hsiung, Sherchin C.	Hupei	Chem.	Box 1011, Johns Hopkins Univ.
~~Hsu, Tseng Ying~~	~~Shangtung~~	~~An. Hus.~~	~~c/o Wyoming Hereford Ranch, Cheyenne Wyoming~~
Hsu, Yin Chi		Entom.	Dept of Entom., Cornell Univ.
? Hu, Stephen M. K.		Entom.	615 N. Wolfe St., Baltimore, Md.
Huang (Hui), T. S. (Y.)	Kwangtung	E. E.	c/o A. F. Djang 509 Huntington Ave., Boston, Mass.
Huong, Miss S. S.			Sch. of Medicine, Boston Univ.
Jen, Chih Kung	Shansi	Physics	~~16 Wendell St.~~ 57 Gorham St., Cambridge, Mass.
Kuan, F. C.	Kiangsu	C. E.	Sch. of C. E., Cornell Univ.
Kwan, Chia Chi	Chekiang	Plant Brd.	Dept of Plant Breeding, Cornell U
Lee, Pui Man	Kiangsu	Pomol.	Cornell Univ.
Lee, T. Y.			923 W. Johnson St., Madison, Wis.
Li, Liang Ching		Plant Morph.	157 W. 8th Ave., Columbus, Ohio
Li, Tehying	Chekiang	Statis.	~~823 W. Johnson St.,~~ 436 Frances St., Madison, Wis.
Liang, Ching Chun		Econ.	10 Trowbridge St., Cambridge, Mass.
Liu, Hu	Hupei	Bio-Chem.	Bio-Chem. Dept., St. Paul, Minn.
Liu, T.	Kwangtung	Chem.	21 Fall Creek Dr., Ithaca, N. Y.
Lou, Chao Mien	Chekiang	E. E.	Purdue Univ. Lafayette, Ind.
Mar, Peter	Kwangtung	Geo.	~~296 Ellen St., Winnipeg~~ Gordon Bell Research Laboratory, Medical College, Winnipeg, Man. Canada
Ohn, Miss Asta			1632 Le Roy Ave., Berkeley, Calif.
Pan, L. C.	Kiangsu	Ch. Eng.	419 W. 115th St., N. Y. C.
Penn, Amos B.	Szechun	Bio.	Box 95, Johns Hopkins Univ.
Tai, An Pang		Chem.	John Jay Hall, Columbia Univ.
Tang, Pei Sung	Hupei	Plant Physio.	Lab. of General Physio., Harvard
Tao, Philip T.	Kiangsu	Chem.	~~5711 Maryland Ave.~~ 1414 E. 59th St., Chicago, Ill.
Ting, Supao	Anhwei	Physics	~~c/o H. H. Ting~~ Institute of Applied Optics, Univ. of Rochester, Roch. N. Y.
Ting, Hsu Huai	Anhwei	Ch. Eng.	531 Forest Ave., Ann Arbor, Mich.
Tsai, Liu Sheng	Fukien	Chem.	5738 Drexel Ave., Chicago, Ill.
Tsao, Miss Chien Yu		Bio-Chem.	~~803 S. Goler St., Urbana Ill.~~ 602 Busey St. Urbana Ill.
Tsou, Tseng Hou		Econ.	823 W. Johnson St., Madison, Wis.
Twiss, G. R.	U. S. A.	Physics	2595 Summit St., Columbus, Ohio
Wang, George T. C. (correct add. below)			550 Riverside Dr., N. Y. C.
Wang, Pao Ho	Hopei	E. E.	c/o Dr. C. K. Jen
Wang, Sherman R.	Hupei	E. E.	1360 Madison St. N. W., Washington, D.C
Woodworth, C. W.	U.S.A.		Univ. of Calif., Berbeley, Calif.
? Wu, Ju Lin			521 W. 123rd St., N. Y. C.
Yang, S. C.	Anhwei	Math.	~~84 Ellery St., Cambridge, Mass.~~ 63 Charles Field St. Providence R. I.
Yang, Shou Chen	Liaonien	Chem.	Cornell Univ.
Ying, Yu Chang	Shansi	Med.	St. Luke's Hospital, Bethlehem, Pa.
Young, C. C.	Shangtung	Bio-Chem.	307 N. Orchard St., Madison, Wis.
Yuan, Han Ching	Kiangsu	Chem.	Box 94 Univ. Station, Urbana, Ill.
Yang, P. S.			66th and N. Y. Ave., N. Y. C.
~~Tsai~~ Yang, L. S. (~~S.~~ C.)		Chem.	Jones Chemical Lab., Univ. of Chie Chicago
Li, C. C.			Box 641 Station A., Champaign, Ill.
Wang, George T. C.			c/o Vulcan Detinning Co., Sewaren, N. J.
Feng, H. Y.			351 Harvard St. Camb. Mass.

Total no. 66

71

DIRECTORY OF THE MEMBERS OF SCIENCE SOCIETY OF CHINA AMERICAN BRANCH (REVISED OCTOBER 16, 1932)

Name	Province	Field	Address
Chai, Ho Cheng	Hupei	C. E.	105 Oxford Pl., Ithaca, N.Y.
Chang, Ho Tseng		Bot.	Dept. of Plant Physio., Cornell U.
Chang, Tsung Han		Physio.	49 Snell Hall, U. of Chicago
Chang, Wei C.			208 Delware Ave., Ithaca, N.Y.
Chao, Bu Wei Yang	Anhwei	Med. Sc.	1360 Madison St. N.W. Washington, D.C.
Chao, Iping	Kiangsi	Physio.	5738 Drexel Ave., Chicago, Ill.
Chao, Robert F. H.	Kiangsu	E.E.	10 Trowbridge St., Cambridge, Mass.
Chao, Ting Ping			129 Linden Ave., Ithaca, N.Y.
Chao, Yuen Ren	Kiangsu	Philo.	1360 Madison St. N.W. Washington, D.C.
Chen, Huang			c/o M.H.kan, Box 104 Univ. Station, Urbana, Ill.
Chen, Wei	Fukien	Chem.	317 College Ave., Ithaca, N.Y.
Cheo, Ming Tsung		Entom	Dept. of Entomology, Cornell U.
Chiu, A. Kaiming			Oriental Library, Harvard U., C.,M.
Chou, Cheng Yao	Kiangsu	Plant Brd.	104 Harvard Pl., Ithaca, N.Y.
Chou, Yung Tiao	Hunan	Bio-Chem.	Box 6182 Univ. of Minn.
Chow, Bacon F.	Fukien	Chem.	24 Chauncy St., Cambridge, Mass.
Chow, Tung Ching	Kiangsu	Physics	Palmer Physical Lab., Princeton U.
Djang, G. F.			304 Ithaca Rd. Ithaca, N.Y.
Feng, H. Tang		Entom.	208 Delware Ave., Ithaca, N.Y.
Hou, T. P.		Chem	c/o Y.C.Hou, Box 522, W. Lafayette, Ind.
Hsiang, C. C.			1752 17th St. N.W., Washington, D.C.
Hsiung, Sherchin	C. Hupei	Chem.	Box 1011, Johns Hopkins Univ.
Hsu, Yin Chi		Entom.	Dept. of Entm., Cornell Univ.
Hu, Stephen M. K.		Entom.	615 N. Wolfe St., Baltimore, Md.
Huang, T. S.	Kwangtung	E. E.	509 Huntington Ave., Boston, Mass.
Hui, C. Y.			203 Linden Ave., Ithaca, N.Y.
Huong, Miss S. S.			Sch. of Medicine, Boston Univ.
Jen, Chih Kung	Shansi	Physics	16 Wendell St., Cambridge, Mass.
Kuan, F. C.	Kiangsu	C. E.	Sch. of C. E., Cornell Univ.
Koo, Eugene			M.I.T. Dorms., Cambridge, Mass.
Kwan, Chia Chi	Chekiang	Pl. Brd.	Dept. of Plant Breeding, Cornell U.
Lee, Pui Man	Kiangsu	Pomol.	Cornell Univ.
Lee, T. Y.			923 W. Johnson St., Madison, Wisc.
Li, Liang Ching		Plant Morph.	157 W. 8th Ave., Columbus, Ohio.
Li, Tehying	Chekiang	Statis	436 Frances St., Madison, Wisc.
Liang, Ching Chun		Econ.	10 Trowbridge St., Cambridge, Mass.
Liu, Hu	Hupei	Bio-Chem.	Bio-Chem., Dept., St. Paul, Minn.
Liu, T.	Kwangtung	Chem.	Baker lab. Cornell Univ. Ithaca, N.Y.
Lou, Chao Mien	Chekiang	E. E.	Purdue Univ., Lafayette, Ind.
Mar, Peter	Kwangtung	Geo.	Gordon Bell Res. Lab., Medical College Winnipeg, Canada
Ohn, Miss Asta			1362 Le Roy Ave., Berkeley, Calif.
Pan, L. C.	Kiangsu	Ch. Eng.	419 W. 115th St., N.Y.C.
Penn, Amos B.	Szechun	Bio.	Box 95, Johns Hopkins Univ.
Tai, An Pang		Chem.	Johns Jay Hall, Columbia Univ.
Tang, Pei Sung	Hupei	Pl. Physio.	Lab. of General Physio., Harvard
Tao, Philip T.	Kiangsu	Chem.	1414 E. 59th St., Chicago, Ill.
Ting, Supao	Anhwei	Physics	Institute of Applied optics, Univ. of Rochester, Rochester, N.Y.
Ting, Hsu Huai	Anhwei	Ch. Eng.	531 Forest Ave., Ann. Arbor, Mich.

72

2

Mark	Name	Province	Field	Address
o§	Tsai, Liu Sheng	Fukien	Chem.	5738 Drexel Ave., Chicago, Ill.
	Tsao, Miss Chien Yu		Bio-Chem.	602 Busey St., Urbana, Ill.
x*	Tsou, Tseng Hou		Eco.	823 W. Johnson St., Madison, Wisc.
x§	Twiss, G. R.	U.S.A.	Physics	2595 Summit St., Columbus, Ohio
	Wang, George T. C.			~~c/o Vulcan Detinning Co., Sewaren, N.J.~~
	Wang, Pao Ho	Hopei	E. E.	c/o Dr. C. K. Jen
o	Wang, Sherman R.	Hupei	E. E.	1360 Madison St. N.W. Washington, D.C.
x§	Woodworth, C. W.	U.S.A.		Univ. of Calif., Berkeley, Calif.
x*	Wu, Ju Lin			521 W. 123rd St., N.Y.C.
o§	Yang, P.S.			66th St. & N.Y. Ave., N.Y.C.
	Yang, S. C.	Anhwei	Math.	63 Charles Field St., Providence, R.I.
§	Yang, Shou Chen	Liaonien	Chem.	Cornell Univ.
(§)	Yin, Yu Chang	Shangsi	Med.	St. Luke's Hospital, Bethlehem, Pa.
§	Young, C. C.	Shangtung	Bio-Chem.	307 N. Orchard St., Madison, Wis.
(§)	Yuan, Han Ching	Kiangsu	Chem.	Box 94 Univ. Station, Urbana, Ill.
§	Yang, P. S.			66th St. And N. Y. Ave., N.Y.C.
§	Tsai, L.S. (=蔡镏生?)		Chem.	Johnes Chemical Lab., Univ. of Chicago
§	Li, C. C.			Box 641 Station A., Champaign, Ill.

Richard Biben

Explanation of signs:

§ ballots sent, but did not vote for 1932-33 officers, addresses doubtful.

(§) same as above, but addresses quite authentic.

° Applications sent to Shanghai.

* ballots sent, but returned by P. O. undelivered.

x names for which verification of standing by Home Society is requested.

73

The 68 districts of Hupeh Province are used as examples. The data are from the Directorate of Budget and Statistics and the Hupeh Department of Civil Affairs.

The method is first a weighing of the value of cultivated land per capita of farm population and of the value of farm crops per capita of farm population. A combined unit measure is then devised. The product moment correlation method is applied. It is found that tax revenue has a negative correlation with the value of cultivated land. The r is —.14. The r between the unit values of land and crops is +.59.

There are the following assumptions:

1. The value of land of China constitutes about 82% of her total wealth.
2. The value of subsidiary agricultural industries (which is not included in this study) has a high correlation with the value of farm crops, the ratio of the two being 68.34:100.
3. This method measures only the relative or comparative ability of the districts and not their absolute ability. It measures the ability of the farmers of the districts, since urban wealth is left out of consideration.
4. Both the technique and findings are held tentative until better data are available.

CARBONIZATION OF COAL IN BULK

By C. S. LOMAX

Carbonization of Coal in Bulk is now the world's preferred method for the production of gas for domestic use and a smokeless burning domestic and metallurgical fuel—coke.

The purpose of the paper is to show the growth of the process in plant size, in the number and value of its products, and hence the economic value to the country.

THE FUTURE DEVELOPMENT OF INCANDESCENT LAMP AND VACUUM TUBE INDUSTRIES IN CHINA

By CHAI YEH
Cruft Laboratory, Harvard University

This paper begins with a short discussion of the possibility and necessity of the future development of incandescent lamp and vacuum tube industries in China. The present situation of Chinese manufacturers and the market condition in China are briefly described. The raw materials used for the manufacture of lamps and tubes are mentioned and the mining of Chinese tungsten is described. Following are brief descriptions of the processes of manufacture of both incandescent lamps and vacuum tubes. A factory design is outlined and briefly discussed. At last, the author makes a few suggestions as to the development of these industries.

THE EFFECT OF TEMPERATURE ON THE CONTRACTILE VACUOLE OF CERTAIN CILIATES

By HARRY GAW
Yale University

The rate of pulsation of the anterior contractile vacuole of four species of Paramecium (P. multimicronucleata, P. aurelia, P. caudatum and P. polycaryum) has been determined over a temperature range of about 16° C. The temperature

A. K. Chiu
THE CHINESE INSTITUTE OF ENGINEERS
AMERICAN SECTION
THE SCIENCE SOCIETY OF CHINA
AMERICAN BRANCH
I
CE
SCS
JOINT
ANNUAL CONVENTION
NEW YORK CITY
AUGUST 24-28, 1933
PROGRAM & ABSTRACTS OF PAPERS
165

CONDENSED PROGRAM

Thursday, August 24

4:00 P. M.— 6:00 P. M.	Registration

Friday, August 25

9:00 A. M.—10:00 A. M.	Registration
10:00 A. M.—12:00 A. M.	Opening Session
12:00 Noon— 1:30 P. M.	Luncheon
2:00 P. M. — 5:00 P. M.	Technical Paper Session
6:00 P. M. — 8:00 P. M.	Informal Dinner
8:30 P. M. —11:00 P. M.	Social Meeting

Saturday, August 26

9:00 A. M.—12:00 Noon	Technical Paper Session
12:00 Noon— 1:30 P. M.	Luncheon
2:00 P. M. — 5:00 P. M.	Business Meetings
7:00 P. M. —11:00 P. M.	Convention Banquet

Sunday, August 27

9:00 A. M.—12:00 Noon	Symposium—"Industrialization of China"
12:00 Noon— 1:30 P. M.	Luncheon
2:00 P. M. — 5:00 P. M.	Sight Seeing
7:00 P. M. —11:00 P. M.	Tour to Radio City

Monday, August 28

9:00 A. M.—12:00 Noon	Inspection Trip to Sperry Gyroscope Company, Brooklyn, New York
12:00 Noon— 1:00 P. M.	Luncheon
2:00 P. M. — 5:00 P. M.	Inspection Trip to Ford Motor Plant, Edgewater, New Jersey
6:30 P. M. — 8:30 P. M.	Informal Farewell Dinner

166

CONTENTS

JOINT CONVENTION COMMITTEES

Thomas T. Eoyang, Chairman

Representatives

American Branch of S. S. C.

B. F. Chow
S. C. Hsiung
General Secretaries

Ting Supao
Paper Session Chairman

American Section of C. I. E.

Kwang H. Chang
Convention Chairman

George C. Chou
Executive Secretary

P. H. Wang
Paper Session Chairman

Social Committee

Mrs. C. N. Li, Chairman

Miss Mao-Lan Kung
Mrs. Geo. C. Chou
Miss Chu-Sen Yen
Miss Lellie Lee

Publication Committee

Edward W. Fong, Chairman

Kwang H. Chang
George C. Chou

167

10. Controllable-Pitch Propeller
Yih-Chow Mar, University of Michigan

11. 做反射镜面之新法
T. L. Ho, California Institute of Technology

12:00 Noon— 1:30 P.M.—LUNCHEON
Sin Kee Garden, 500 West 125th Street

2:00 P.M.— 5:00 P.M.—BUSINESS MEETING
The Science Society of China, American Branch
Room "AB"; Chairman, Dr. B. F. Chow
The Chinese Institute of Engineers, American Section
Room "C"; Chairman, Thomas T. Eoyang

7:00 P.M.—11:00 P.M.—BANQUET
Chin Lee Restaurant—Broadway at 49th Street
Toastmaster, Richard S. M. Lee
Speakers:
DR. A. D. BROWN
Honorary Chairman of International China Relief
MR. K. C. LI
President, Wah Chang Trading Company, New York, N. Y.

Sunday, August 27

9:00 A.M.—12:00 Noon—SYMPOSIUM
"Industrialization of China"
Presiding Officers: Ting Supao, Thomas T. Eoyang

1. Where China Stands in the Course of Industrialization
Thomas T. Eoyang, Columbia University
2. The Problems of Chinese Coal Mining Industry
Y. L. Chu, University of Illinois
3. Protecting the Eye in Industry
Dr. Eugene Chan, Wilmer Institute, Johns Hopkins Hospital and University

General Discussions

12:00 Noon— 1:30 P.M.—LUNCHEON
Sin Kee Garden, 500 West 125th Street

2:00 P.M.— 5:00 P.M.—SIGHT SEEING
Trip to George Washington Bridge
180th Street, New York City

5:30 P.M.— 7:00 P.M.—DINNER
Lotus Village, 143 West 47th Street, New York City

7:00 P.M.—11:00 P.M.—TOUR TO RADIO CITY
Leader, Kwang H. Chang

Monday, August 28

9:00 A.M.—12:00 Noon—Inspection Trip to Sperry Gyroscope Company, Brooklyn, New York
Leaders: Kwang H. Chang, George C. Chou
Directions: Starting from International House, first take 125th Street I. R. T subway to Times Square, then change to B. M. T. downtown trains for Brighton Beach or West End and get off at the first stop after the Manhattan Bridge and walk back two blocks, & you will find the Sperry Gyroscope Company.

12:00 Noon— 1:30 P.M.—LUNCHEON
Lee's Restaurant, 36 Pell Street

2:00 P.M.— 5:00 P.M.—Inspection Trip to Ford Motor Plant, Edgewater, N. J.
Leaders: Kwang H. Chang, Thomas T. Eoyang
Directions: Walk from the International House to 129th Street Ferry, take Ferry Boat to get over to New Jersey side, then take street car. Get off at Edgewater, ask for Ford Plant.

6:30 P.M.— 8:30 P.M.—INFORMAL FAREWELL DINNER PARTY
Sin Kee Garden, 500 West 125th Street

172

THE RELATION BETWEEN THE RATE OF REACTION AND THE POTENTIAL OF THE SYSTEM.

I. The Rate of Absorption of Linseed Oil.

II. The Nitrogen Evolution of Hydrozine.

B. F. Chow
Harvard University

ABSTRACT—In the series of two papers a general equation has been found to relate the rate of a reaction catalyzed by substances of different oxidation-reduction potentials with the normal potentials.

I. The rate of absorption of oxygen by Linseed oil in presence of different catalysts. The net reaction involved is:

$$\left.\begin{array}{l}\text{Linseed Oil} + (OH^-) + O_2 + C \\ \text{L} \qquad\qquad (\text{oxidized form})\end{array}\right\} \longrightarrow \left\{\begin{array}{l}LO_n \text{ (complex)} \\ + C^- + \frac{1}{2}H_2O \\ (\text{reduced form})\end{array}\right.$$

The rate of the reaction is followed by the decrease of the O_2 pressure. The equation found is:

$$-\frac{do_2}{dt} = k\ (L)\ (OH^-)\ (O_2)\ (C) \quad f(E)$$

Where f(E) is a function of the potential of the system.

A mechanism of the chemical reaction has been proposed, from which a similar equation can be derived from purely kinetic and thermodynamic considerations. The evidences for the chain reaction are also given. A thorough study of the inhibition of the reaction is also included.

II. The evolution of nitrogen when hydrozine is oxidized by potassium ferricyanide and other molybidinum has long been known. The rate of evolution of nitrogen is also related to the normal potential of the catalyst, as required by the equation derived in paper I. Thus an additional evidence for the general applicability of the equation is furnished. This reaction has the advantages that the reaction takes place in a homogeneous aqueous medium and is free from the uncertainties inherent to a three phase-system as in the case of the Linseed oil.

EXPERIMENTAL STUDY OF SUPER-REGENERATIVE DETECTION

Yorke Chang
Harvard University

ABSTRACT—The super-regenerative detection was studied at two different frequencies; one being long wave (750 m.) and the other short wave (63 m.) Different signal strengths were applied to the detector from a modulator, the voice frequency of which is 1,000 cycles. The output voltages of the detector were balanced by equal and opposite voltages from the 1,000 cycles source through a bridge system. The balancing points were obtained by using a pair of phones through a multistage audio frequency amplifier and a 1,000 cycle band pass filter. The balancing system was calibrated so that the voltage output or the "voltage detection coefficient" can be calculated and plotted under different conditions.

The supersonnic frequency used in the long wave experiments was 30 kc. while that used in the short wave experiments was 50 kc. In the short wave experiments all the frequencies were controlled by crystals; so that they were constant—which is important in order to obtain accurate results. Due to the fact that the apparatus were near to one another, exceedingly careful shielding and grounding system were resorted to eliminate local pick up.

A number of curves were obtained under different circuit arrangements and tube voltages. The results show the advantage of the superregeneration over the plain regeneration especially at short waves.

CHEMICAL PLANT ENGINEERING ORGANIZATION

R. L. Holliday
Consulting Chemist and Chemical Engineer, New York City

ABSTRACT—This paper is to deal with the general organization of the engineering department of a chemical plant. An organization chart shows the relationship between the chief engineer who is the head of the department and various divisions such as design and construction division, etc.

The project engineer who is the head of the design division and the construction superintendent who is the man to take charge of actual construction of a new project are two essential engineers really on the job. So they must be well equipped with adequate training and knowledge in both mechanical and chemical engineering. The proper functioning of the department is illustrated by the flow sheet and follow up routing sheet.

STUDIES OF AIR RESISTANCE IN MODERN FAST AIRPLANES

George C. Chou
Aero E., Vice-Pres. and Chief Eng., Cosmic Aircraft Corp.

OUTLINE—Keynote on high speed and effectiveness in finishing an errand.

- Resistance (commonly called drag) constants of whole airplanes and their derivations.
- Drag of airplane parts,
  - Wing drag (1) Form drag,
    - (2) Induced drag,
    - (3) Drag due to lift,
    - (4) Skin friction.
  - Body drag (1) Form drag, (bases on area and volume),
    - (2) Skin drag.
  - Drag of other airplane components,
    - (1) Strut forms,
    - (2) Wires,
    - (3) Wheels,
    - (4) Motors, motor cowls, etc.,
    - (5) Interference.
- Troubles of excessive lift in high speed airplanes.
- Complexities of aviation research.
- Economy studies (fuel) of high speed and weight lifted.
- Conclusions.

TOOLS, GAUGES AND METHODS REQUIRED TO INSURE INTERCHANGEABLE MANUFACTURE OF SMALL ARMS

F. J. Root
Major, Ordnance Dept., U.S.A., 1917-1919; Supervisor in charge of Design and Tool Dept., Adriance Machine Works, Brooklyn, N. Y., 1931

ABSTRACT—This paper gives an outline of the tools, gauges and methods required to insure interchangeable manufacture of small arms. In order to insure interchangeable manufacture of small arms a large amount of accurate tools and gauges which are correct to a few thousandths of an inch are required.

In the manufacture of fire arms rigid inspection of all raw materials entering into the manufacture of all component parts is both essential and absolutely necessary. Methods of testing and processes of inspection to insure the interchangeability and accuracy are also outlined and illustrated with a chart.

創辦中國科學儀器廠意見書

何增祿
CALIFORNIA INSTITUTE OF TECHNOLOGY
丁緒寶
UNIVERSITY OF ROCHESTER

要目：
一. 宗旨
二. 事業
三. 開辦資本
四. 賣價原則
五. 銷場預計
六. 儀器廠組織
七. 款項保障
八. 盈餘分配
九. 廠址選擇原則

附件：
一. 開辦機料估價單
二. 儀器廠佈置畧圖
三. 總技師合同要點
四. 薪工估數單

BRIEF HISTORICAL ACCOUNT OF THE VECTOR CALCULUS WITH REFERENCE TO ELECTRICAL ENGINEERING

Si-Ping Cheo
University of Michigan

ABSTRACT—The methods of vector calculus have, since their introduction within recent years, been pursued with such success in the various fields of physical sciences and now appearing so generally in the literature and in the text-books that it seems appropriate to consider their increasing importance in the training of a group of men likely to be very nearly affected by them, either directly or indirectly, namely the electrical engineering students. With this intent a brief inquiry into the recent history of vector calculus with reference to electrical engineering will be made in this paper. The vector calculus itself will, for the purpose of this treatment, be divided on three levels: (1) the elementary concept of vector and its simple treatment based on graphical addition and subtraction, on this level the subject is familiar to all engineering students and need not be further considered; (2) a more advanced treatment, such as that offered in the first formal course in vector analysis, this involves the scalar and vector products, simple differentiation and integration and a more extended literal treatment; (3) a still more advanced treatment involving the so-called differential operations, tensor analysis, and the like.

THE QUANTUM DEFECTS OF f STATES OF HEAVY ATOMS

Ta-You Wu
University of Michigan

ABSTRACT—The expression for the eigenvalues of the problem of two unequal potential valleys obtained by the author is applied to the calculation of the f states of heavy atoms, the Fermi potential for positive ions being used. The calculation explains the fact that the quantum defects of these states are all close to unity.

175

To the oriental world, which is still rich in philosophical thought and sound in its ethical principles, the present rapid advancement will give a good lesson to avoid mistakes. It is hoped that every attempt will be made to preserve and promote activities of men endowed with minds so ably described by Francis Bacon as follows:

> "A mind nimble and versatile enough to catch the resemblances of things, and at the same time steady enough to fix and distinguish their subtle differences; endowed by nature with the desire to seek, the patience to doubt, fondness to meditate, slowness to ascert, readiness to reconsider, carefulness to dispose and set in order; and neither affecting what is new nor admiring what is old, hating every kind of impotence."

THE CURTISS "HAWK" PURSUIT PLANE

Structural Design Conditions and Performance

J. A Lo

Curtiss Aeroplane & Motor Company

ABSTRACT—

General Description

ABSTRACT—The "Hawk" is a single seater pursuit with a single bay biplane wing. The **wing cellule** is made up of one upper panel continuous across the center section and two lower panels. The beams and ribs are made of spruce; the panels are fabric covered. **Fuselage** is built of welded steel tubing, fabric covered. **Landing gear** is of the single strut type, equipped with oleo shock absorbing units. **Tail surfaces** have steel tube beams and dural ribs, fabric covered. The export planes are powered with Wright R-1820 **engine** rated 640 HP at 1900 RPM.

Design Conditions for Airplane Structures

I. FLYING CONDITIONS

A—Dive and pull-up

1. Dive at Terminal Velocity at angle of zero lift; Dynamic Lift=1; factor of safety = 1.5; load factor (L.F.) = 1x1.5 = 1.5.
2. Movement of center of pressure of air forces on wings towards leading edge and increase of air load as angle of attack increases in pulling out of dive.
   (a) At +4° from zero lift, center of pressure at 53% chord, Load Factor = 8
   (b) At +19° from zero lift, center of pressure at 31% chord, maximum dynamic load = 9, factor of safety = 1.33, LF=9x1.33=12

B—Dive and negative pull-out

1. Negative bump-cross wind of 20 mph in terminal dive Load Factor = 4.4
2. Inverted flight conditions Load Factor = 4

C—Rolling conditions—Unsymmetrical load on wings, 100% on one side and 75% on the other.

II—LANDING CONDITIONS

Free drop = 24 inches; load factor = 7

III—CONTROL SURFACE LOADINGS

1. Stabilizer and elevator ....35 lbs. per sq. ft. area
2. Fin and rudder ....30 lbs. per sq. ft. area
3. Ailerons ....35 lbs. per sq. ft. area

Static Test of Airplane

	L. F. Required	L. F. Supported Without Failure	L. F. at Failure
Wing cellule	12	12	
Wing beams			
Upper front	12	12	13.2
Upper rear	8	8.8	8.8
Lower front	4.4	7.5	7.9
Lower rear	8	9.6	10.4
Fuselage	12	12	12.25

178

Performance

(gross weight = 3500#; Wing area = 252 sq. ft; Airfoil Clark Y)

High speed at sea level	=	192 m.p.h.
Stalling speed		60 m.p.h.
Rate of climb		2300 ft./min.
Service ceiling		25,000 ft.

RECENT DEVELOPMENTS OF TUNG OIL INDUSTRY AND ITS PRESENT ECONOMIC TRENDS

M. R. Bhagwat
Consulting Chemical Engineer, New York City

ABSTRACT—Tung oil is a great factor in the varnishing industry. The nuts of the tung-tree produce the tung oil. Growth and life of the tree 25 years.

Tung nut statistics: 326 pounds oil per 5 acre lot, 150 trees per acre. The seed is 59% of a nut, and oil is from the seed.

Uses: It completely revolutionized the varnish industry in the United States. It is used also in high voltage insulation, brake-lining, steam-pipe gaskets, oil cloth, artificial leather, and so forth.

Chemical compounds: (No summary).

Economic trends: Realizing its value, the United States in 1905 started planting tung trees. In 1932, 3200 acres of tung trees existed in the gulf coast and their neighboring states.

Prices: 1919, 4 cents to 40 cents, 53 million lbs. came to U. S.
1920-1928, 27 to 109 million lbs.
1929, 120 million lbs.
1930, 126 million lbs., price at 5 to 8 cents only.

CONTINUOUS RECORDING OF KENNELLY-HEAVISIDE LAYER HEIGHTS

Dr. Pao Ho Wang
Harvard University

ABSTRACT—A new method of recording continuously and automatically the apparent heights of the Kennelly-Heaviside layers has been developed. Two recorders, one for the permanent use in laboratory and one for field tests have been built and used.

A new modulator used to "key" the crystal controlled transmitter for this work is made. Powerful pulses are generated from a thyratron circuit.

Nearby reception is made possible by using a balanced receiving circuit. Satisfactory results have been obtained with the receiving apparatus about 4 meters from the transmitter.

Records covering a total time of 6000 hours have been obtained since June 10, 1932. Most pieces are long time records showing the slow diurnal changes. High speed records are useful in studying the "splitting" of the layers, the effect of magnetic storm, the effect of solar eclipse, etc.

TOOL PLANNING AND INSPECTION FOR MUNITION PRODUCTION

Herbert James Keating
Chief Engineer, Thomas A. Edison, Inc., Orange, N. J., 1931

ABSTRACT—Part I. Introduction to the organization, modern and efficient, capable of producing 1,345 pieces of work daily, 3.67 cutters and 92 cents per man employed.

This type of modern organization has not only blood veins and arteries, but also nerves and dynamic life.

Part II. Tool Planning and Inspection for Munition Production; Procedure: Definite steps are outlined as to the giving of orders, flow of work, and perfect Central Control. Inspection is carried on to check up the flow of work in each branch and each step of the manufacturing unit.

Part III. Tool Shop Planning: This part of the paper outlines the exact manners in which the shops are marked, tools marked, operation and machine symbols given so that the workers can follow quickly and the whole system fits into the plan. The exact manner to operate the Central Control tells why this system is most efficient.

179

Part IV. Duties of Inspectors. The Chief Inspector of a section is responsible for the condition of work passing from one hand to another. A higher inspector applies judgment on conditions of work, a detail inspector applies exactness of workmanship.

The last part of this paper relates of remarkable results of firms employing this type of organization.

20 Order Forms are given.

ANALYTIC GRADIENT FUNCTIONS

Si-Ping Cheo
University of Michigan

ABSTRACT—The purpose of this paper is to investigate a fundamental property of a vector function obtained from taking the gradient of a harmonic function. Examples of such analytic vector function will be given.

CAPILLARY PHENOMENA OF COMMERCIAL CELLULOSE

Yi Ou'Yang
Ohio State University

ABSTRACT—The purposes of this work were to find the relationship between the "rise" method and "drop" method for determining the capillarity of paper in order to compare the degree of correctness of them; to find the factors which may affect the measurement of capillarity of paper; to find the effect of sizing materials on the capillarity of paper; and to find the relationship between the capillarity of paper and the nature of liquid.

In laying a foundation for such an investigation, the modified procedures of these two methods—"rise" and "drop"—by which the conditions can be better controlled, were used. Three kinds of unsized paper, blotter, filter and newsprint, were used as samples in determining the relationship between these two methods and the factors which may affect the measurement of capillarity. Two kinds of sized papers, white bond typing paper and superfine typewriter paper, were used for determining the effect of sizing materials on the capillarity of paper. Aqueous solutions of ethyl alcohol of different concentrations were used for determining the relationship between the capillarity of paper and the nature of liquid.

It was found that the result by "rise" method does not agree with that by "drop" method, but can be converted into the latter by using the following formula:

$$C^d = 0.86\pi\ (C^r\ T\ P)^2$$

where C^d = Capillarity by "drop" method in cc/sec.
C^r = Capillarity by "rise" method in cm/10 min.
T = Thickness of paper
P = Porosity of paper
π = 3.1416;

measurement of capillarity is affected by temperature, evaporation of the liquid and air current; capillarity of paper strips along the machine direction is always higher than that across the machine direction; relationships between the capillarity and bulk density of paper and capillarity and porosity of paper can not be found; capillarity of felt side of paper is not considerably different from that of wire side; the width of paper strips in "rise" method does not affect the measurement of capillarity; capillarity of paper can be completely removed by the sizing process; and the capillarity of paper is inversely proportional to the viscosity of the liquid

THE INFRARED ABSORPTION SPECTRUM OF CARBON DIOXIDE

Ta-You Wu
University of Michigan

ABSTRACT—With a grating spectrometer the infrared absorption spectrum of CO_2 is studied with an absorption tube of 7 meters containing the gas at atmospheric pressure. New bands are found at 4860, 4982, 5110, 6079, 6233, 6353, 6512, 6978 cm^{-1}. These bands are identified as v_3+4v_2, $v_3+2v_2+v_1$,; v_3+2v ; v_3+6v_2, $v_3+4v_2+v_1$, $v_3+2v_2+2v_1$, v_3+3v_1; and $3v_3$ respectively of Dennison's scheme. The observed positions of these bands agreed exceedingly well with the values 4852, 4982, 5109, 6078, 6233, 6352, 6512, 6974 obtained by Adel and Dennison by a second order energy correction calculation.

做反射鏡面之新法

T. L. HO
California Institute of Technology

提要—此新法係指金屬在真空中加熱使蒸發而凝結於磨光之玻璃或其他固體面上而言。用此法做反射鏡面，手續簡單，所需時間不長，可應用於大部分金屬及合金，並所成反射面頗精確，易持久，易保護。文中備述作者所試驗儀器之裝置，與作者對於做巨大反射鏡面之理論設計。

WHERE CHINA STANDS IN THE COURSE OF INDUSTRIALIZATION

Thomas T Eoyang
Columbia University

ABSTRACT—By graphical representation this paper indicates the present trend of national industrialization in China. By means of statistical analysis I have tried to show that it is no longer true that China has vast territory with rich resources. She has lost very greatly by imperialistic exploitation.

Preliminary to proceeding on any course of industrialization, we should not overlook the appraisal of our national wealth. Some of the figures and charts are plain enough to show how much wealth is at our disposal for the purpose of industrialization and which route we should take to industrialize our country.

This paper deals with five main topics; namely, power and fuel, mineral resources, communications, agricultural products and foreign trade. Since the subject of the industrialization of China is so broad and has so many phases, it can be adequately covered only by a comprehensive study. However, the writer hopes that the facts here set forth by illustration will throw some light on the big problem that we are facing.

THE PROBLEMS OF CHINESE COAL MINING INDUSTRY

Y. L. Chu
Illinois University

ABSTRACT—

A. Economical Problems

I. The development of coal mining industry and its present situation in the most important coal producing countries.

II. The geographical coal distribution and the probable coal reserve in China.

III. Character of coal in each field as adapted to (1) steam generation (2) metallurgical coke, (3) gas and by-products, (4) domestic consumption.

IV. Availability of each field to probable point of consumption.

V. Availability of other primary resources such as iron ore, lumber, aluminum, antimony, etc., to coal field.

VI. Increasing the market demands

1. The earning power of the people
2. The price of coal
3. The distribution system
4. The transportation facilities
5. The development of power and allied industries
6. The development of new uses of coal
7. The development of irrigation system
8. The development of smelting plants
9. The export trade
10. The development of domestic furnace
11. The increased use of powdered coal

181

AUTHOR INDEX

F indicates Friday session.
S " Saturday "
Su " Sunday "

The numbers 1, 2, 3, ... indicate the order of presentation.
Abstracts of papers F9, F10, S10, not available at the time of printing, do not actually appear in the section "Abstracts"

聯合年會特刊

年會會程
論文提要

科學與工程

中國工程師學會美洲分會
中國科學社美洲分社

民國二十二年八月二十五至二十八日紐約

K. H. Chang
457 W. 123 St.
Apt. 2

CONDENSED PROGRAM

Friday, August 31

4:00 P.M.— 6:00 P.M.	Registration
6:30 P.M.— 7:30 P.M.	Informal Dinner
8:00 P.M.—11:00 P.M.	Opening Session

Saturday, September 1

9:00 A.M.—12:00 Noon	Technical Session
12:00 Noon— 1:30 P.M.	Luncheon
2:00 P.M.— 5:00 P.M.	Visit to the New York Museum of Science and Industry
6:00 P.M.— 8:00 P.M.	Informal Dinner
8:30 P.M.—11:00 P.M.	Social Meeting

Sunday, September 2

9:00 A.M.—12:00 Noon	Technical Paper Session
12:30 P.M.— 1:30 P.M.	Luncheon
2:30 P.M.— 6:00 P.M.	Business Meeting
7:00 P.M.—11:00 P.M.	Annual Banquet

Monday, September 3

9:00 A.M.—12:00 Noon	Symposium on the Industrialization of China
2:00 P.M.— 6:00 P.M.	Sight-Seeing
6:30 P.M.— 8:30 P.M.	Informal Dinner

190

FOREWORD

The pressing need in China for men and women trained in sciences and engineering is generally recognized. From testimonials by individuals as well as by organizations the consensus of opinion points to the acute shortage of trained abilities as the foremost difficulty in our national reconstruction.

It is apparent, however, that the problem of developing our national resources could not and should not be faced by each engineer or each scientist in isolation. Unaided, he will fall far short of his usefulness no matter how proficient he may be in his line. Our engineers and scientists can contribute most to our country by banding ourselves together as intellectual comrades against one common enemy — the economic backwardness of our country.

It is with this object in view that the two societies have never failed to call once every year a joint convention. In the most congenial and stimulating atmosphere provided by such a gathering, we are given the opportunity not only to discuss problems of common interest but to form an esprit de corps that may permeate all future enterprises in which we participate.

Recognizing the divergent interests of members as well as nonmembers, the Committee has constantly borne in mind the necessity of making the program as varied and interesting as possible. Special care has been taken to make the papers, speeches and motion pictures representative of a wide range of subject matter and to balance technical sessions with gatherings that are purely social and recreational in nature.

It is hoped that those who will see this program will realize that, by attending this Convention, they will not only reap for themselves the benefits of the sessions, but make it possible for others to reap the benefits to which they are entitled.

THE JOINT CONVENTION COMMITTEE.

171

JOINT CONVENTION COMMITTEES

General Committee

Dr. Chen-nan Li, *Chairman*

Edward W. Fong, *Secretary and Treasurer*

Dr. Bacon F. Chow
Thomas T. Eoyang
Kwang H. Chang
Harry Lee
Dr. Ronald Y. S. Cheng

Committee on Technical Papers

Thomas T. Eoyang, *Chairman*
Dr. Bacon F. Chow
Dr. P. T. Young
George C. Chow
Chai Yeh

Committee on Publication

Kwang H. Chang, *Chairman*
Dr. Chen-nan Li
Wing Y. Wong
Dr. Farn B. Chu
Richard S. M. Li

Committee on Finance

Edward W. Fong, *Chairman*
Richard W. C. Kuo
Dr. Ronald Y. S. Cheng
Harry Lee
C. P. Wong

Social Committee

Mrs. Chen-nan Li, *Chairman*
Miss Daisy Lew
Richard W. C. Kuo
Mrs. Richard S. M. Li
K. S. Lee

Banquet Committee

Dr. Ronald Y. S. Cheng, *Chairman*

Wing Y. Wong
Dr. Farn B. Chu
C. P. Wong
Dr. T. S. Jung

• • •

4

PROGRAM OF 1934 JOINT CONVENTION
of
The Chinese Institute of Engineers, American Section
and
The Science Society of China, American Branch

Headquarters: 500 Riverside Drive, New York, N. Y.

AUGUST 31 to SEPTEMBER 3

Friday Afternoon, August 31

3:00 P.M.—6:00 P.M.—REGISTRATION *Room C*

Registrars: Thomas T. Eoyang, Harry Lee, Kim S. Lee, Dr. Ronald Y. S. Cheng

Friday Evening, August 31

INFORMAL DINNER

At New China Restaurant, Broadway and La Salle

8:00 P.M.—11:00 P.M.—OPENING SESSION *Room ABC*

Chairman, Edward W. Fong.

OPENING REMARKS

Introduction of Officers of both Societies.

Official Welcome by Kwang H. Chang and Dr. Chen-nan Li.

ADDRESSES.

1. Iron Casting in China.
   Prof. T. T. Read (Former Professor of Peiyang University, China) Professor of Mining Engineering, Columbia University.
2. The High-Pressure Chemical Industries in China.
   T. P. Hou, Ph.D., Chief Engineer and Works Manager, Pacific Alkali Co., Ltd., Tangku, Hopei, China.

Saturday Morning, September 1

9:00 A.M.—12:00 Noon—TECHNICAL PAPER SESSION *Room AB*

Presiding Officers: Dr. T. S. Jung, George C. C. Chou.

1. The Financial Burden and Livelihood of the Chinese Farmer.
   A. Kaiming Chiu, Ph.D., Honorary Consultant to the Directorate of Statistics, National Government of China, Nanking.
2. Transient Phenomenon in Synchronous Machines.
   Hsu-Yun Fan, Massachusetts Institute of Technology.

3. A Suggested Trend Number for Airplanes and a Wider Meaning of Aviation Economy.
   George C. C. Chou, Aeronautical Engineer.

4. Studies on the Electrolysis of Brine with Mercury Cathode.
   W. I. Liao, Chemical Engineering, The Ohio State University.

5. Design of a Rigid Frame Bridge.
   M. L. Loh, Civil Engineering, Massachusetts Institute of Technology.

6. Chemical Control of One Bath Chrome Tannage.
   Dean Shoo-Tze and Yun-Hwong Chen, Chemistry Department, Science College, National Peking University, Peiping, China.

7. General Survey of the Field of Synthetic Resins.
   M. R. Bhagwat, Consulting Chemical Engineer.

12:00 P.M.—1:30 P.M.—LUNCHEON
Lotus Village, 143 West 47th Street
Edward W. Fong in charge.

2:00 P.M.—6:00 P.M.—Trip to New York Museum of Science and Industry
Ronald Y. S. Cheng and Kwang H. Chang in charge.

6:00 P.M.—7:00 P.M.—INFORMAL DINNER
Sin Kee Garden, 500 West 125th Street
T. T. Eoyang in charge.

7:30 P.M.—11:00 P.M.—SOCIAL MEETING *Room ABC*
Chairman, Mrs. Chen-nan Li.

Address:
Present Conditions in China.
Dr. Francis C. M. Wei, President of Central China College, Wu-Chang, Hupeh, China.

Talking Pictures:
1. Sound
2. Fundamentals of Acoustics
3. Molecular Theory of Matter

Paper:
A Suggested Program Audio Visual Education for China.
Ronald Y. S. Cheng, Columbia University.

Entertainment and Refreshments

Sunday, September 2

9:00 A.M.—12:00 Noon—TECHNICAL PAPER SESSION *Room AB*
Presiding Officers: Thomas T. Eoyang, Dr. A. Kaiming Chiu.

1. Summation Method Adapted to Fitting Parabolic Curves and Calculating the Index of Correlation with Data Plotted in a Scatter Diagram.
   Dr. Chen-nan Li, Economic Statistician, Research Department, The Standard Statistics Company, New York City.

6

2. A Study of Theory and Practice of the Application of Pulverized Coal Firing in the Modern Steam-Generating Stations.
   Jenney Kang, Cornell University.

3. Carbonization of Coal in Bulk.
   C. S. Lomax, Consulting Chemical Engineer.

4. The Measurement of Economic Ability of the Local Districts in China.
   Dr. Ronald Y. S. Cheng, Columbia University.

5. The Future Development of Incandescent Lamp and Vacuum Tube Industries in China.
   Chai Yeh, Craft Laboratory, Harvard University.

6. The Effect of Temperature on the Contractile Vacuole of Certain Ciliates.
   Harry Gaw, Yale University.

12:30 P.M.—1:30 P.M.—LUNCHEON
College Inn, 3100 Broadway
Richard W. C. Kao in charge.

2:00 P.M.—6:00 P.M.—BUSINESS MEETING *Room C*
Chinese Institute of Engineers, American Section
Presiding Officer: Kwang H. Chang.

2:00 P.M.—6:00 P.M.—BUSINESS MEETING *Room AB*
Science Society of China, American Branch
Presiding Officer: Dr. Chen-nan Li.

7:00 P.M.—11:00 P.M.—ANNUAL BANQUET
Port Arthur Restaurant, 7-9 Mott Street
Toastmaster, Dr. Chen-nan Li

SPEAKERS:
Mr. R. S. Grene, Vice-Director, Peking Union Medical College, Peiping.
Mr. K. C. Li, President, Wah Chang Trading Co., New York City.

Monday, September 3

9:00 A.M.—12:00 Noon—SYMPOSIUM ON THE INDUSTRIALIZATION OF CHINA *Room AB*

Presiding Officers: Thomas T. Eoyang, George C. Chou.

1. Man Power in Modern Industry.
   William W. Coutts, Former Engineer, Guardbridge Paper Mills, Scotland.

2. An Appraisal of Economic Planning in China.
   Ronald Y. S. Cheng, Columbia University.

3. The Present Status of the Industrialization of China and Its Major Considerations.
   Thomas T. Eoyang, Columbia University.

4. General Discussions
   Led by: George C. C. Chou, Harry Lee, Dr. Chen-nan Li, Kwang H. Chang.

12:30 P.M.—1:45 P.M.—LUNCHEON
Lee's Restaurant, 36 Pell Street
Edward W. Fong in charge.

2:00 P.M.—6:00 P.M.—SIGHT-SEEING
A Boat Trip Around New York.
Harry Lee in charge.

7:00 P.M.—8:30 P.M.—INFORMAL FAREWELL DINNER
Port Arthur, 7-9 Mott Street
James Hu in charge.

ABSTRACTS OF TECHNICAL PAPERS

THE FINANCIAL BURDEN AND LIVELIHOOD OF THE CHINESE FARMER

By A. KAIMING CHIU, Ph.D.

Formerly Research Fellow of the Institute of Social Research, Peiping, and Honorary Consultant to the Directorate of Statistics, National Government of China, Nanking

This is a chapter in a report of an economic survey of 184 farms in Shentze County, Hupei Province, conducted by the writer in 1930-31. It attempts to portray by statistical method the economic conditions of Chinese farmers in an inland village comparatively unaffected by "Western influence." The full report deals with such subjects as general physical characteristics and economic conditions of the locality, population, education, farm organization, land utilization, capital investment, type of farming, factors affecting financial success, farm indebtedness and rural credit, and family living. In this paper, only the last two topics will be taken up. The data for the study were secured by the "Representative Method" of sampling with prepared and tested individual farm and household schedules, and the results were analyzed and summarized by employing the usual statistical methods.

TRANSIENT PHENOMENON IN SYNCHRONOUS MACHINES

By HSU-YUN FAN

Massachusetts Institute of Technology

The paper begins with a general outline of the transient phenomenon in synchronous machines. Short-circuit current is briefly mentioned. The main discussion is devoted to the transient oscillations. The resultant equations are given, the approximations being carefully explained. Brief description of the M.I.T. Differential Analyzer and its application to the solution of the differential equation of transient oscillations conclude the theoretical discussions. A laboratory experiment to check the analytical solutions by the differential analyzer is described and followed by a discussion of the obtained results.

A SUGGESTED TREND NUMBER FOR AIRPLANES AND A WIDER MEANING OF AVIATION ECONOMY

By GEORGE CHUAN-CHANG CHOU

Aeronautical Engineer

This paper contains: (I) A suggested Trend Number for new airplanes based on the Lift coefficient of the finished airplane, Drag or resistance coefficient, from both the finished airplane and the power input calculations. Then the ratio of Lift coefficient over the Drag coefficient will represent the FINENESS of the airplane. Finally, the WING POWER in horsepower per square foot of wing area, when multiplied by the Fineness, will give the SUGGESTED TREND NUMBER FOR AIRPLANES. This Trend Number is much simpler to use and gives quick results in keeping airplane statistics. It is also easier for the general public to comprehend the Trend Number than the "High Speed Number" by Everling and others in Europe. (II) A wider meaning of Aviation Economy in: 1—Methods of airplane production; 2—Methods of airplane construction; 3—Coordination of maintenance problems; 4—Speed regulation of airplane team operations.

The 68 districts of Hupeh Province are used as examples. The data are from the Directorate of Budget and Statistics and the Hupeh Department of Civil Affairs.

The method is first a weighing of the value of cultivated land per capita of farm population and of the value of farm crops per capita of farm population. A combined unit measure is then devised. The product moment correlation method is applied. It is found that tax revenue has a negative correlation with the value of cultivated land. The r is —.14. The r between the unit values of land and crops is +.59.

There are the following assumptions:

1. The value of land of China constitutes about 82% of her total wealth.
2. The value of subsidiary agricultural industries (which is not included in this study) has a high correlation with the value of farm crops, the ratio of the two being 68.34:100.
3. This method measures only the relative or comparative ability of the districts and not their absolute ability. It measures the ability of the farmers of the districts, since urban wealth is left out of consideration.
4. Both the technique and findings are held tentative until better data are available.

CARBONIZATION OF COAL IN BULK

By C. S. LOMAX

Carbonization of Coal in Bulk is now the world's preferred method for the production of gas for domestic use and a smokeless burning domestic and metallurgical fuel—coke.

The purpose of the paper is to show the growth of the process in plant size, in the number and value of its products, and hence the economic value to the country.

THE FUTURE DEVELOPMENT OF INCANDESCENT LAMP AND VACUUM TUBE INDUSTRIES IN CHINA

By CHAI YEH

Cruft Laboratory, Harvard University

This paper begins with a short discussion of the possibility and necessity of the future development of incandescent lamp and vacuum tube industries in China. The present situation of Chinese manufacturers and the market condition in China are briefly described. The raw materials used for the manufacture of lamps and tubes are mentioned and the mining of Chinese tungsten is described. Following are brief descriptions of the processes of manufacture of both incandescent lamps and vacuum tubes. A factory design is outlined and briefly discussed. At last, the author makes a few suggestions as to the development of these industries.

THE EFFECT OF TEMPERATURE ON THE CONTRACTILE VACUOLE OF CERTAIN CILIATES

By HARRY GAW

Yale University

The rate of pulsation of the anterior contractile vacuole of four species of Paramecium (P. multimicronucleata, P. aurelia, P. caudatum and P. polycaryum) has been determined over a temperature range of about 16° C. The temperature characteristics calculated are nearly the same: below 16° + or — 1° the u value is around 25,000. Between 16° + or — 1° and 22.5° + or — 1° around 16,000. Above 22.5° + or — 1° around 12,000.

The rate of pulsation of the contractile vacuole of Blepharisma undulans has been determined over a temperature range of about 18° C. There is considerable difference between individuals from old and new cultures, and between individuals in the same old culture in the rate of pulsation and in u values. The temperature characteristic of the individuals from the new culture is constant; namely, between 14.9° + or — .5° and 28.8° + or — .5° it is 16,700.

The rate of pulsation of the contractile vacuole of Spirostomum ambiguum has been determined over a temperature range of about 18° C. The temperature characteristic is 12,000 between 13.6° and 32.1°.

Most of the u values are very close to Crozier's values for oxidative processes and some are close to one of McCutcheon and Lucke's u values for water permeability. It seems if either or both oxidation and water permeability might control the rate of pulsation in Paramecium and Blepharisma.

ABSTRACTS OF TECHNICAL PAPERS

Industrialization of China

MAN-POWER IN MODERN INDUSTRY

By WILLIAM W. COUTTS
Former Engineer, Guardbridge Paper Mills, Scotland

With the introduction of modern technique and machinery, requiring, as they do, something more than the natural ingenuity of the workman, there arises what is probably the greatest problem in any program of industrialization—that of creating a sufficiency of adequately trained mechanics.

This study was made with the object of answering the following questions:

1. What is the best method, during the present period of transition from handicraft to modern methods, of preparing mechanics in modern technique?
2. How may this training be obtained?
3. What is the inducement for employer cooperation?
4. What would be the probable immediate cost and return to the employer?

A comparison of American and British training methods, based upon personal observation, and a study of cost, based upon industrial wage rates in Great Britain, lead to the conclusion that the best method of preparation is by extension courses in vocational training and that these courses could be financed by employers at little or no cost to them.

HIGH GRADE PRESS

GENERAL PRINTERS
and
MENU SPECIALISTS
for the Chinese Trade

929 Third Avenue
Bet. 55th & 56th Sts.
New York

ELdorado 5-8788

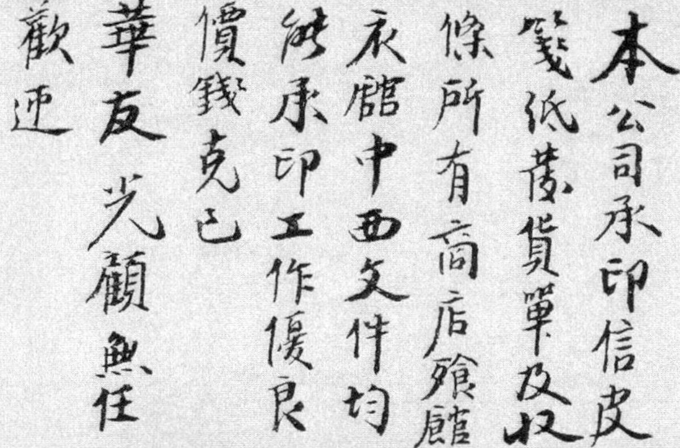

Phone MEdallion 3-8947

蓮 Lotus Village 洞

143 WEST 47th ST. - NEW YORK

Featuring

Chinese Barbecues and Egg Rolls
Real Chinese Foods

DAILY LUNCHEON 35c
Served from 11 to 3:30 P.M.
EXCEPT SUNDAY & HOLIDAYS

DAILY DINNER 50c
Served from 5 to 9:30 P.M.

UNiversity 4-8330

興 記
SING, KEE GARDEN

American and Chinese Restaurant

Special Luncheon 11 a. m. to 3 p.m. - 30c
Special Dinner 5 p. m to 9 p. m. - 45c
THE ONLY SHANGHAI RESTAURANT
IN THE U. S.

500 WEST 125th STREET New York City

Tel. WOrth 2-5890

PORT ARTHUR RESTAURANT, Inc.

旅順樓

Special Arrangement for Parties
FIRST CLASS
CHINESE RESTAURANT
Open From 11 A. M. to 1 A. M. — Sat. to 4 A. M.

7-9 MOTT STREET NEW YORK CITY

$70-80 advertise

$100 Printing

$100-200 Convention expenses

PRINTED BY
929 Third Ave., N. Y. C.—HIGH GRADE PRESS—Phone ELdorado 5-8788

211

FINANCIAL STATEMENT

of the

AMERICAN BRANCH OF THE SCIENCE SOCIETY OF CHINA
(Ending April 30, 1934)

Dear Members:

The following is an itemized statement of the financial condition of the American Branch of the Science Society of China ending April 30, 1934:

Cash Receipts:

Balance from Dr. Bacon F. Chow.	$47.23
Permanent Membership Fees	45.45
Initiation Fees	40.00
Annual Dues (1934)	33.00
TOTAL . .	$165.68

Cash Disbursements:

Chairman Dr. Bacon F. Chow's expenses	$ 1.00
Treasurer's expenses	3.03
TOTAL . .	$ 4.03
Balance on hand in cash.	161.65
TOTAL . .	$ 165.65

Those members who have not yet paid their initiation fee of $2.50 please pay the said amount at your ear'iest convenience. The annual dues of $1.50 for 1934 for the American Branch of the Science Society is also due. As I am leaving this country the middle of May, I have asked Dr. Bacon F. Chow to take charge of the treasury for the remaining term. Please pay your initiation fee and dues to Dr. Chow whose address is: Hospital of Rockefeller Institute, East 66th Street and York Avenue, New York City, New York.

I take this opportunity to thank those who have cooperated with me and also for their prompt attention.

Yours sincerely,

Shorchin C. Hsiung, treasurer.

April 30, 1934,
3011 Abell Avenue,
Baltimore, Maryland.

34

444 E. 66th St.
Apt. 2 KK
New York City
Sept. 28, 1934

Dear Member,

The Election Committee takes pleasure in submitting the following nominees for officers of the Science Society of China, American Branch, for the year 1934-35. Please indicate your choice for each office on the enclosed card, sign and return before Oct. 15.

For President:

1. Chen-nan Li, Statistics, N.Y. City
2. Alfred Kaiming Chiu, Economics, Harvard
3. Richard Bien, Physics, M.I.T.
4. Chin-Chih Jao, Botany, Michigan
5. Tze-Ching Huang, Prof. of Chemistry at Tsing Hua on furlough doing research at M.I.T.

For Secretary:

1. Miss Daisy L. Lau, Psychology, Columbia
2. Y. Cheng, Zoology, Pennsylvania
3. Richard Bien, Physics, M.I.T.
4. Thomas T. Eoyang, Engineering, Columbia
5. S. C. Chen, Physics, Pennsylvania 陳世昌 Rm 41 Physics Laboratory Research Section

For Treasurer:

1. H.Y. Feng, Anthropology, Pennsylvania
2. S. C. Chen, Physics, Pennsylvania
3. Harry Gaw, Zoology, Yale
4. Miss Yuan Kuan-shih, Physics, Michigan
5. I-ping Chao, Physiology, Chicago

Respectfully submitted,

Bacon F. Chow
Alfred Kaiming Chiu

Election Committee

35

敬啟者：二十四年五月七日晚上，丁在君先生在中央廣播電台講演，元任因爲常常在實驗室裏用鋁片收灌廣播講演，作爲語言的參考材料，這一次也把這講演收灌下來了。

在君先生死後，我們談到各種紀念他的方式，因而想到無意中留下來他的聲音，如果能複製，豈不是好給大家朋友做一個絕好的紀念物？但是最後一面已經糟蹋了。於是又想法把這面外圈的講演部分轉灌在一張新片子上，餘下來的新空白就請了翁詠霓先生說了幾句關於在君先生的生平的話，把這四面兩片的材料送到上海百代公司複製出來，就成了現在的這兩張片子。

現在百代公司來信說，這兩張片子約在四月十日可以製成。估計的價錢是每套國幣六元三角；京滬以外的各地加裝寄費七角。

在君先生的朋友們如願得這一套「在君遺音片」，請趕快通知上海白利南路中央研究院丁燮林，或南京北極閣中央研究院歷史語言研究所趙元任，以便預定爲要。此請

大安！

丁燮林
趙元任

同啓

二十五年四月七日

37

茲擬定購丁在君先生講演遺音片一套價洋（六元二角（京滬）七元正（外埠））俟接到出片通知時即當匯上此致

丁燮林
趙元任先生

簽名：

住址：

中國科學社用箋

逕復者接奉五月百 大示承 分神代收社費並往佩蔵先將此向記賬情形開列備核並祈將分擾歸如錢入美分社賬冊及收據以備考

收社費撥入93	$10.00
收〃〃〃常329-333	$25.00
收寶通匯餘元接匯票補分墊收	$0.03
(+)	$35.03
支社費撥入93賠水	$4.68
支〃〃〃常329-333又	$3.70
支〃〃〃入93除賠水扣四成分社經費	$2.13
(−) 支社費撥常329-333又	$8.52
實收寶通匯票#149915	$16.00

式中所收項已分數入賬計共收卅元〇三分（內多匯三分即前接匯百廿日代領書二元半之一部分另墊二元五角）所支項亦已分數出帳計共支九元〇三分兩抵為十六元今如

總辦事處 上海亞爾培路五三三號 電話七一二五五一號

27/6/35

63

中國科學社用箋

前通之敬函二月二十日敬函所述周名字錯
誤暫留之D.D.V.o.2.9該文社費業會社
費撥入「70」帳「263」頁銷號並已將函知陝字第
號記室共收支情形開列下頁不
再逐述此致
高尚三陰先生 中國科學社總社事務室 廿年二月廿八日
撥社費撥入93帳329-333六頁社存查
此出為高君已酬復計
美分社代理會計振周存卷

總辦事處 上海亞爾培路五三三號 電話七一五五一號

64

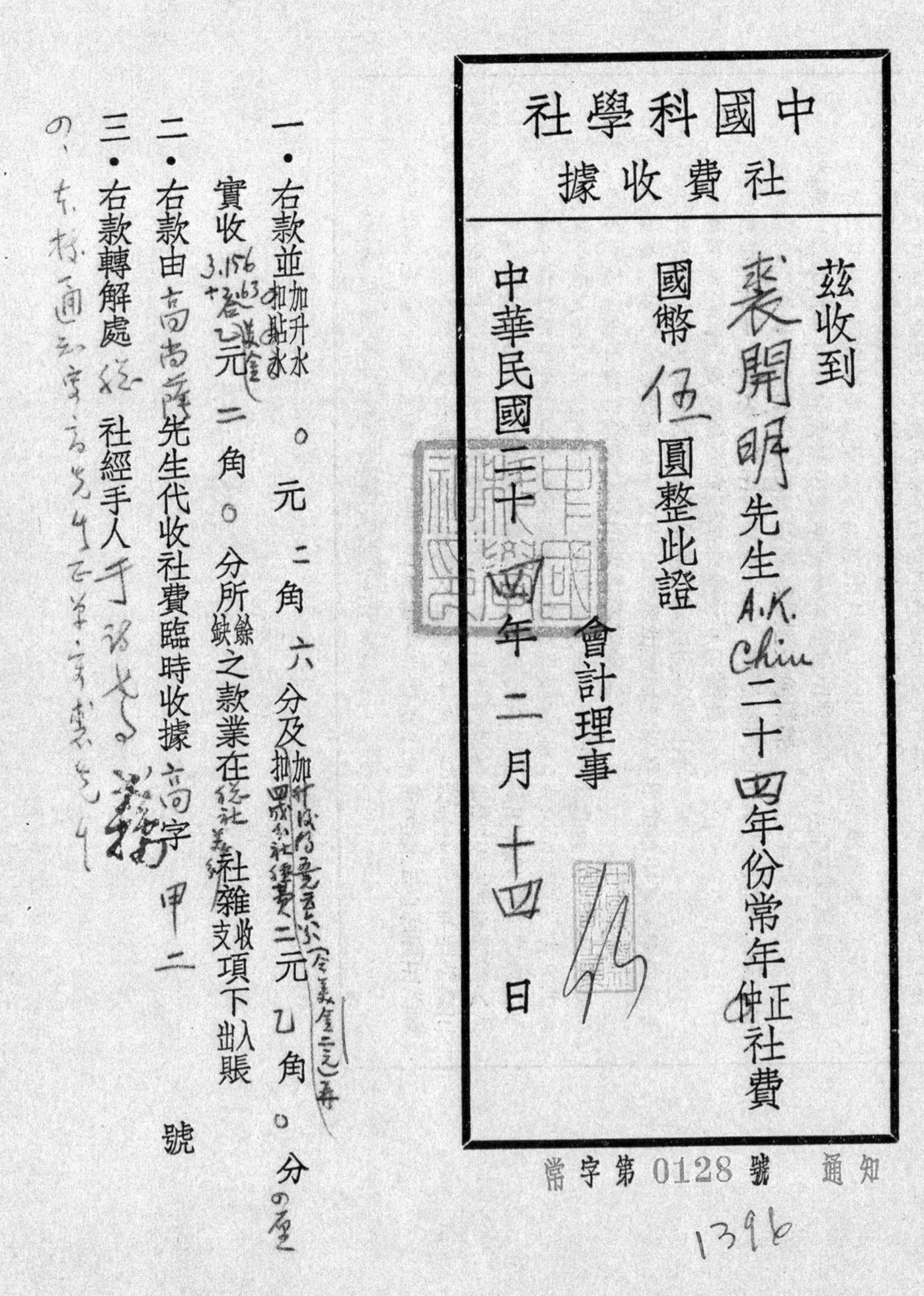

中國科學社
社費收據

茲收到
裘開明先生 A.K. Chiu 二十四年份常年(正)社費
國幣伍圓整此證
會計理事
中華民國二十四年二月十四日

常字第0128號　通知

一、右款並加升水／扣貼水〇元二角六分及加升水／扣回成社經費二元乙角〇分
實收 3.156 +.163 叁元二角〇分所餘／缺之款業在總社美洲社雜收／支項下入／出賬
二、右款由高尚蔭先生代收社費臨時收據高字甲二號
三、右款轉解處總社經手人
四、本條通知寄高先生

1396

105

中國科學社社費徵收簡則 廿三年七月一日訂正

一 本社常年社費以每年一月一日至十二月三十一日爲一年份凡屬(甲)普通正社員[子]在上半年經理事會選決入社者除入社費收十元外再收本年份常年正社費三元次年起每年份收常年正社費五元[丑]在下半年經理事會選決入社者祗收入社費十元不收本年份常年正社費次年起每年份收常年正社費五元(乙)仲社員每年份收常年仲社費三元其入社費俟補實正社員時補收(丙)永久社員總收永久社費一百元不收其他費用如不能一次繳足則每次至少繳廿五元並須在三年內繳清

二 社費收到概由本社會計理事簽發正式社費收據爲憑

三 代收社費須俟代收者將款彙集轉到方能將社費正據簽奉在社費正據未簽奉前由各代收者出具社費臨時收據該項臨時收據由代收者完全負責

四 社員應享各種權利須自應繳各種社費繳清之日開始

五 社員對社費事項如有查詢請正式專函上海亞爾培路五三三號中國科學社總社事務室轉會計理事以便答復其他事項請勿並列以免延誤

六 社費正據分編常字入字永字三種各依徵費性質三疊複塡(甲)存根留簿存查(乙)通知專供本社內部記賬及交代收者存查之用(丙)正單掣交繳費者或由代收者轉交繳費者舊用白色硬片式收據廿三年七月起一律廢止

七 社費據上社員姓名均寫最近社員錄中正名社員錄中尚未印入者寫其入社願書上正名社費金額均塡所繳各費全額如有代收者預扣各費憑其彙轉款項時隨附之扣費單據另賬付出並在社費正據之存根通知兩單附註內塡明其他損益依此類推

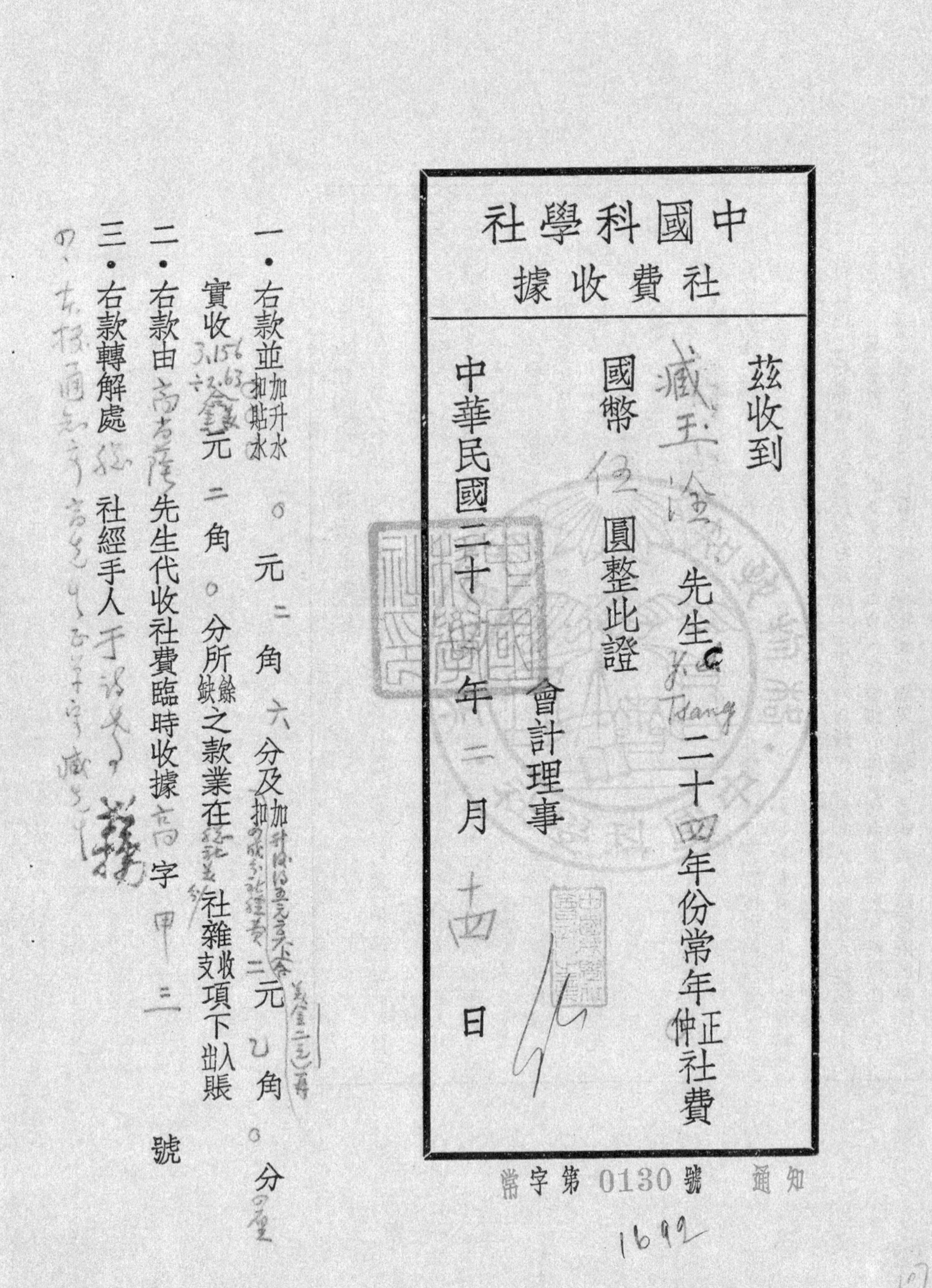

中國科學社
社費收據

茲收到
臧玉淦 先生 Y. C. Tsang 二十四年份常年正社費
國幣 伍 圓整此證
會計理事
中華民國二十 年 二 月 十四 日

常字第 0130 號 通知

1692

一、右款並加升水扣貼水 ○ 元 二 角 六 分及加升水扣貼水 二 元 乙 角 ○ 分
實收 元 二 角 ○ 分所餘缺之款業在 社雜收支項下出入賬
二、右款由 高君藩 先生代收社費臨時收據 高 字 甲 二 號
三、右款轉解處 總社經手人

中國科學社社費徵收簡則 廿三年七月一日訂正

一 本社常年社費以每年一月一日至十二月三十一日為一年份凡屬（甲）普通正社員［子］在上半年經理事會選決入社者除入社費收十元外再收本年份常年正社費三元次年起每年份收常年正社費五元［丑］在下半年經理事會選決入社者祇收入社費十元不收本年份常年正社費次年起每年份收常年正社費五元（乙）仲社員每年份收常年仲社費三元其入社費俟補實正社員時補收（丙）永久社員總收永久社費一百元不收其他費用如不能一次繳足則每次至少繳廿五元並須在三年內繳清

二 社費收到概由本社會計理事簽發正式社費收據為憑

三 代收社費須俟代收者將款彙集轉到方能將社費正據簽奉在社費正據未簽奉前由各代收者出具社費臨時收據該項臨時收據由代收者完全負責

四 社員應享各種權利須自應繳各種社費繳清之日開始

五 社員對社費事項如有查詢請正式專函上海亞爾培路五三三號中國科學社總社事務室轉會計理事以便答復其他事項請勿並列以免延誤

六 社費正據分編常字入字永字三種各依徵費性質三疊複填（甲）存根留簿存查（乙）通知專供本社內部記賬及交代收者存查之用（丙）正單掣交繳費者或由代收者轉交繳費者舊用白色硬片式收據廿三年七月起一律廢止

七 社費據上社員姓名均寫最近社員錄中正名社員錄中尚未印入者寫其入社願書上正名社費金額均填所繳各費全額如有代收者預扣各費憑其彙轉款項時隨附之扣費單據另賬付出並在社費正據之存根通知兩單附註內填明其他損益依此類推

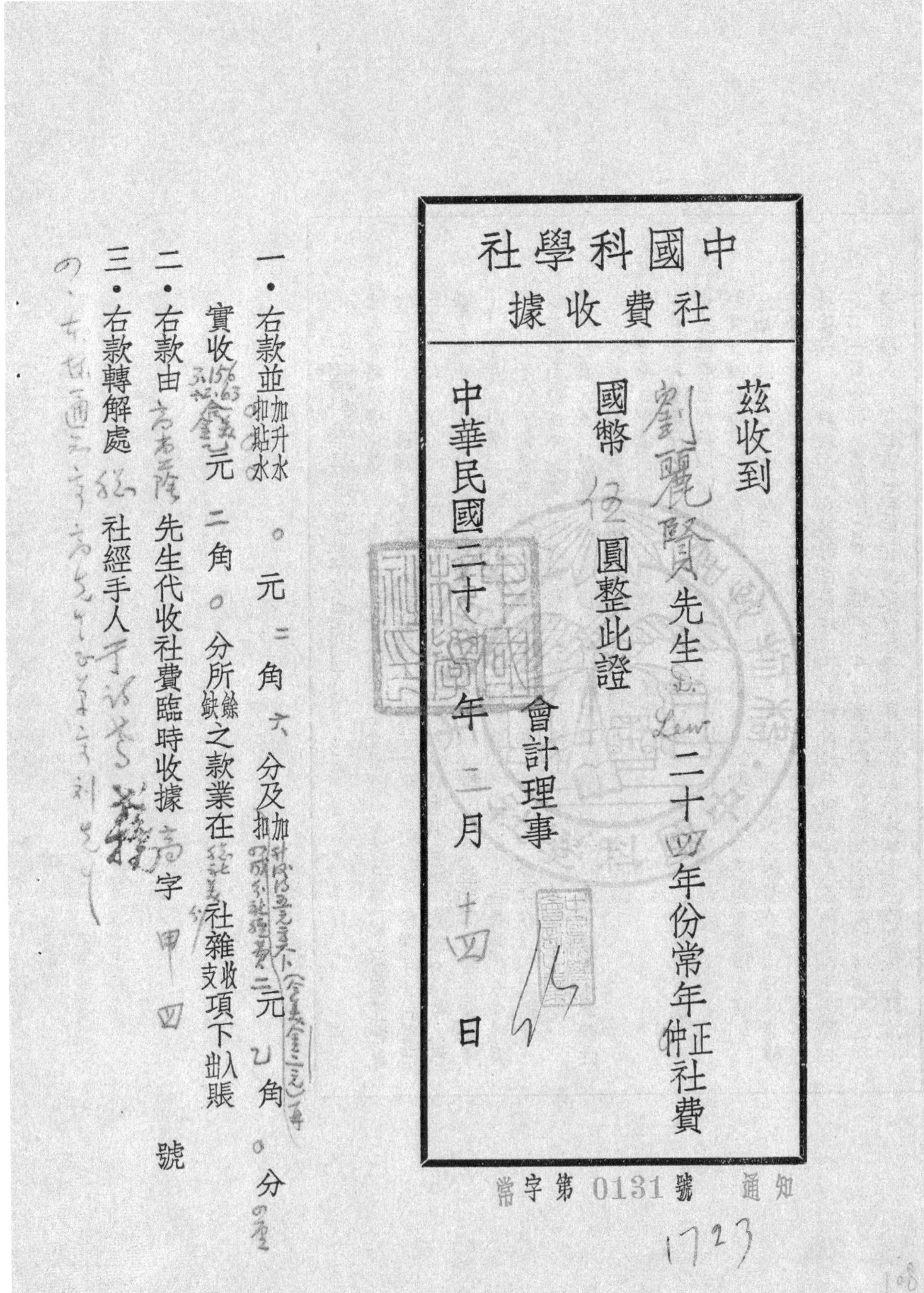

中國科學社
社費收據

茲收到
劉麗賢先生 Lew 二十四年份常年(仲正)社費
國幣伍圓整此證
會計理事
中華民國二十年三月十四日

常字第0131號　通知

1723

一、右款並加升水/扣貼水 ○元二角六分及加升水/扣貼水 二元乙角○分
實收 合洋 元二角○分所餘/缺之款業在 社雜收項下出/入賬
二、右款由高尚蔭先生代收社費臨時收據高字甲四號
三、右款轉解處 總社經手人

中國科學社社費徵收簡則 廿三年七月一日訂正

一　本社常年社費以每年一月一日至十二月三十一日爲一年份凡屬〔甲〕普通正社員〔子〕在上半年經理事會選決入社者除入社費收十元外再收本年份常年正社費三元次年起每年份收常年正社費五元〔丑〕在下半年經理事會選決入社者祗收入社費十元不收本年份常年正社費次年起每年份收常年正社費五元〔乙〕仲社員每年份收常年仲社費三元其入社費俟補實正社員時補收〔丙〕永久社員總收永久社費一百元不收其他費用如不能一次繳足則每次至少繳廿五元並須在三年內繳清

二　社費收到概由本社會計理事簽發正式社費收據爲憑

三　代收社費須俟代收者將款彙集轉到方能將社費正據簽奉在社費正據未簽奉前由各代收者出具社費臨時收據該項臨時收據由代收者完全負責

四　社員應享各種權利須自應繳各種社費繳清之日開始

五　社員對社費事項如有查詢請正式專函上海亞爾培路五三三號中國科學社總社事務室轉會計理事以便答復其他事項請勿並列以免延誤

六　社費正據分編常字入字永字三種各依徵費性質三疊複塡〔甲〕存根留簿存查〔乙〕通知專供本社內部記賬及交代收者存查之用〔丙〕正單掣交繳費者或由代收者轉交繳費者舊用白色硬片式收據廿三年七月起一律廢止

七　社費據上社員姓名均寫最近社員錄中正名社員錄中尙未印入者寫其入社願書上正名社費金額均塡所繳各費全額如有代收者預扣各費憑其彙轉款項時隨附之扣費單據另賬付出並在社費正據之存根通知兩單附註內塡明其他損益依此類推

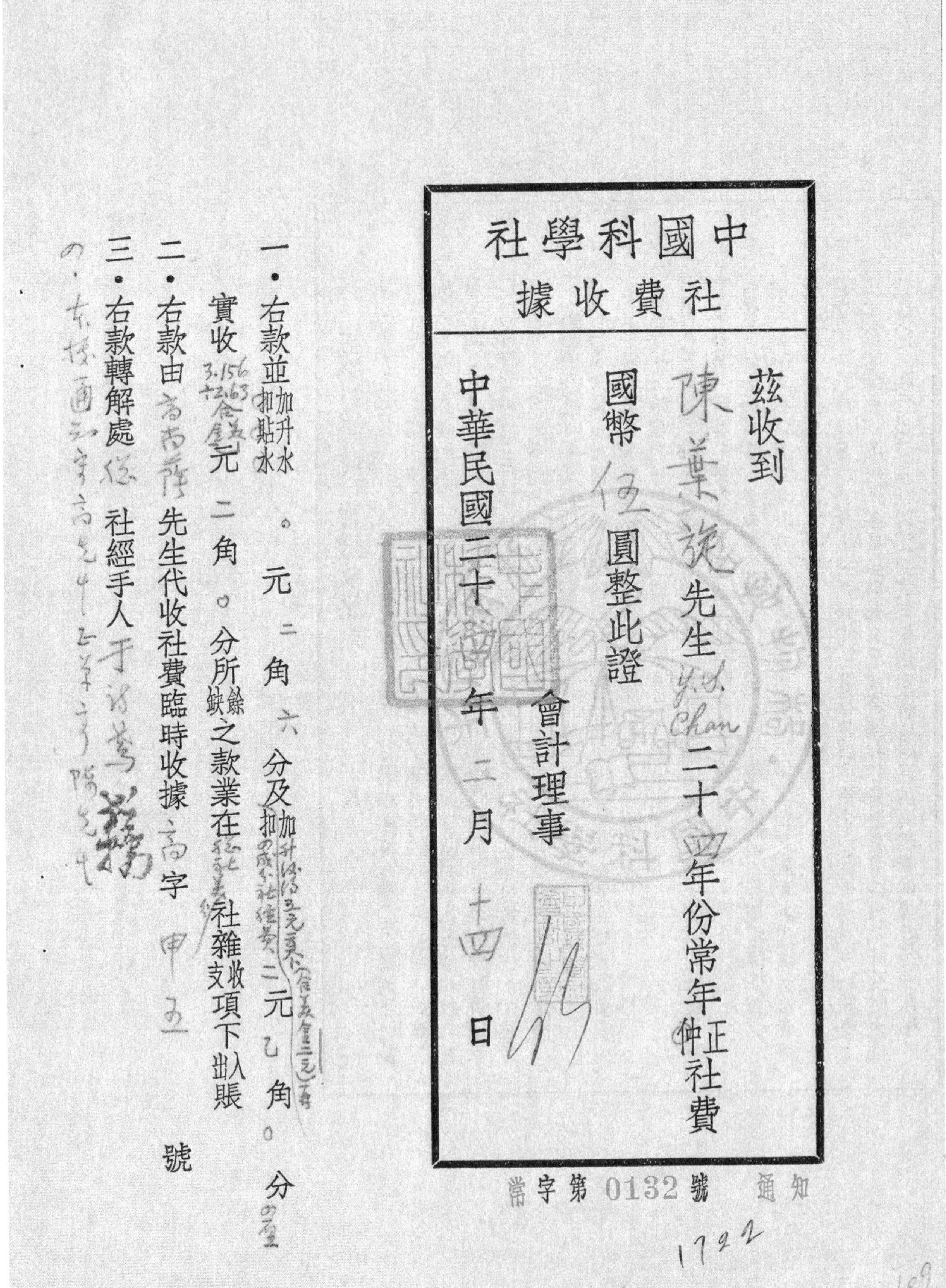

中國科學社
社費收據

茲收到
陳華旋先生 Y.H. Chan 二十四年份常年仲正社費
國幣伍圓整此證
會計理事
中華民國二十年三月十四日

常字第 0132 號　通知

一、右款並加升水扣貼水〇元二角六分及扣加升水等…二元乙角〇分
實收 3.156 +2.63 合金洋元二角〇分所餘缺之款業在…社雜收支項下出入賬
二、右款由高尚蔭先生代收社費臨時收據高字申五一號
三、右款轉解處總社經手人…

1722

109

中國科學社社費徵收簡則 廿三年七月一日訂正

一　本社常年社費以每年一月一日至十二月三十一日為一年份凡屬(甲)普通正社員[子]在上半年經理事會選決入社者除入社費收十元外再收本年份常年正社費三元次年起每年份收常年正社費五元[丑]在下半年經理事會選決入社者祇收入社費十元不收本年份常年正社費次年起每年份收常年正社費五元(乙)仲社員每年份收常年仲社費三元其入社費俟補實正社員時補收(丙)永久社員總收永久社費一百元不收其他費用如不能一次繳足則每次至少繳廿五元並須在三年內繳清

二　社費收到概由本社會計理事簽發正式社費收據為憑

三　代收社費須俟代收者將款彙集轉到方能將社費正據簽奉在社費正據未簽奉前由各代收者出具社費臨時收據該項臨時收據由代收者完全負責

四　社員應享各種權利須自應繳各種社費繳清之日開始

五　社員對社費事項如有查詢請正式專函上海亞爾培路五三三號中國科學社總社事務室轉會計理事以便答復其他事項請勿並列以免延誤

六　社費正據分編常字入字永字三種各依徵費性質三疊複填(甲)存根留簿存查(乙)通知專供本社內部記賬及交代收者存查之用(丙)正單掣交繳費者或由代收者轉交繳費者舊用白色硬片式收據廿三年七月起一律廢止

七　社費據上社員姓名均寫最近社員錄中正名社員錄中尚未印入者寫其入社願書上正名社費金額均填所繳各費全額如有代收者預扣各費憑其彙轉款項時隨附之扣費單據另賬付出並在社費正據之存根通知兩單附註內填明其他損益依此類推

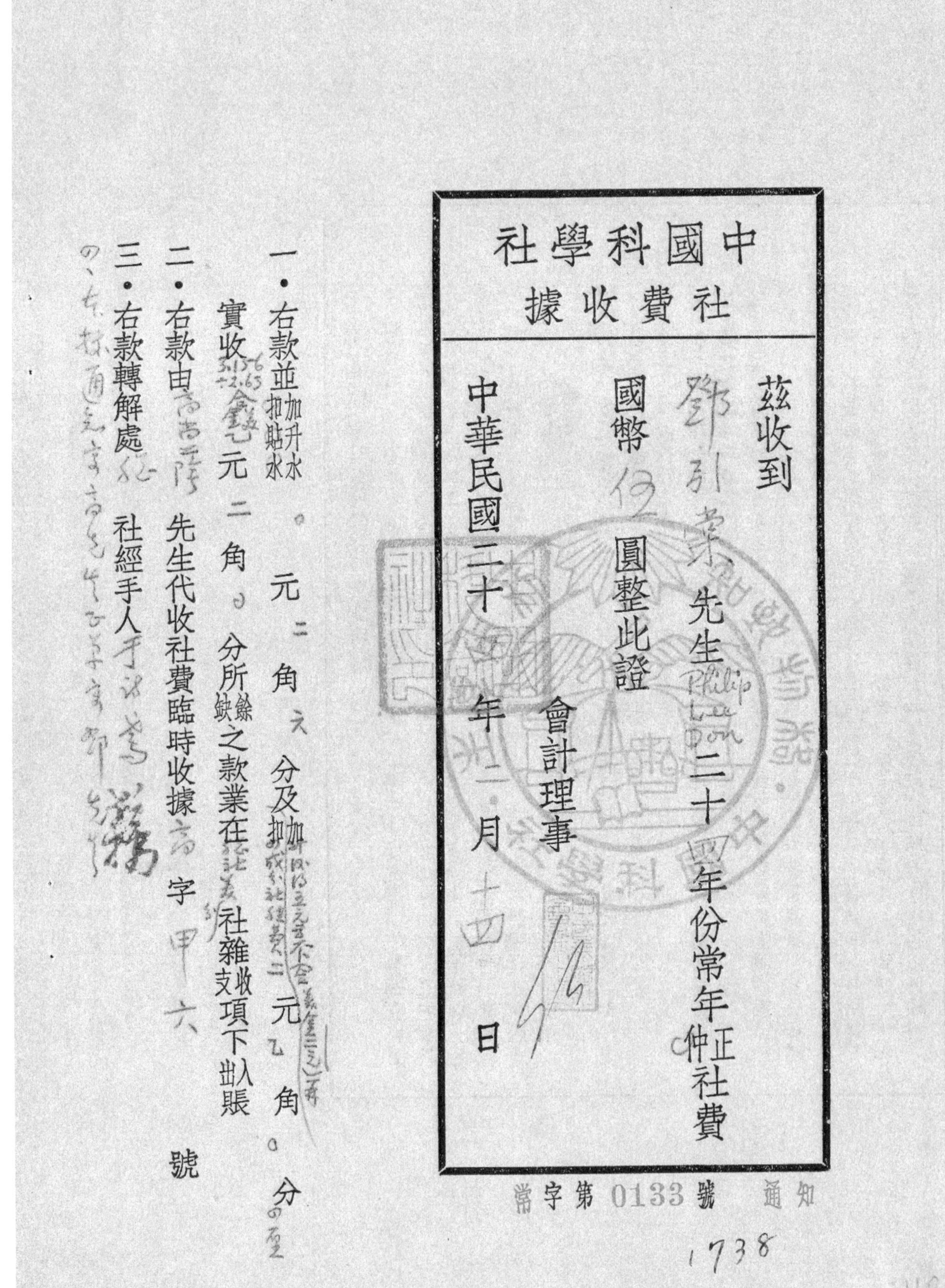

中國科學社
社費收據

茲收到
鄧引棠先生 Philip L. Den 二十四年份常年仲正社費
國幣伍圓整此證
會計理事
中華民國二十五年一月十四日

常字第0133號　通知

1738

一、右款並加升水、加貼水　○元二角九分及加[illegible]　元乙角○分
實收[illegible]　元二角○分所餘缺之款業在社雜收支項下出入賬
二、右款由[illegible]先生代收社費臨時收據[illegible]字甲六號
三、右款轉解處[illegible]社經手人[illegible]

110

中國科學社社費徵收簡則 廿三年七月一日訂正

一 本社常年社費以每年一月一日至十二月三十一日爲一年份凡屬〔甲〕普通正社員〔子〕在上半年經理事會選決入社者除入社費收十元外再收本年份常年正社費三元次年起每年份收常年正社費五元〔丑〕在下半年經理事會選決入社者祇收入社費十元不收本年份常年正社費次年起每年份收常年正社費五元〔乙〕仲社員每年份收常年仲社費三元其入社費俟補實正社員時補收〔丙〕永久社員總收永久社費一百元不收其他費用如不能一次繳足則每次至少繳廿五元並須在三年內繳清

二 社費收到概由本社會計理事簽發正式社費收據爲憑

三 代收社費須俟代收者將款彙集轉到方能將社費正據簽奉在社費正據未簽奉前由各代收者出具社費臨時收據該項臨時收據由代收者完全負責

四 社員應享各種權利須自應繳各種社費繳清之日開始

五 社員對社費事項如有查詢請正式專函上海亞爾培路五三三號中國科學社總社事務室轉會計理事以便答復其他事項請勿並列以免延誤

六 社費正據分編常字入字永字三種各依徵費性質三疊複填〔甲〕存根留簿存查〔乙〕通知專供本社內部記賬及交代收者存查之用〔丙〕正單掣交繳費者或由代收者轉交繳費者舊用白色硬片式收據廿三年七月起一律廢止

七 社費據上社員姓名均寫最近社員錄中正名社員錄中尚未印入者寫其入社願書上正名社費金額均填所繳各費全額如有代收者預扣各費憑其彙轉款項時隨附之扣費單據另賬付出並在社費正據之存根通知兩單附註內填明其他損益依此類推

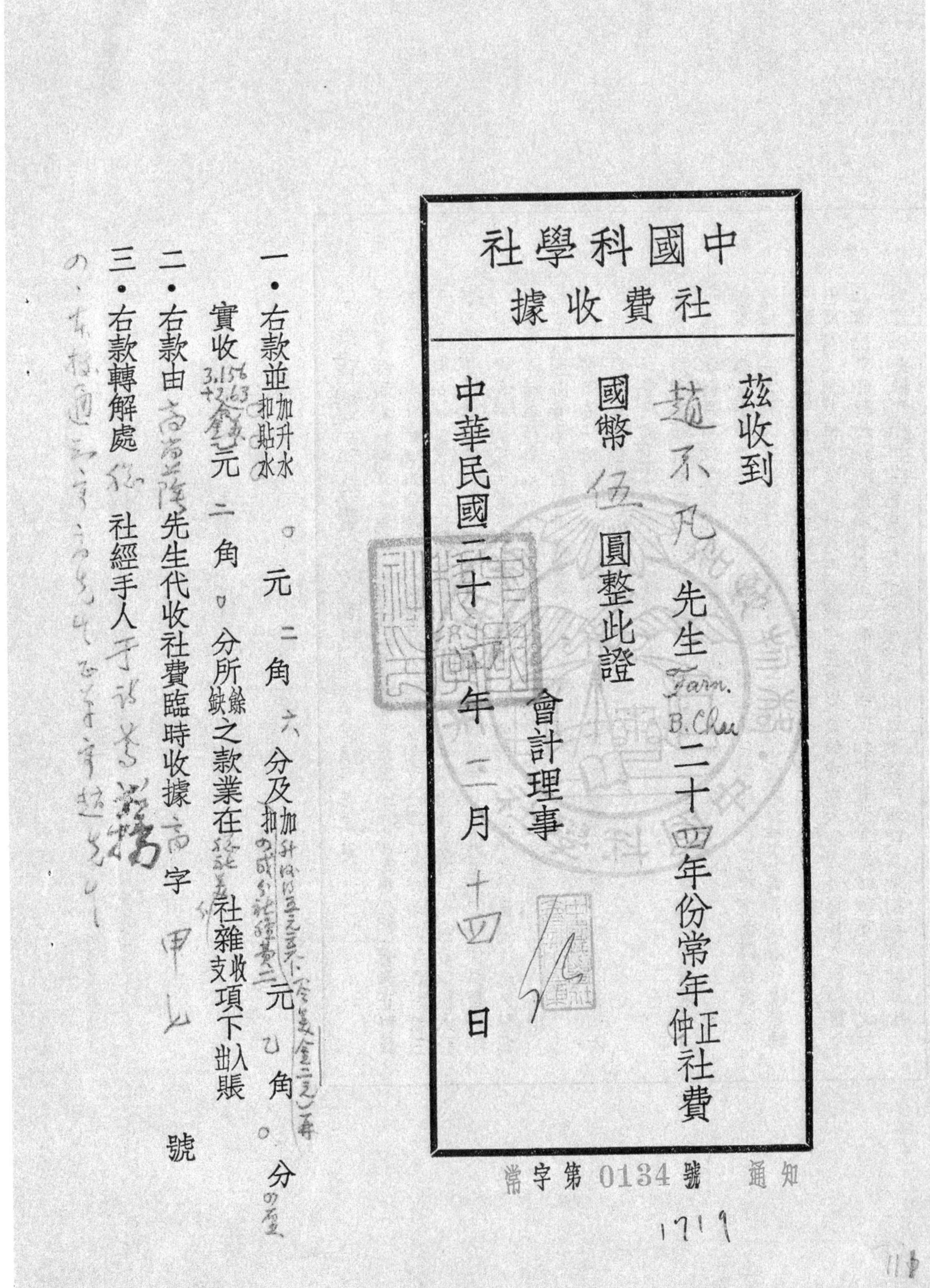

中國科學社
社費收據

茲收到
趙不凡先生 Farn. B. Chao 二十四年份常年仲正社費
國幣伍圓整此證
會計理事
中華民國二十四年二月十四日

常字第 0134 號 通知

一、右款並加升水扣貼水 0 元二角六分及加升扣貼 …… 元乙角 0 分
二、右款由 …… 先生代收社費臨時收據 …… 字 甲 …… 號
實收 …… 元二角 0 分所餘缺之款業在 …… 社雜收支項下出入賬
三、右款轉解處 …… 社經手人

1719

中國科學社社費徵收簡則 廿三年七月一日訂正

一　本社常年社費以每年一月一日至十二月三十一日爲一年份凡屬（甲）普通正社員（子）在上半年經理事會選決入社者除入社費收十元外再收本年份常年正社費三元次年起每年份收常年正社費五元（丑）在下半年經理事會選決入社者祇收入社費十元不收本年份常年正社費次年起每年份收常年正社費五元（乙）仲社員每年份收常年仲社費三元其入社費俟補實正社員時補收（丙）永久社員總收永久社費一百元不收其他費用如不能一次繳足則每次至少繳廿五元並須在三年內繳清

二　社費收到概由本社會計理事簽發正式社費收據爲憑

三　代收社費須俟代收者將款彙集轉到方能將社費正據簽奉在社費正據未簽奉前由各代收者出具社費臨時收據該項臨時收據由代收者完全負責

四　社員應享各種權利須自應繳各種社費繳清之日開始

五　社員對社費事項如有查詢請正式專函上海亞爾培路五三三號中國科學社總社事務室轉會計理事以便答復其他事項請勿並列以免延誤

六　社費正據分編常字入字永字三種各依徵費性質三疊複塡（甲）存根留簿存查（乙）通知專供本社內部記賬及交代收者存查之用（丙）正單掣交繳費者或由代收者轉交繳費者舊用白色硬片式收據廿三年七月起一律廢止

七　社費據上社員姓名均寫最近社員錄中正名社員錄中尚未印入者寫其入社願書上正名社費金額均塡所繳各費全額如有代收者預扣各費憑其彙轉款項時隨附之扣費單據另賬付出並在社費正據之存根通知兩單附註內塡明其他損益依此類推

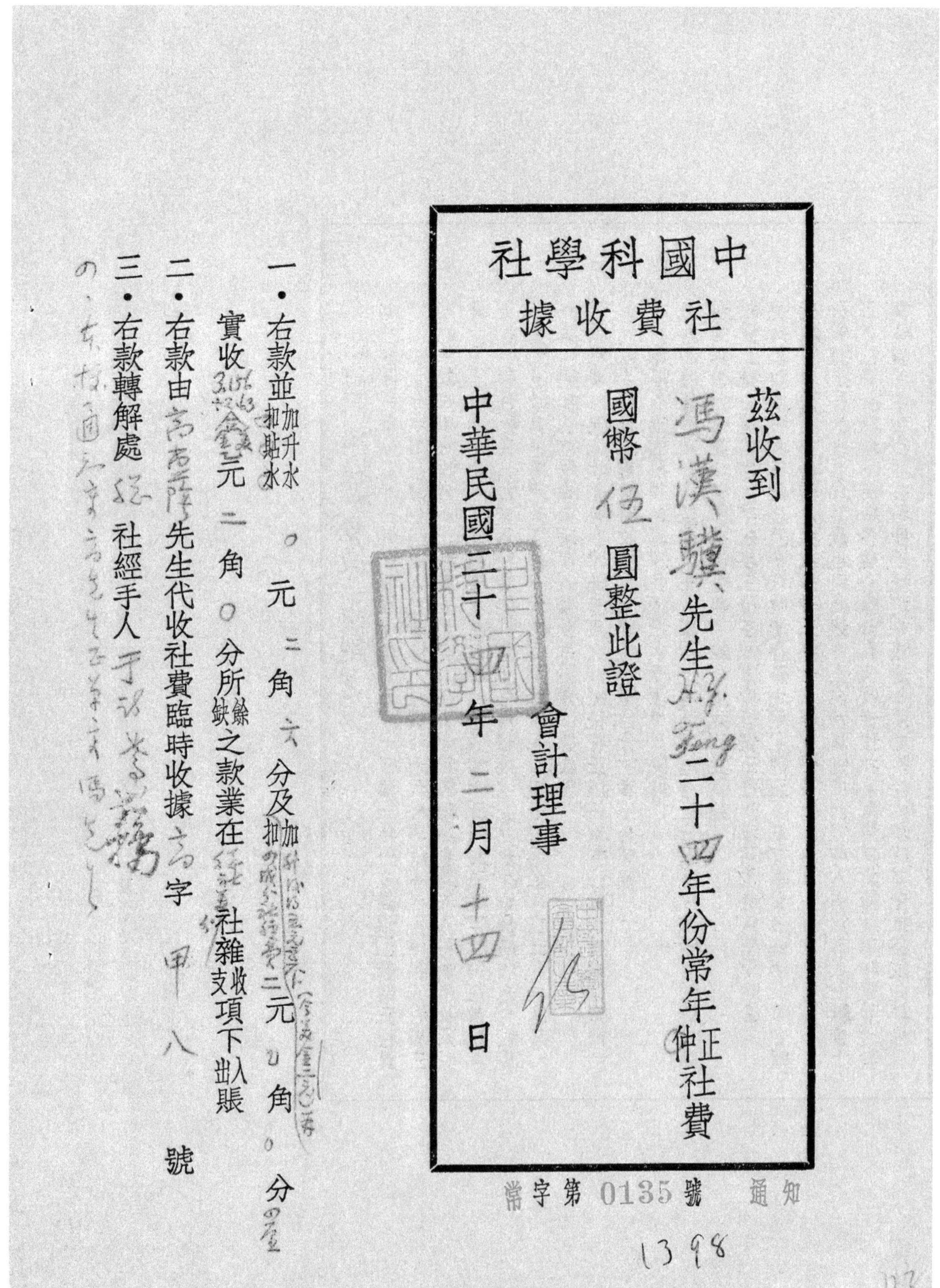
中國科學社
社費收據

茲收到
馮漢驥先生 H. Y. Feng 二十四年份常年仲正社費
國幣伍圓整此證
會計理事
中華民國二十四年二月十四日

常字第0135號 通知

一、右款並加升水扣貼水 ○元二角六分及加扣 二元七角○分
二、右款由高君陶先生代收實收 元二角○分所缺餘之款業在 社雜支收項下出入賬
三、右款轉解處 社經手人 社費臨時收據 字甲八號

1398

中國科學社社費徵收簡則 廿三年七月一日訂正

一 本社常年社費以每年一月一日至十二月三十一日爲一年份凡屬(甲)普通正社員(子)在上半年經理事會選決入社者除入社費收十元外再收本年份常年正社費三元次年起每年份收常年正社費五元(丑)在下半年經理事會選決入社者祇收入社費十元不收本年份常年正社費次年起每年份收常年正社費五元(乙)仲社員每年份收常年仲社費三元其入社費俟補實正社員時補收(丙)永久社員總收永久社費一百元不收其他費用如不能一次繳足則每次至少繳廿五元並須在三年內繳清

二 社費收到概由本社會計理事簽發正式社費收據爲憑

三 代收社費須俟代收者將款彙集轉到方能將社費正據簽奉在社費正據未簽奉前由各代收者出具社費臨時收據該項臨時收據由代收者完全負責

四 社員應享各種權利須自應繳各種社費繳清之日開始

五 社員對社費事項如有查詢請正式專函上海亞爾培路五三三號中國科學社總社事務室轉會計理事以便答復其他事項請勿並列以免延誤

六 社費正據分編常字入字永字三種各依徵費性質三疊複塡(甲)存根留簿存查(乙)通知專供本社內部記賬及交代收者存查之用(丙)正單掣交繳費者或由代收者轉交繳費者舊用白色硬片式收據廿三年七月起一律廢止

七 社費據上社員姓名均寫最近社員錄中正名社員錄中尚未印入者寫其入社願書上正名社費金額均塡所繳各費全額如有代收者預扣各費憑其彙轉款項時隨附之扣費單據另賬付出並在社費正據之存根通知兩單附註內塡明其他損益依此類推

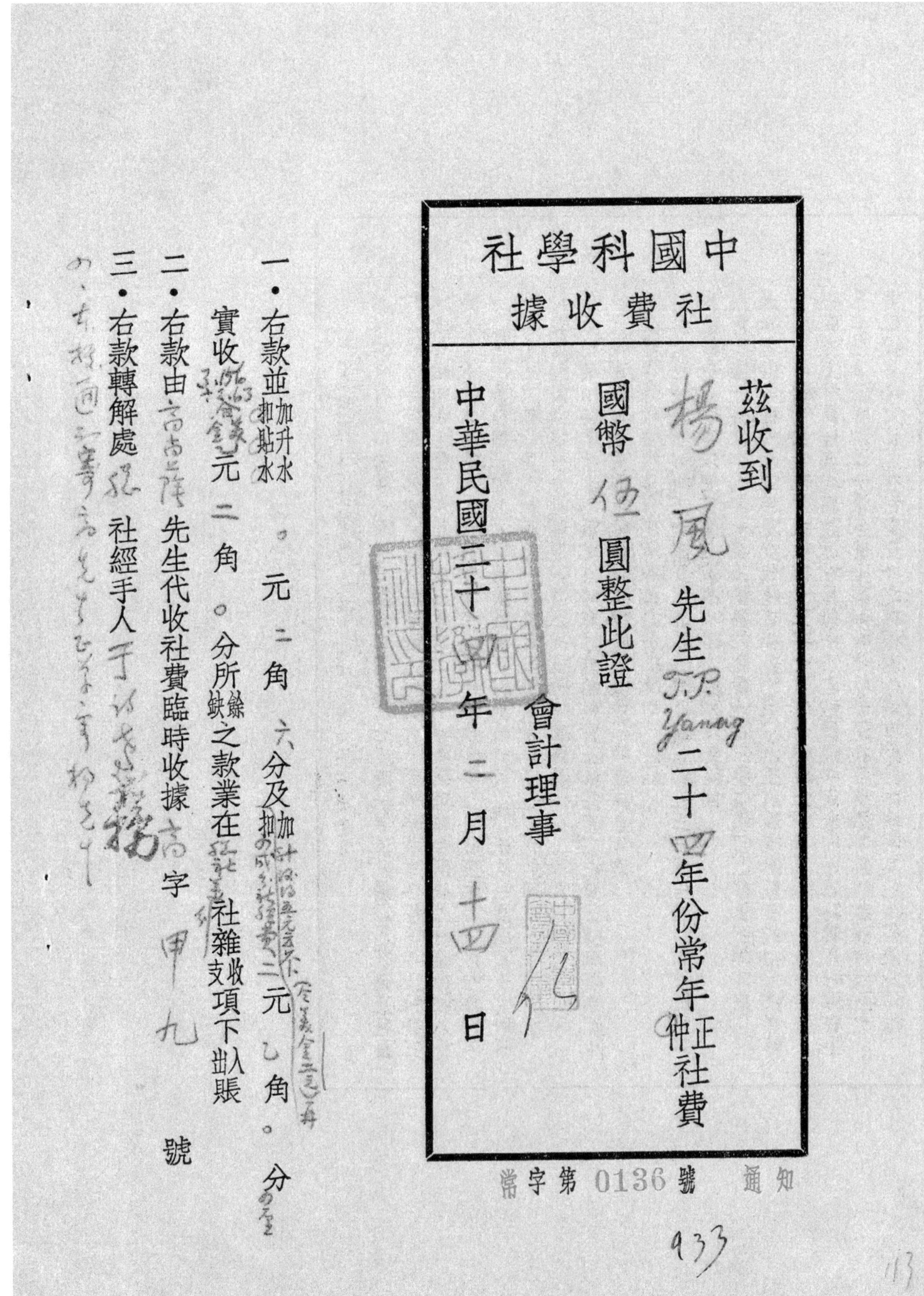

中國科學社
社費收據

茲收到楊風先生 T. P. Yang 二十四年份常年仲正社費

國幣伍圓整此證

會計理事

中華民國二十四年二月十四日

常字第 0136 號　知通

一·右款並加升水扣貼水 ○元二角六分及加扣……二元乙角○分

實收……元二角○分所餘……之款業在……社雜收項下出入賬

二·右款由……先生代收社費臨時收據……字甲九號

三·右款轉解處……社經手人……

933

113

中國科學社社費徵收簡則 廿三年七月一日訂正

一 本社常年社費以每年一月一日至十二月三十一日為一年份凡屬(甲)普通正社員[子]在上半年經理事會選決入社者除入社費收十元外再收本年份常年正社費三元次年起每年份收常年正社費五元[丑]在下半年經理事會選決入社者祗收入社費十元不收本年份常年正社費次年起每年份收常年正社費五元(乙)仲社員每年份收常年仲社費三元其入社費俟補實正社員時補收(丙)永久社員總收永久社費一百元不收其他費用如不能一次繳足則每次至少繳廿五元並須在三年內繳清

二 社費收到概由本社會計理事簽發正式社費收據為憑

三 代收社費須俟代收者將款彙集轉到方能將社費正據簽奉在社費正據未簽奉前由各代收者出具社費臨時收據該項臨時收據由代收者完全負責

四 社員應享各種權利須自應繳各種社費繳清之日開始

五 社員對社費事項如有查詢請正式專函上海亞爾培路五三三號中國科學社總社事務室轉會計理事以便答復其他事項請勿並列以免延誤

六 社費正據分編常字入字永字三種各依徵費性質三疊複填(甲)存根留簿存查(乙)通知專供本社內部記賬及交代收者存查之用(丙)正單製交繳費者或由代收者轉交繳費者舊用白色硬片式收據廿三年七月起一律廢止

七 社費據上社員姓名均寫最近社員錄中正名社員錄中尚未印入者寫其入社願書上正名社費金額均填所繳各費全額如有代收者預扣各費憑其彙轉款項時隨附之扣費單據另賬付出並在社費正據之存根通知兩單附註內填明其他損益依此類推

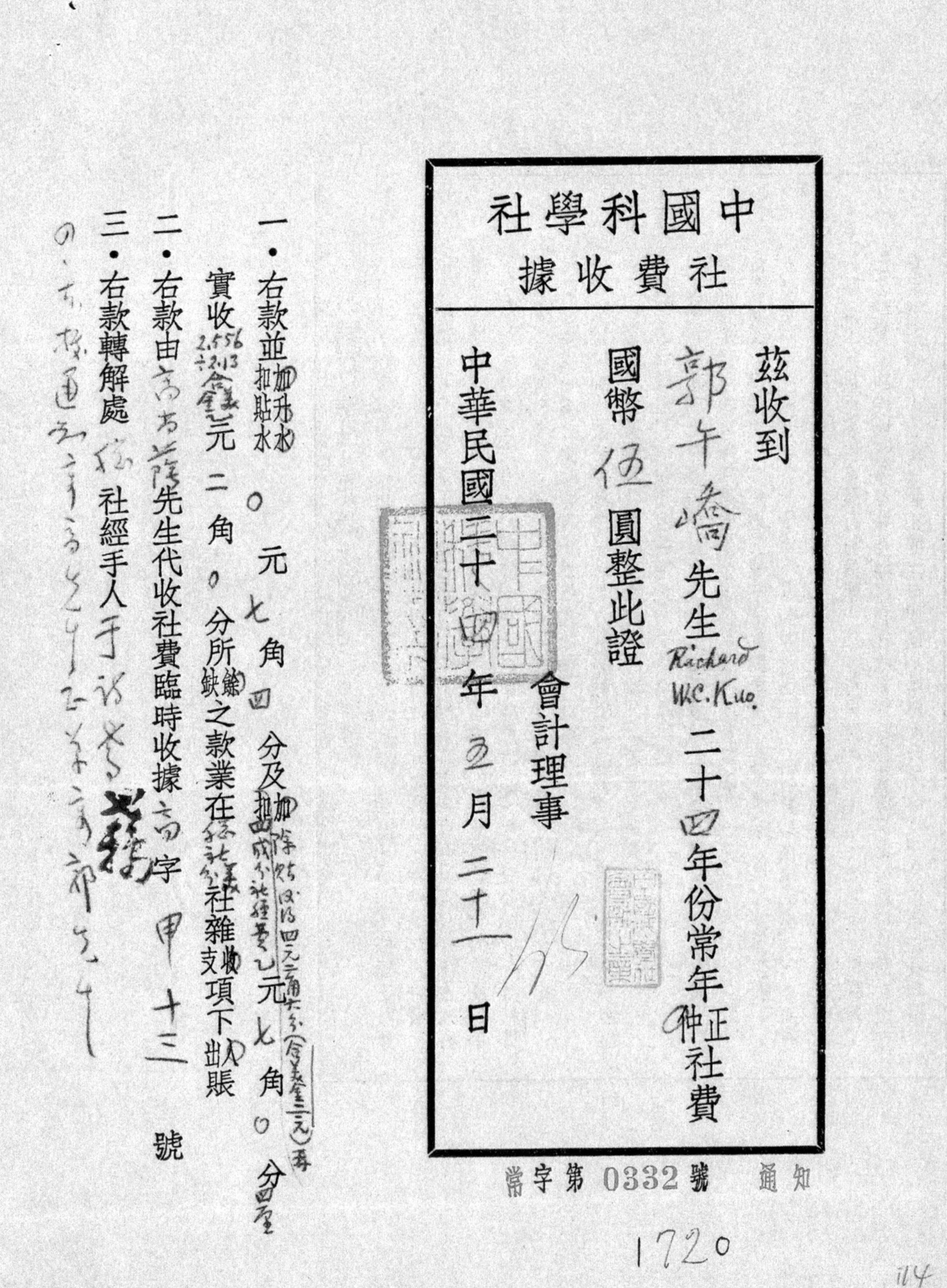

中國科學社
社費收據

茲收到郭午嶠先生 Richard W.C. Kuo 二十四年份常年正社費
國幣伍圓整此證
會計理事
中華民國二十四年五月二十一日

常字第0332號　通知

一、右款並加升水／扣貼水 ○元七角四分及加／扣[illegible]元七角○分
實收[illegible]元二角○分所餘／缺之款業在[illegible]社雜收／支項下出／入賬
二、右款由[illegible]先生代收社費臨時收據[illegible]字甲十三號
三、右款轉解處[illegible]社經手人[illegible]

[illegible]

1720

114

中國科學社社費徵收簡則

廿三年七月一日訂正

一　本社常年社費以每年一月一日至十二月三十一日爲一年份凡屬(甲)普通正社員[子]在上半年經理事會選決入社者除入社費收十元外再收本年份常年正社費三元次年起每年份收常年正社費五元[丑]在下半年經理事會選決入社者祇收入社費十元不收本年份常年正社費次年起每年份收常年正社費五元(乙)仲社員每年份收常年仲社費三元其入社費俟補實正社員時補收(丙)永久社員總收永久社費一百元不收其他費用如不能一次繳足則每次至少繳廿五元並須在三年內繳清

二　社費收到概由本社會計理事簽發正式社費收據爲憑

三　代收社費須俟代收者將款彙集轉到方能將社費正據簽奉在社費正據未簽奉前由各代收者出具社費臨時收據該項臨時收據由代收者完全負責

四　社員應享各種權利須自應繳各種社費繳清之日開始

五　社員對社費事項如有查詢請正式專函上海亞爾培路五三三號中國科學社總社事務室轉會計理事以便答復其他事項請勿並列以免延誤

六　社費正據分編常字入字永字三種各依徵費性質三疊複填(甲)存根留簿存查(乙)通知專供本社內部記賬及交代收者存查之用(丙)正單掣交繳費者或由代收者轉交繳費者舊用白色硬片式收據廿三年七月起一律廢止

七　社費據上社員姓名均寫最近社員錄中正名社員錄中尚未印入者寫其入社願書上正名社費金額均填所繳各費全額如有代收者預扣各費憑其彙轉款項時隨附之扣費單據另賬付出並在社費正據之存根通知兩單附註內填明其他損益依此類推

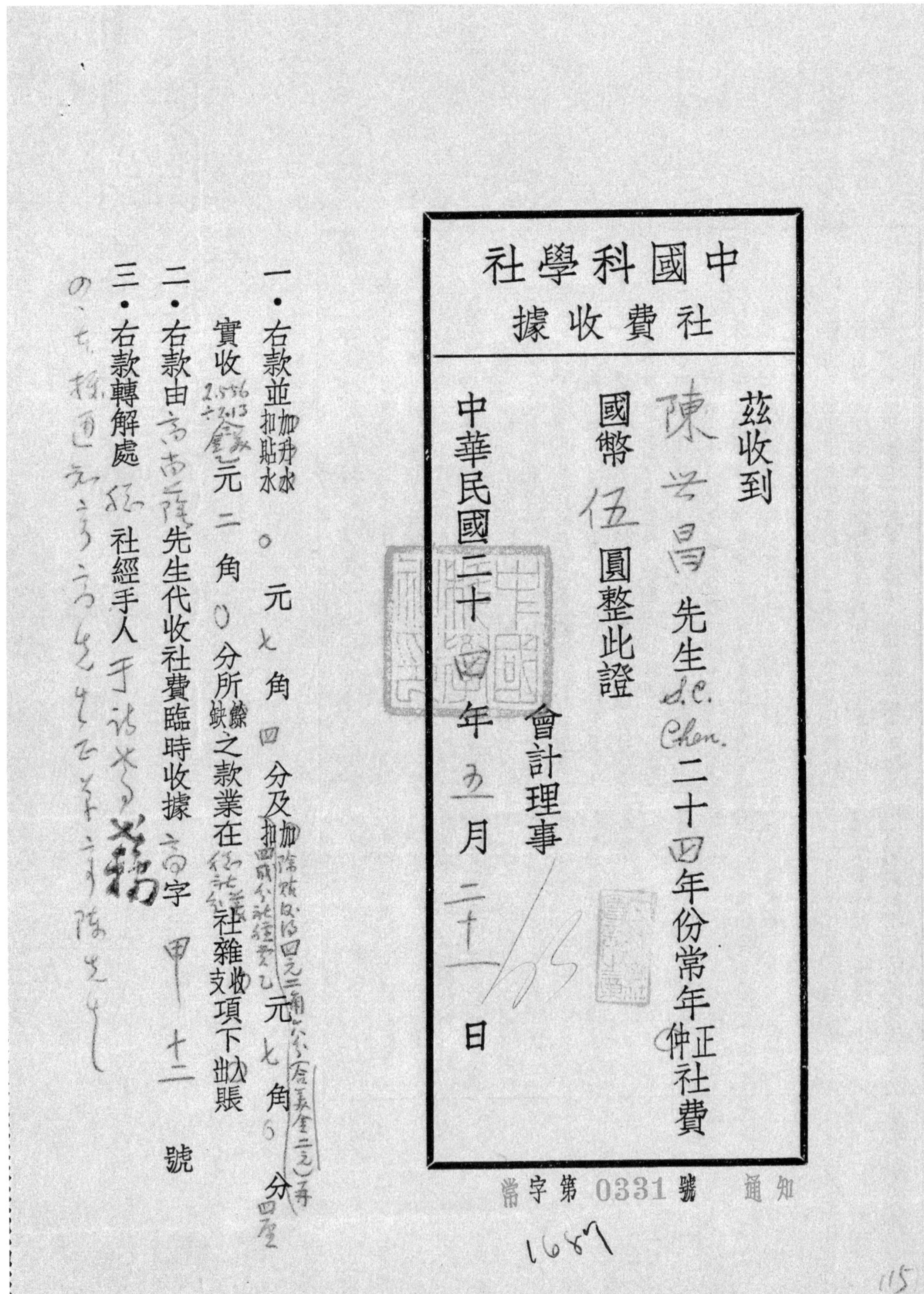

中國科學社
社費收據

茲收到
陳學昌先生 S.C. Chen.
二十四年份常年仲正社費
國幣伍圓整此證
會計理事
中華民國二十四年五月二十一日

知通 常字第0331號

一、右款並加升水加貼水〇元七角四分及加……元七角6分
實收……元二角〇分所餘缺之款業在……社雜收支項下出入賬
二、右款由……先生代收社費臨時收據……字甲十二號
三、右款轉解處……社經手人……

1687

115

中國科學社社費徵收簡則 廿三年七月一日訂正

一 本社常年社費以每年一月一日至十二月三十一日爲一年份凡屬（甲）普通正社員[子]在上半年經理事會選決入社者除入社費收十元外再收本年份常年正社費三元次年起每年份收常年正社費五元[丑]在下半年經理事會選決入社者祇收入社費十元不收本年份常年正社費次年起每年份收常年正社費五元（乙）仲社員每年份收常年仲社費三元其入社費俟補實正社員時補收（丙）永久社員總收永久社費一百元不收其他費用如不能一次繳足則每次至少繳廿五元並須在三年內繳清

二 社費收到概由本社會計理事簽發正式社費收據爲憑

三 代收社費須俟代收者將款彙集轉到方能將社費正據簽奉在社費正據未簽奉前由各代收者出具社費臨時收據該項臨時收據由代收者完全負責

四 社員應享各種權利須自應繳各種社費繳清之日開始

五 社員對社費事項如有查詢請正式專函上海亞爾培路五三三號中國科學社總社事務室轉會計理事以便答復其他事項請勿並列以免延誤

六 社費正據分編常字入字永字三種各依徵費性質三疊複填（甲）存根留簿存查（乙）通知專供本社內部記賬及交代收者存查之用（丙）正單掣交繳費者或由代收者轉交繳費者舊用白色硬片式收據廿三年七月起一律廢止

七 社費據上社員姓名均寫最近社員錄中正名社員錄中尚未印入者寫其入社願書上正名社費金額均填所繳各費全額如有代收者預扣各費憑其彙轉款項時隨附之扣費單據另賬付出並在社費正據之存根通知兩單附註內填明其他損益依此類推

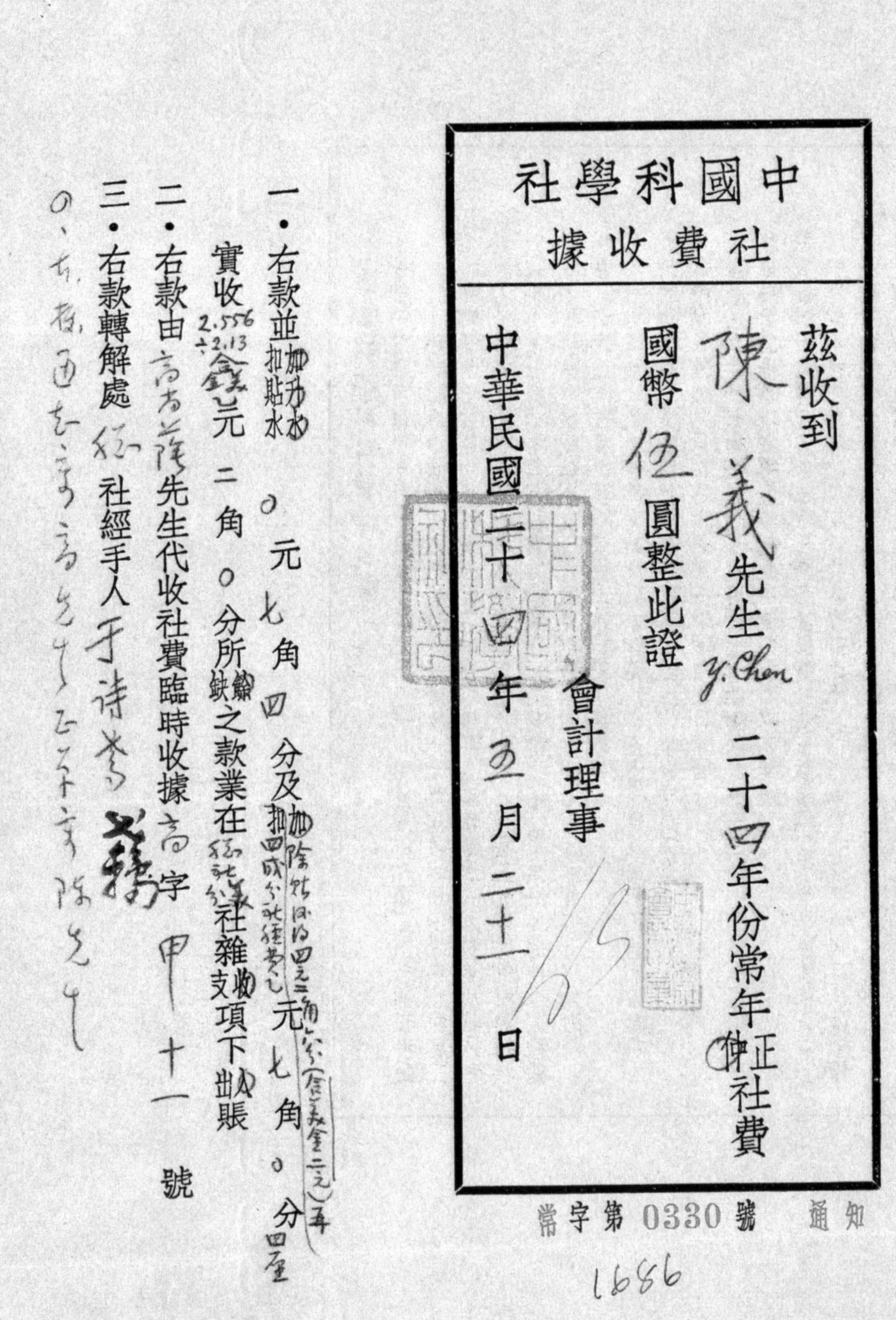

中國科學社
社費收據

茲收到
陳義先生 Y. Chen
二十四年份常年（仲）正社費
國幣伍圓整此證
會計理事
中華民國二十四年五月二十一日

常字第0330號　通知

一、右款並加貼水 0 元七角四分及加除
實收 金元二角 0 分所缺之款業在社雜支項下出賬

二、右款由　先生代收社費臨時收據　字甲十一號

三、右款轉解處　社經手人

1686

116

中國科學社社費徵收簡則 廿三年七月一日訂正

一　本社常年社費以每年一月一日至十二月三十一日為一年份凡屬（甲）普通正社員〔子〕在上半年經理事會選決入社者除入社費收十元外再收本年份常年正社費三元次年起每年份收常年正社費五元〔丑〕在下半年經理事會選決入社者衹收入社費十元不收本年份常年正社費次年起每年份收常年正社費五元（乙）仲社員每年份收常年仲社費三元其入社費俟補實正社員時補收（丙）永久社員總收永久社費一百元不收其他費用如不能一次繳足則每次至少繳廿五元並須在三年內繳清

二　社費收到概由本社會計理事簽發正式社費收據為憑

三　代收社費須俟代收者將款彙集轉到方能將社費正據簽奉在社費正據未簽奉前由各代收者出具社費臨時收據該項臨時收據由代收者完全負責

四　社員應享各種權利須自應繳各種社費繳清之日開始

五　社員對社費事項如有查詢請正式專函上海亞爾培路五三三號中國科學社總社事務室轉會計理事以便答復其他事項請勿並列以免延誤

六　社費正據分編常字入字永字三種各依徵費性質三疊複填（甲）存根留簿存查（乙）通知專供本社內部記賬及交代收者存查之用（丙）正單製交繳費者或由代收者轉交繳費者舊用白色硬片式收據廿三年七月起一律廢止

七　社費據上社員姓名均寫最近社員錄中正名社員錄中尚未印入者寫其入社願書上正名社費金額均填所繳各費全額如有代收者預扣各費憑其彙轉款項時隨附之扣費單據另賬付出並在社費正據之存根通知兩單附註內填明其他損益依此類推

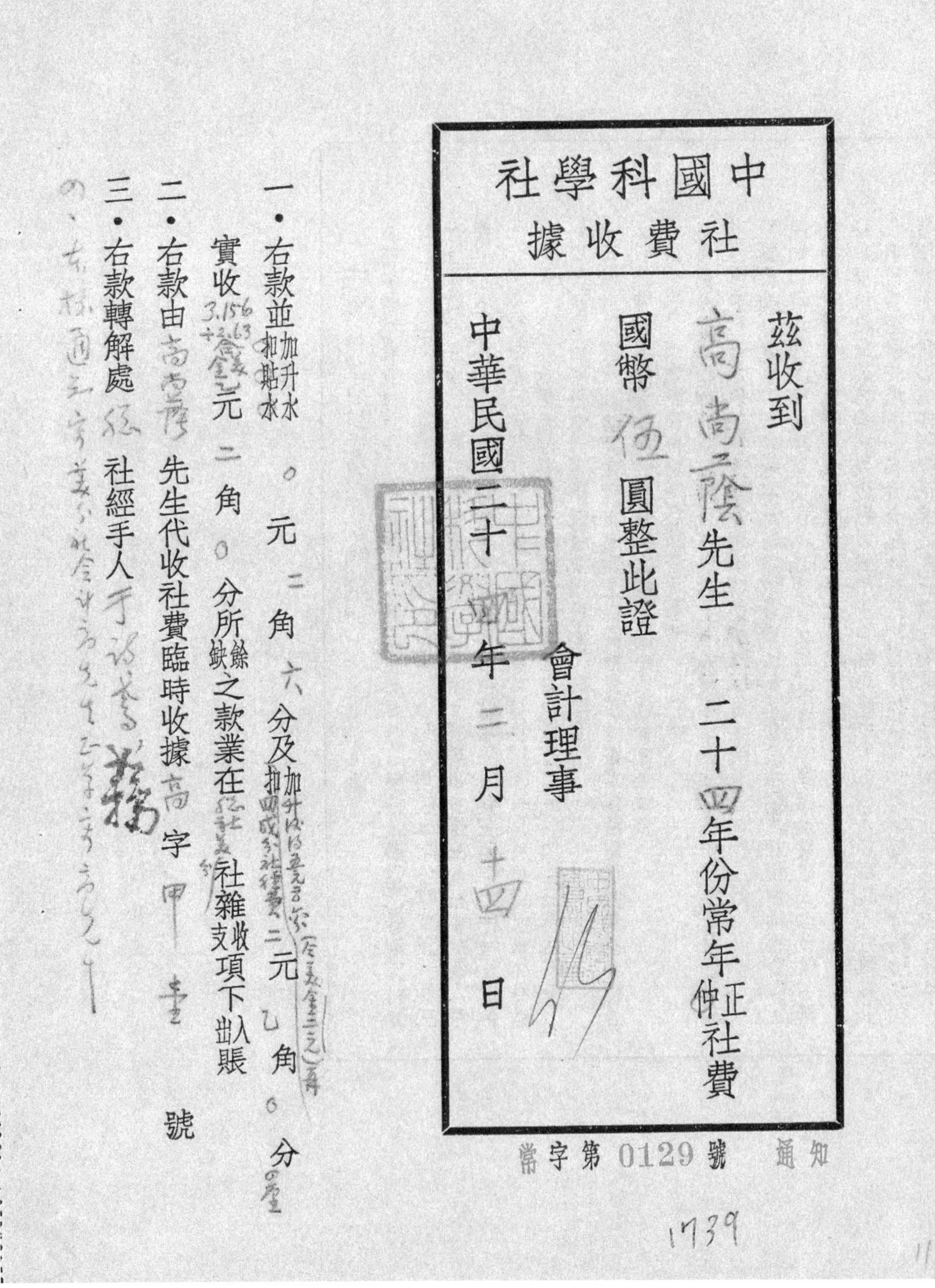
中國科學社
社費收據

茲收到高尚蔭先生二十四年份常年[正]社費
國幣伍圓整此證
會計理事
中華民國二十四年二月十四日

常字第0129號　通知

一、右款並加[扣]貼[升]水〇元二角六分及加升水[illegible]元二角〇分
實收[illegible]元二角〇分所餘之款業在社雜收項下出入賬
二、右款由高尚蔭先生代收社費臨時收據高字甲壹號
三、右款轉解處[illegible]社經手人[illegible]
四、[illegible]

1739

117

中國科學社社費徵收簡則 廿三年七月一日訂正

一 本社常年社費以每年一月一日至十二月三十一日爲一年份凡屬〔甲〕普通正社員〔子〕在上半年經理事會選決入社者除入社費收十元外再收本年份常年正社費三元次年起每年份收常年正社費五元〔丑〕在下半年經理事會選決入社者祇收入社費十元不收本年份常年正社費次年起每年份收常年正社費五元〔乙〕仲社員每年份收常年仲社費三元其入社費俟補實正社員時補收〔丙〕永久社員總收永久社費一百元不收其他費用如不能一次繳足則每次至少繳廿五元並須在三年內繳清

二 社費收到概由本社會計理事簽發正式社費收據爲憑

三 代收社費須俟代收者將款彙集轉到方能將社費正據簽奉在社費正據未簽奉前由各代收者出具社費臨時收據該項臨時收據由代收者完全負責

四 社員應享各種權利須自應繳各種社費繳清之日開始

五 社員對社費事項如有查詢請正式專函上海亞爾培路五三三號中國科學社總社事務室轉會計理事以便答復其他事項請勿並列以免延誤

六 社費正據分編常字入字永字三種各依徵費性質三疊複塡〔甲〕存根留簿存查〔乙〕通知專供本社內部記賬及交代收者存查之用〔丙〕正單製交繳費者或由代收者轉交繳費者舊用白色硬片式收據廿三年七月起一律廢止

七 社費據上社員姓名均寫最近社員錄中正名社員錄中尚未印入者寫其入社願書上正名社費金額均塡所繳各費全額如有代收者預扣各費憑其彙轉款項時隨附之扣費單據另賬付出並在社費正據之存根通知兩單附註內塡明其他損益依此類推

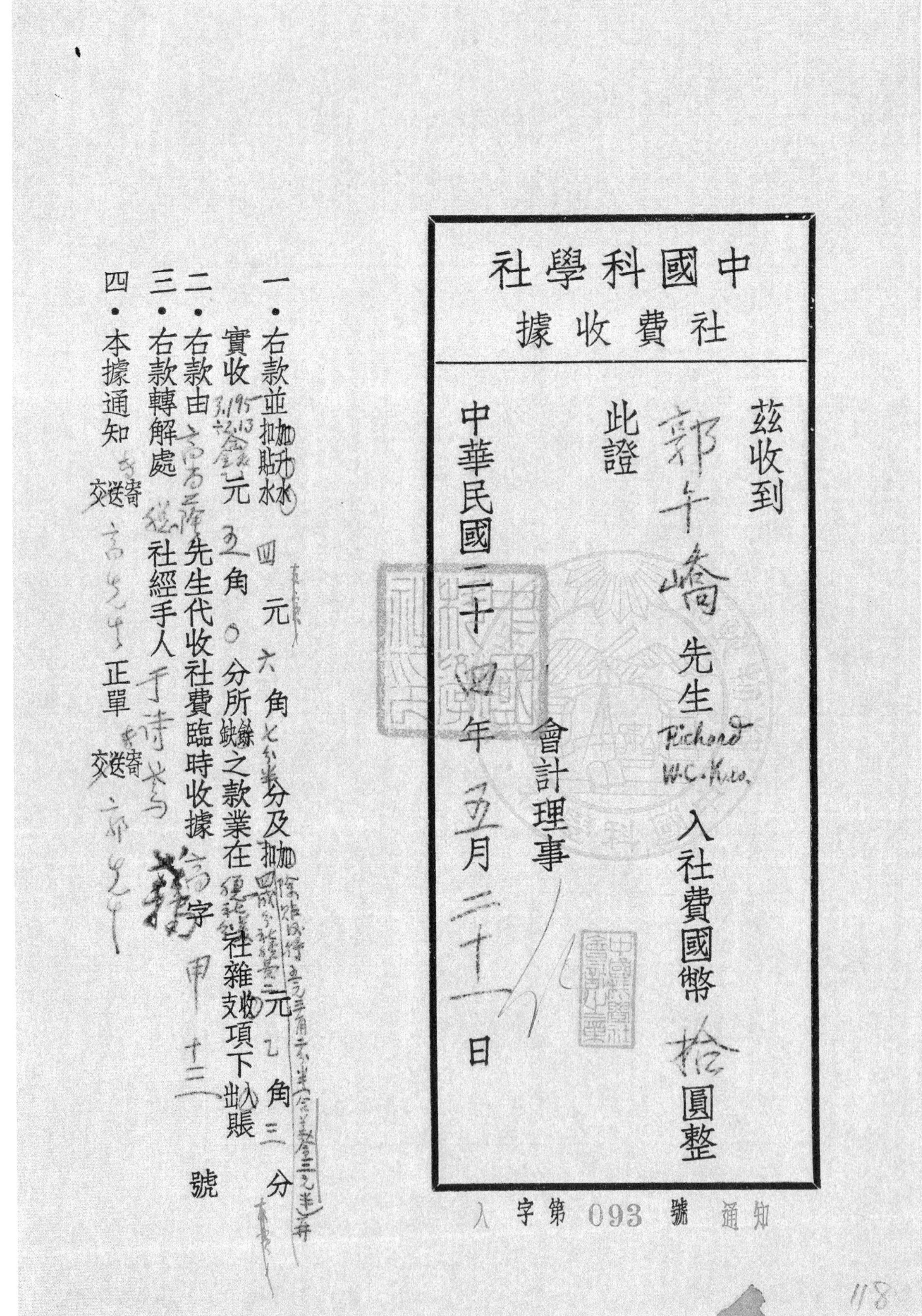

中國科學社
社費收據

茲收到 郭午嶠 先生 Richard W.C. Kuo 入社費國幣 拾 圓整

此證

會計理事

中華民國二十四年五月二十一日

入字第093號通知

一、右款並加扣貼升水 四 元 六 角 七分半 分及加扣除 元 乙 角 三 分

實收 元 五 角 〇 分所缺餘之款業在 社雜收支項下出入賬

二、右款由 高君韋 先生代收社費臨時收據 字 甲 十二 號

三、右款轉解處 總社經手人

四、本據通知寄送交 高君韋先生 正單寄送交

118

中國科學社社費徵收簡則 廿三年七月一日訂正

一 本社常年社費以每年一月一日至十二月三十一日爲一年份凡屬(甲)普通正社員(子)在上半年經理事會選決入社者除入社費收十元外再收本年份常年正社費三元次年起每年份收常年正社費五元(丑)在下半年經理事會選決入社者祇收入社費十元不收本年份常年正社費次年起每年份收常年正社費五元(乙)仲社員每年份收常年仲社費三元其入社費俟補實正社員時補收(丙)永久社員總收永久社費一百元不收其他費用如不能一次繳足則每次至少繳廿五元並須在三年內繳清

二 社費收到概由本社會計理事簽發正式社費收據爲憑

三 代收社費須俟代收者將款彙集轉到方能將社費正據簽奉在社費正據未簽奉前由各代收者出具社費臨時收據該項臨時收據由代收者完全負責

四 社員應享各種權利須自應繳各種社費繳清之日開始

五 社員對社費事項如有查詢請正式專函上海亞爾培路五三三號中國科學社總社事務室轉會計理事以便答復其他事項請勿並列以免延誤

六 社費正據分編常字入字永字三種各依徵費性質三疊複塡(甲)存根留簿存查(乙)通知專供本社內部記賬及交代收者存查之用(丙)正單製交繳費者或由代收者轉交繳費者舊用白色硬片式收據廿三年七月起一律廢止

七 社費據上社員姓名均寫最近社員錄中正名社員錄中尚未印入者寫其入社願書上正名社費金額均塡所繳各費全額如有代收者預扣各費憑其彙轉款項時隨附之扣費單據另賬付出並在社費正據之存根通知兩單附註內塡明其他損益依此類推

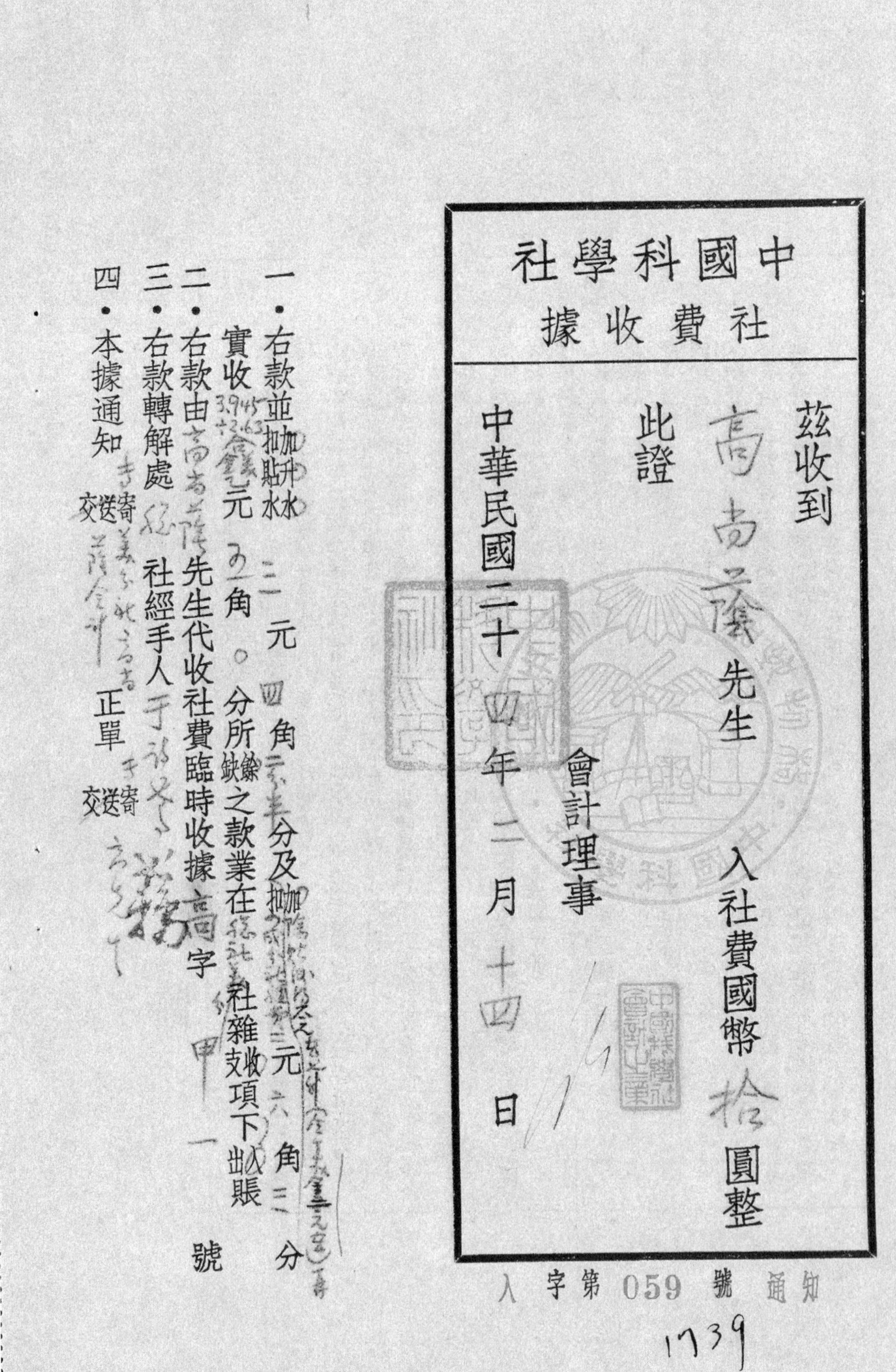

中國科學社
社費收據

茲收到
高尚蔭先生入社費國幣拾圓整
此證
會計理事
中華民國二十四年二月十四日

入字第059號通知

1739

一、右款並加貼水二元四角三分及加貼水……三元六角三分
實收3.945 +3.63 合金元五角〇分所缺之款業在總社雜支項下出賬
二、右款由高尚蔭先生代收社費臨時收據高字第一號
三、右款轉解處總社經手人
四、本據通知 寄送交 正單 寄送交

119

中國科學社社費徵收簡則 廿三年七月一日訂正

一 本社常年社費以每年一月一日至十二月三十一日為一年份凡屬〔甲〕普通正社員〔子〕在上半年經理事會選決入社者除入社費收十元外再收本年份常年正社費三元次年起每年份收常年正社費五元〔丑〕在下半年經理事會選決入社者祇收入社費十元不收本年份常年正社費次年起每年份收常年正社費五元〔乙〕仲社員每年份收常年仲社費三元其入社費俟補實正社員時補收〔丙〕永久社員總收永久社費一百元不收其他費用如不能一次繳足則每次至少繳廿五元並須在三年內繳清

二 社費收到概由本社會計理事簽發正式社費收據為憑

三 代收社費須俟代收者將款彙集轉到方能將社費正據簽奉在社費正據未簽奉前由各代收者出具社費臨時收據該項臨時收據由代收者完全負責

四 社員應享各種權利須自應繳各種社費繳清之日開始

五 社員對社費事項如有查詢請正式專函上海亞爾培路五三三號中國科學社總社事務室轉會計理事以便答復其他事項請勿並列以免延誤

六 社費正據分編常字入字永字三種各依徵費性質三疊複塡〔甲〕存根留簿存查〔乙〕通知專供本社內部記賬及交代收者存查之用〔丙〕正單掣交繳費者或由代收者轉交繳費者舊用白色硬片式收據廿三年七月起一律廢止

七 社費據上社員姓名均寫最近社員錄中正名社員錄中尚未印入者寫其入社願書上正名社費金額均塡所繳各費全額如有代收者預扣各費憑其彙轉款項時隨附之扣費單據另賬付出並在社費正據之存根通知兩單附註內塡明其他損益依此類推

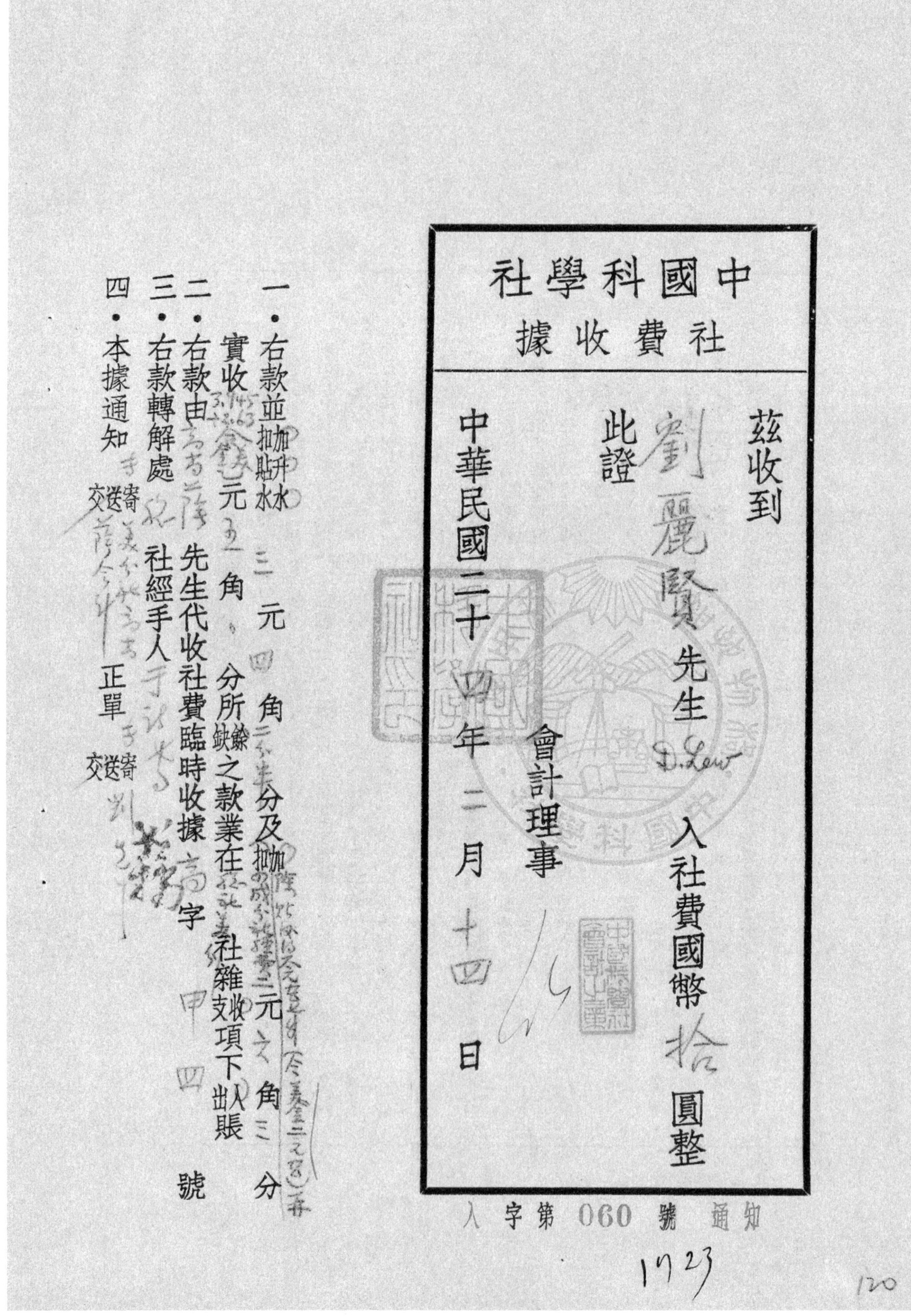

中國科學社
社費收據

茲收到
劉麗賢先生 L. Law
入社費國幣拾圓整
此證
會計理事
中華民國二十四年二月十四日

入字第060號通知

一、右款並加貼水 三元四角二分七分及加 陸 分 共計三元六角三分
實收 元五角 分所餘之款業在社雜支項下出賬
二、右款由 先生代收社費臨時收據 字 號
三、右款轉解處 社經手人
四、本據通知 寄送交 正單 寄送交

1723

120

中國科學社社費徵收簡則

廿三年七月一日訂正

一　本社常年社費以每年一月一日至十二月三十一日爲一年份凡屬(甲)普通正社員(子)在上半年經理事會選決入社者除入社費收十元外再收本年份常年正社費三元次年起每年份收常年正社費五元(丑)在下半年經理事會選決入社者祇收入社費十元不收本年份常年正社費次年起每年份收常年正社費五元(乙)仲社員每年份收常年仲社費三元其入社費俟補實正社員時補收(丙)永久社員總收永久社費一百元不收其他費用如不能一次繳足則每次至少繳廿五元並須在三年內繳清

二　社費收到概由本社會計理事簽發正式社費收據爲憑

三　代收社費須俟代收者將款彙集轉到方能將社費正據簽奉在社費正據未簽奉前由各代收者出具社費臨時收據該項臨時收據由代收者完全負責

四　社員應享各種權利須自應繳各種社費繳清之日開始

五　社員對社費事項如有查詢請正式專函上海亞爾培路五三三號中國科學社總社事務室轉會計理事以便答復其他事項請勿並列以免延誤

六　社費正據分編常字入字永字三種各依徵費性質三疊複填(甲)存根留簿存查(乙)通知專供本社內部記賬及交代收者存查之用(丙)正單製交繳費者或由代收者轉交繳費者舊用白色硬片式收據廿三年七月起一律廢止

七　社費據上社員姓名均寫最近社員錄中正名社員錄中尚未印入者寫其入社願書上正名社費金額均塡所繳各費全額如有代收者預扣各費憑其彙轉款項時隨附之扣費單據另賬付出並在社費正據之存根通知兩單附註內塡明其他損益依此類推

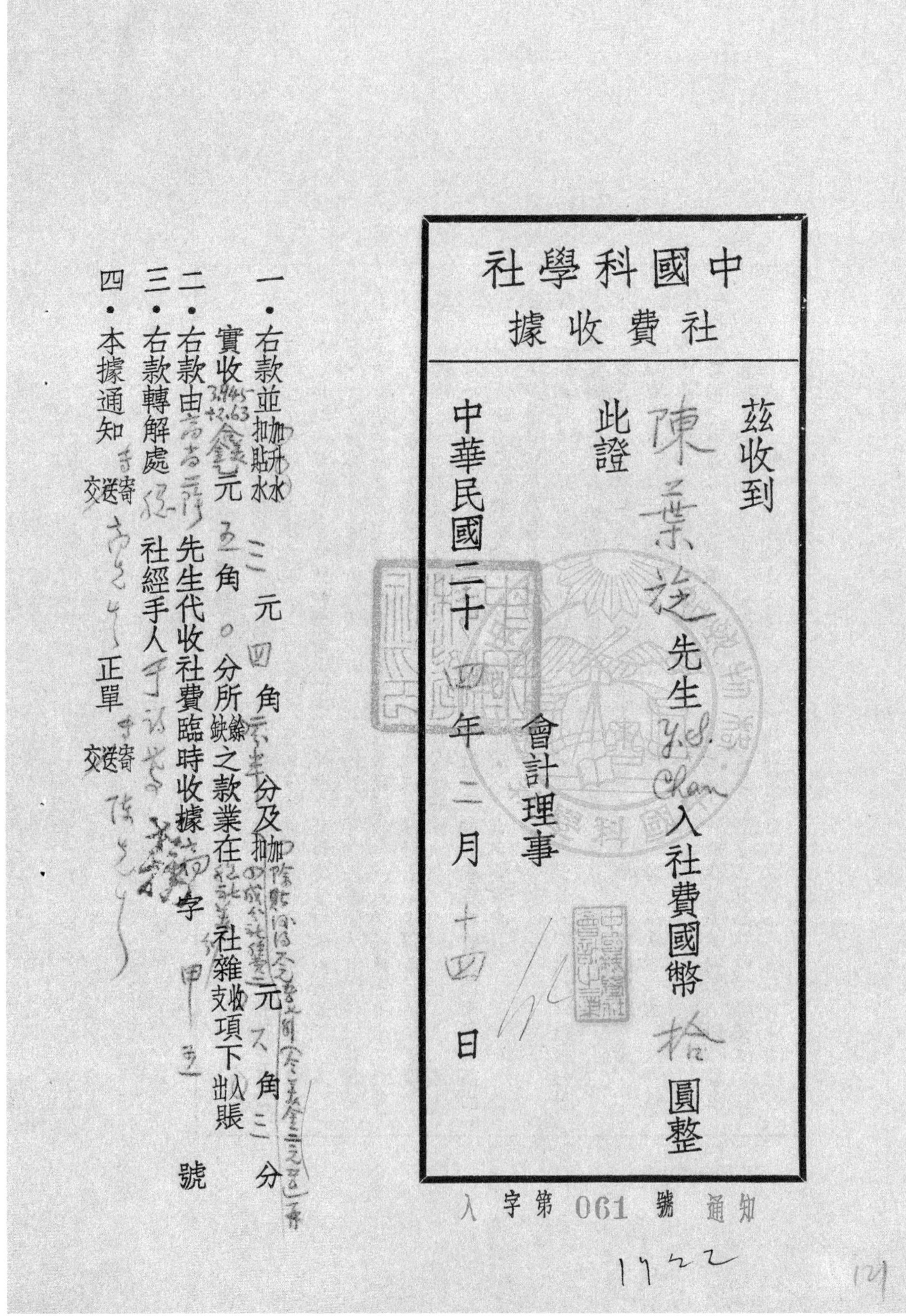

中國科學社
社費收據

茲收到
陳葉詒之先生 Y.S. Chan 入社費國幣拾圓整
此證
會計理事
中華民國二十四年二月十四日

入字第 061 號通知

一、右款並加扣匯水 三元四角二分
二、實收 3.945 +2.63 金 元 五角 〇 分所餘之款業在 社雜收項下出賬
三、右款由 高士其 先生代收社費臨時收據 字 號
四、本據通知寄送交 正單寄送交

1722

121

中國科學社社費徵收簡則

廿三年七月一日訂正

一　本社常年社費以每年一月一日至十二月三十一日爲一年份凡屬（甲）普通正社員（子）在上半年經理事會選決入社者除入社費收十元外再收本年份常年正社費三元次年起每年份收常年正社費五元（丑）在下半年經理事會選決入社者祇收入社費十元不收本年份常年正社費次年起每年份收常年正社費五元（乙）仲社員每年份收常年仲社費三元其入社費俟補實正社員時補收（丙）永久社員總收永久社費一百元不收其他費用如不能一次繳足則每次至少繳廿五元並須在三年內繳清

二　社費收到概由本社會計理事簽發正式社費收據爲憑

三　代收社費須俟代收者將款彙集轉到方能將社費正據簽奉在社費正據未簽奉前由各代收者出具社費臨時收據該項臨時收據由代收者完全負責

四　社員應享各種權利須自應繳各種社費繳清之日開始

五　社員對社費事項如有查詢請正式專函上海亞爾培路五三三號中國科學社總社事務室轉會計理事以便答復其他事項請勿並列以免延誤

六　社費正據分編常字入字永字三種各依徵費性質三疊複塡（甲）存根留簿存查（乙）通知專供本社內部記賬及交代收者存查之用（丙）正單掣交繳費者或由代收者轉交繳費者舊用白色硬片式收據廿三年七月起一律廢止

七　社費據上社員姓名均寫最近社員錄中正名社員錄中尚未印入者寫其入社願書上正名社費金額均塡所繳各費全額如有代收者預扣各費憑其彙轉款項時隨附之扣費單據另賬付出並在社費正據之存根通知兩單附註內塡明其他損益依此類推

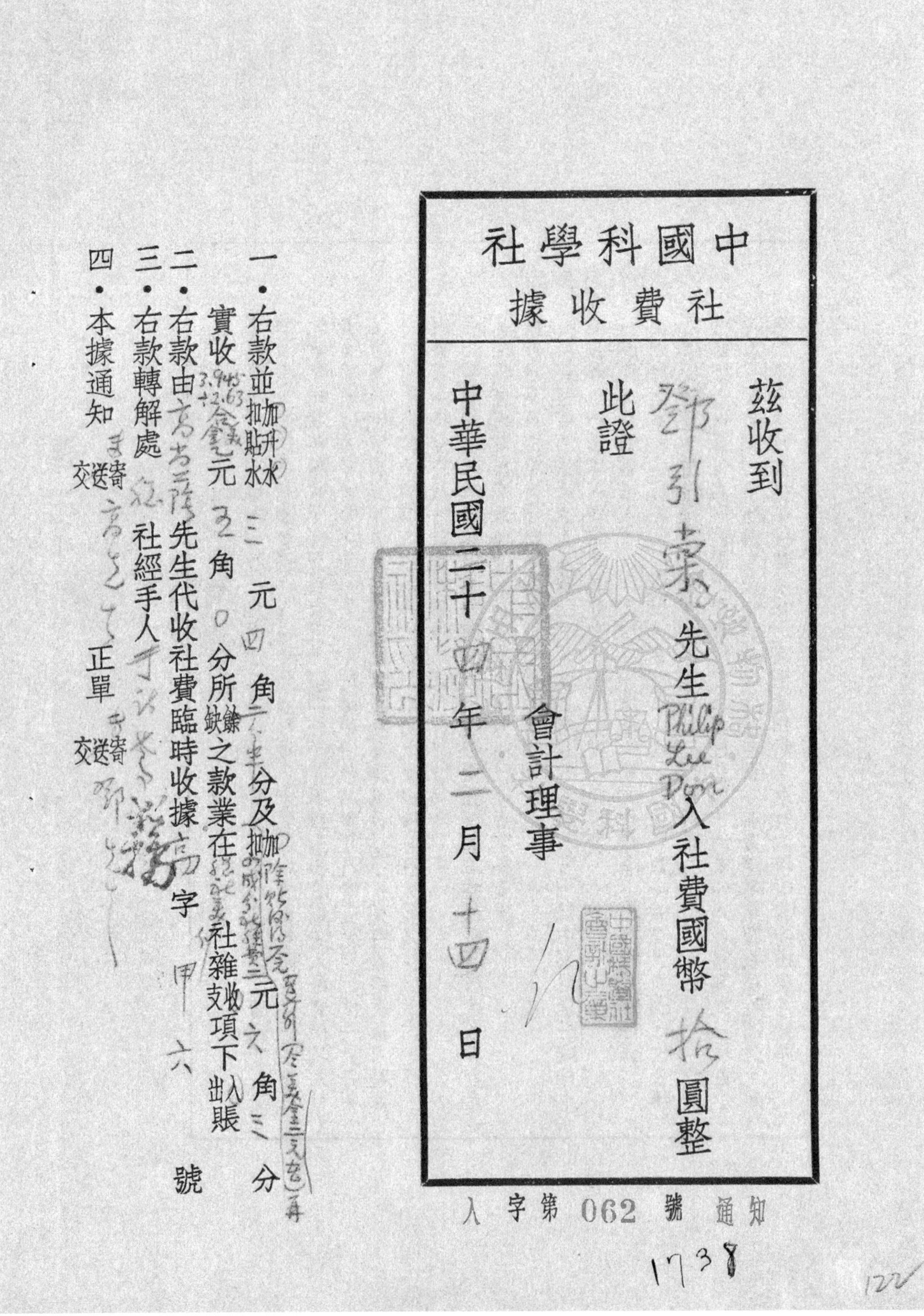

中國科學社
社費收據

茲收到
鄧引棠 先生 Philip Lee Don 入社費國幣 拾 圓整
此證
會計理事
中華民國二十四年二月十四日

入字第062號 通知

一、右款並加扣貼水 三 元 四 角 二 分及加扣除 …… 三元 六 角 三 分
二、實收 3.945 +2.63 金元 五 角 〇 分所缺餘之款業在 …… 社雜支收項下出入賬
三、右款由 …… 先生代收社費臨時收據 …… 字 甲 六 號
四、右款轉解處 …… 社經手人 ……
本據通知 …… 交送寄 …… 正單 …… 交送寄 ……

1738

122

中國科學社社費徵收簡則 廿三年七月一日訂正

一　本社常年社費以每年一月一日至十二月三十一日爲一年份凡屬〔甲〕普通正社員〔子〕在上半年經理事會選決入社者除入社費收十元外再收本年份常年正社費三元次年起每年份收常年正社費五元〔丑〕在下半年經理事會選決入社者祇收入社費十元不收本年份常年正社費次年起每年份收常年正社費五元〔乙〕仲社員每年份收常年仲社費三元其入社費俟補實正社員時補收〔丙〕永久社員總收永久社費一百元不收其他費用如不能一次繳足則每次至少繳廿五元並須在三年內繳清

二　社費收到概由本社會計理事簽發正式社費收據爲憑

三　代收社費須俟代收者將款彙集轉到方能將社費正據簽奉在社費正據未簽奉前由各代收者出具社費臨時收據該項臨時收據由代收者完全負責

四　社員應享各種權利須自應繳各種社費繳清之日開始

五　社員對社費事項如有查詢請正式專函上海亞爾培路五三三號中國科學社總社事務室轉會計理事以便答復其他事項請勿並列以免延誤

六　社費正據分編常字入字永字三種各依徵費性質三疊複塡〔甲〕存根留簿存查〔乙〕通知專供本社內部記賬及交代收者存查之用〔丙〕正單掣交繳費者或由代收者轉交繳費者舊用白色硬片式收據廿三年七月起一律廢止

七　社費據上社員姓名均寫最近社員錄中正名社員錄中尚未印入者寫其入社願書上正名社費金額均塡所繳各費全額如有代收者預扣各費憑其彙轉款項時隨附之扣費單據另賬付出並在社費正據之存根通知兩單附註內塡明其他損益依此類推

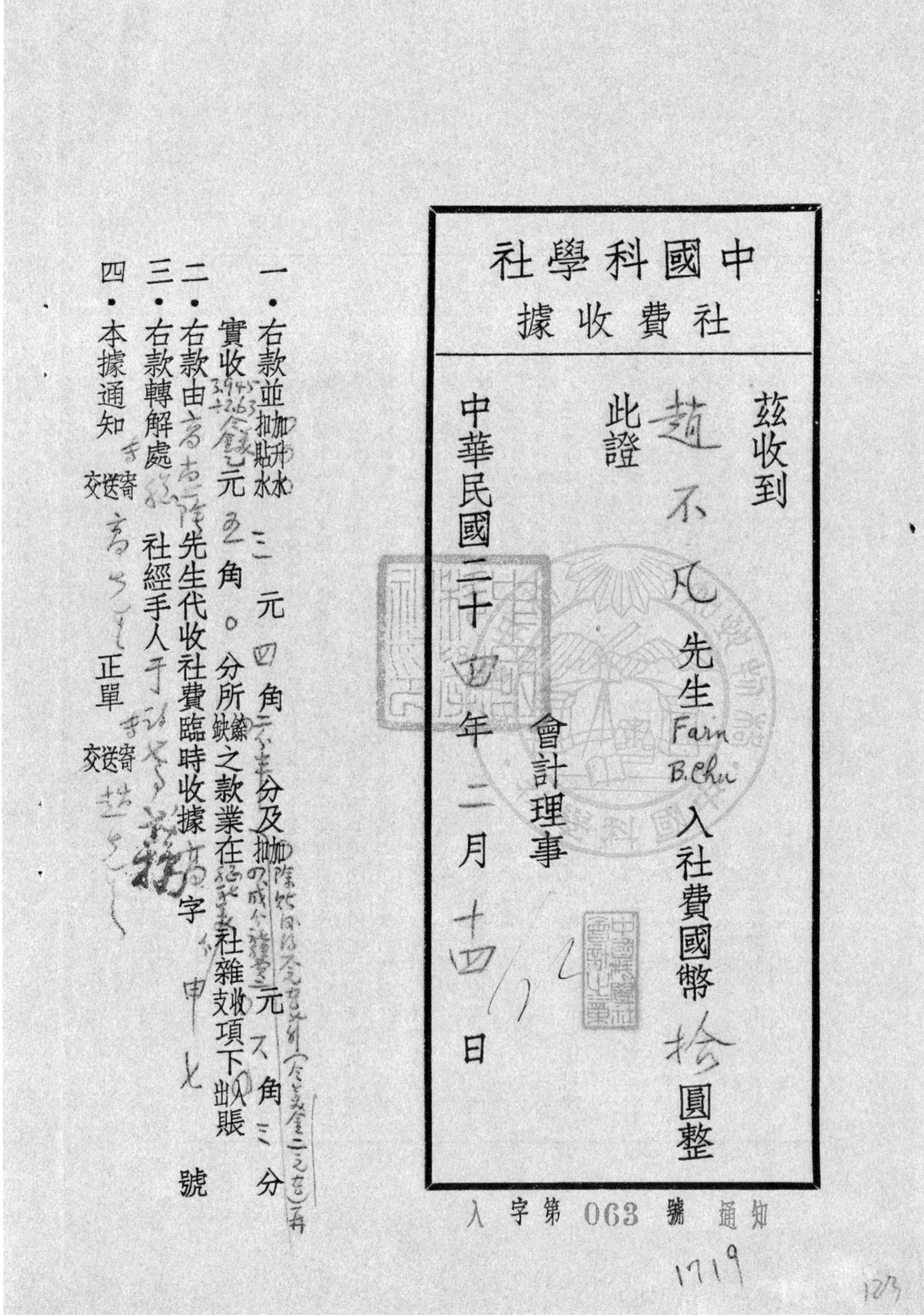
中國科學社
社費收據
茲收到
趙不凡先生 Farn B. Chu
入社費國幣拾圓整
此證
會計理事
中華民國二十四年二月十四日
入字第063號 通知

一·右款並加貼水三元四角三分及加貼水又未分及加除外匯不足…… 元 角 分
實收……元五角○分所缺之款業在……社雜支收項下出賬
二·右款由……先生代收社費臨時收據……字……號
三·右款轉解處……社經手人……
四·本據通知……寄送交 正單 寄送交

1719

中國科學社社費徵收簡則 廿三年七月一日訂正

一 本社常年社費以每年一月一日至十二月三十一日爲一年份凡屬(甲)普通正社員[子]在上半年經理事會選決入社者除入社費收十元外再收本年份常年正社費三元次年起每年份收常年正社費五元[丑]在下半年經理事會選決入社者祇收入社費十元不收本年份常年正社費次年起每年份收常年正社費五元(乙)仲社員每年份收常年仲社費三元其入社費俟補實正社員時補收(丙)永久社員總收永久社費一百元不收其他費用如不能一次繳足則每次至少繳廿五元並須在三年內繳清

二 社費收到概由本社會計理事簽發正式社費收據爲憑

三 代收社費須俟代收者將款彙集轉到方能將社費正據簽奉在社費正據未簽奉前由各代收者出具社費臨時收據該項臨時收據由代收者完全負責

四 社員應享各種權利須自應繳各種社費繳清之日開始

五 社員對社費事項如有查詢請正式專函上海亞爾培路五三三號中國科學社總社事務室轉會計理事以便答復其他事項請勿並列以免延誤

六 社費正據分編常字入字永字三種各依徵費性質三疊複塡(甲)存根留簿存查(乙)通知專供本社內部記賬及交代收者存查之用(丙)正單掣交繳費者或由代收者轉交繳費者舊用白色硬片式收據廿三年七月起一律廢止

七 社費據上社員姓名均寫最近社員錄中正名社員錄中尚未印入者寫其入社願書上正名社費金額均塡所繳各費全額如有代收者預扣各費憑其彙轉款項時隨附之扣費單據另賬付出並在社費正據之存根通知兩單附註內塡明其他損益依此類推

中國科學社入社願書

（姓名）陈.厲剛 今經 袁，高 兩君之

介紹願爲中國科學社　　　　社員如經正式選決

情願遵守社章此上

中國科學社

本人簽名 陳厲剛

介紹人簽名 袁同明，高尚蔭

理事簽名

通過日期：　中華民國　　年　　月　　日

156

（社號）

（姓名）陳勵剛　（字）　（西文名）Chen, Liy-kwong

（籍慣）廣東開平　（生年）　（性別）男

（學科門類）1 Mining Geology

2

（學位）1　學校　年

2　,,　,,

3　,,　,,

（著作）

通信處（永久）廣州市東山啓明路第壹號

（現在）Colorado School of Mines
Golden, Colo. U. S. A.

157

中國科學社入社願書

(姓名) 熊廷柱 今經 袁，高 兩君之

介紹願爲中國科學社　　　社員如經正式選決

情願遵守社章此上

中國科學社

本人簽名 熊廷柱

介紹人簽名 袁同礼，高尚蔭

理事簽名

通過日期：　中華民國　　年　　月　　日

158

（社號）

（姓名）熊廷柱　（字）怡琴　（西文名）T. C. Hsiung

（籍慣）雲南騰衝　（生年）一九〇二　（性別）男

（學科門類）1 園藝

2 農業經濟

（學位）1 國立東南大學 學校 一九二七 年 學士

2 ,, ,,

3 ,, ,,

（著作）

通信處（永久）雲南騰衝綺羅鎮

（現在）626 Remington Street

Fort Collins, Colo. U.S.A.

159

中國科學社入社願書

(姓名) 談家楨 今經 高尚英 陳世昌 兩君之

介紹願爲中國科學社　　　社員如經正式選決

情願遵守社章此上

中國科學社

本人簽名 談家楨

介紹人簽名 陳世昌，高尚蔭

理事簽名

通過日期：　中華民國　　年　　月　　日

160

（社號）

（姓名）談家楨　（字）　（西文名）Chia-chen Tan

（籍慣）浙江鄞縣　（生年）民國前三年　（性別）男

（學科門類）1 生物學 遺傳的，家蠶胚胎的

2

（學位）1 理學士　學校 東吳大學　年 民國十九年

2 理碩士　,, 燕京大學　,, 民國廿一年

3　,,　,,

（著作）① Notes on the Biology of the Lady-bird beetle Hy. axyridis

② Variation in the color pattern of Hy. axyridis

③ Inheritance of the color pattern of Harmonia axyridis

④ Identification of the salivary gland chromosomes in Droso. pseudoobscura

⑤ Salivary gland chromosomes in two races of Dro. pseudoobscura

⑥ Chromosomal difference between races. → to be presented at the Pacific division conference of the American association for the advancement of science.

通信處（永久）浙江寧波南社壇橋六號

（現在）Wm. G. Kerckhoff Laboratories of Biol. Sci.

California Institute of Technology

Pasadena, Calif., U.S.A.

161

REPORT ON THE DEVELOPMENT OF NEW CHEMICAL DYNAMICS

DR. MED. SHAO-KWANG LIU.

Delivered at the Joint Annual Meeting of the Science Society of China and the Chinese Engineering Society American Section, in New York City, Aug. 31, 1930.

Mr. Chairman, Ladies and Gentlemen, our honourable Guests:

The subject which I am going to present to you is ~~announced on the program is a very general one, namely~~ the New Chemical Dynamics, a theory which I have developed in the last two years in the United States. According to the present general conception in physics, dynamics deals with the study of the balanced and unbalanced forces or statics and kinetics. ~~The reason why~~ We denote our theory as New Chemical Dynamics ~~is simply~~ on account of the new development of the classical chemical dynamics which involves the fundamental principles of all branches of chemistry. It is our attempt to extend, to generalize, and to simplify the chemical dynamics. It is also our aim to correlate the chemical kinetics, statics and thermodynamics into one simple form of interpretation.

Chemical dynamics is in many respects like the mechanics in physics. In physics, we have the two ~~most important and~~ fundamental laws of mechanics; namely, Newton's second law of kinetics and his third law of statics. The same thing is true in chemistry. We have also the two ~~most important and~~ fundamental laws; namely, the law of chemical kinetics and of chemical statics. The practical value of the two laws in chemistry is about the same as those ~~laws~~ in physics. Recently the fundamental principle of mechanics has undergone ~~through~~ evolutionary and revolution-

191

ary changes in recent years due to the development of Relativity Theory. Newton's second law of mechanics has become only a special case in Einsteinian mechanics. According to Newtonian mechanics, kinetic energy is equal to

$$K.E. = \frac{1}{2} m_0 v^2$$

where m_0 is the absolute mass and v the velocity of the moving body. According to Einsteinian mechanics, we have

$$m = \frac{m_0}{\sqrt{1 - \frac{v^2}{c^2}}}$$

where m is the apparent mass and C the velocity of light. Thus:

$$K.E. = \frac{1}{2}\left(\frac{m_0}{\sqrt{1 - \frac{v^2}{c^2}}}\right) v^2$$

When the velocity of the moving body is very small, the Einstein-Lorentz's equation can be reduced to Newton's equation. Fortunately ~~enough,~~ we shall find ~~out that the~~ certain ~~same thing will be~~ development ~~in~~ the New Chemical Dynamics ~~that~~ which includes the fundamental law of chemical kinetics ~~and static will be come~~ as special cases. ~~in New Chemical Dynamics.~~

The development of the fundamental laws in chemistry is very gradual. In the year 1850, Wilhemy discovered the fundamental law of chemical kinetics on basis of his experiments on inversion of cane-sugar. The law states that the rate of the chemical reaction is proportional to the momentary concentration of reactants in the solution. For the monomolecular reaction, $A_1 \rightarrow A_2$, Wilhemy's equation is

$$\frac{-d[A]}{dt} = K[A]$$

where A is the reacting substance, [ ] the concentration, and K the reaction coef-

192

ficient or constant of proportionality. For the reversible bimolecular reaction,

$$A + B \rightleftarrows E + F$$

the kinetic equation will be

$$\frac{-d[A]}{dt} = K_1[A][B] - K_2[E][F]$$

For the reversible trimolecular reaction,

$$A + B + C \rightleftarrows E + F + G$$

the kinetic equation will be

$$\frac{-d[A]}{dt} = K_a[A][B][C] - K_b[E][F][G]$$

where K_1 and K_2, K_a and K_b are reaction constants, A, B, C, E, F, G, are reacting substances.

Wilhemy's principle that the rate of the chemical reaction is directly proportional to the product of the momentary concentration of reactants is exceedingly important in chemistry, because it lays not only the foundation for chemical kinetics but also for chemical statics and mass action. Based on Wilhemy's principle, Guldberg and Waage in 1865 established another fundamental law in Chemistry known as law of mass action or better of chemical statics. The law states that when the rates of the reversible reaction reach equilibruim, the ratio of the product of concentration of the direct reactants to that of the reversed reactants is equal to an equilibruim constant of mass action. That is

$$\frac{[A][B]}{[E][F]} = \frac{K_2}{K_1} = K$$

and

$$\frac{[A][B][C]}{[E][F][G]} = \frac{K_b}{K_a} = K$$

193

(4)

where K is the equilibruim constant. In addition to this, Van't Hoff developed another important thermodynamic equation known as Van't Hoff's equation for the maximum chemical work or reaction isochore. From the principles of perfect gas law for very diluted solutions, he obtained chemical work W

$$W = RT \ln \frac{C_2}{C_1}$$

where C_2 and C_1, are two different concentrations of the diluted solutions, R is the gas constant, T is the absolute temperature, ln is the natural logarithm. By setting W equals to nFE, Nernst established the most important potential equation in electrochemistry.

$$E = \frac{RT}{nF} \ln \frac{C_2}{C_1}$$

where E is the potential difference, n is the number of Faradays and F is equal to 96500 Coulombs. Both Van't Hoff and Nernst's equations are widely used in chemistry. Later on, we shall see exactly what they mean in New Chemical Dynamics.

When we separate two sides of permeable and impermeable solutes through a semi-peomeable membrane, we are dealing ~~according to the classical theory~~ with osmosis and ionic distribution. In 1887 Van't Hoff developed the fundamental law of osmosis through his work on diffusion of cane-sugar through a semi-permeable membrane. When the solution reaches equilibrium, the concentration of the diluted solution on both sides is equal to each other. Under such conditions, Donnan in 1910 formulated another important law of ionic distribution that the ratio

94

of the concentration of the distributed diffusible anions of side (1) to that of side (2) is equal to the ratio of the concentration of the diffusible cations of the side (2) to that of side (1). The law has been developed under the assumption that the different diffusible ions would be distributed in one equal ratio, a fact which is hardly justified for all cases. In spite of that, the law of ionic distribution has become exceedingly important in colloidal and biological chemistry. It has been taken for granted that the law can predict the distribution of different diffusible ions between red cells and serum in blood.

This sketch gives only a very short account of the historical development of the most important and useful laws in chemistry. The classical laws have been well established through numerous experiments with very diluted solutions. When the solution is concentrated, we have to introduce the principle of activity, a subject which will not be discussed in this paper, as we shall limit our conditions to very diluted solutions.

The purpose of this paper is to discuss with you an outline of the scope of our work in chemistry. As the subject is exceedingly long and complicated, we cannot possibly go into details here. We can however, discuss with you the main equations which represent the different laws of chemical kinetics and statics.

If we have a reversible isothermic reaction of very diluted solutions

$$aA + bB \rightleftarrows eE + fF$$

195

(6)

so we have according to Wilhemy's law of chemical kinetics

$$\frac{-d[A]}{dt}=K_1[A]^a[B]^b-K_2[E]^e[F]^f \qquad (1)$$

where A, B, E, F, are reacting substances, K_1 and K_2 are reacting coefficients, a, b, e, f, are the definite numbers of molecules going into reaction according to law of *multiple* proportion. This equation is however, not the complete equation for the rate of the chemical reaction, *because the* equation does not express all the chemical facts for the reversible reaction. The reason is that when a molecules of A react with *b* molecules of B to produce e molecules of E and f molecules of F, a molecule of A and b molecules of B will always disappear exactly at the same time. Therefore the complete kinetic equation will be

$$\frac{-(a\,d[A]+b\,d[B])}{dt}=K_1'[A]^a[B]^b-K_2'[E]^e[F]^f \qquad (2)$$

If we simplify the equation further, we get

$$\frac{-d[A]}{dt}=\frac{a}{(a^2-b^2)}K_1'[A]^a[B]^b-\frac{e}{(e^2-f^2)}K_2'[E]^e[F]^f$$

This equation can be transformed into equation (1) by setting

$$K_1=\frac{a}{(a^2-b^2)}K_1'$$

$$K_2=\frac{e}{(e^2-f^2)}K_2'$$

Equation (2) is very important, because it involves the principle of law of *multiple* proportion on the left side of the equation and the principle of mass action on the right side of the equation. *From* equation(1), that is Wilhemy's law, we cannot postulate the fundamental law of chemical kinetics, because the equation represents only part of the important chemical facts of the reaction.

196

But based on equation (2), the complete equation of chemical kinetics, we can now definitely postulate the law of chemical kinetics which, as a matter of fact, has never been completely postulated. The postulation for the fundamental law of chemical kinetics is that the rate of decrease of the total concentration of all reacting substances is proportional to the product of the concentration of reactants raised to the highest powers according to the numbers of molecules going into reaction as determined by the law of definite or multiple proportion.

Equation (1) is really composed of two kinetic equations of direct and reverse reactions.

$$\left(\frac{-a\,d[A]}{dt}\right)_d = K_3 [A]^a [B]^b$$

$$\left(\frac{-e\,d[E]}{dt}\right)_r = K_4 [E]^e [F]^f$$

where subscript d means the direct and r means the reverse reactions. As the reaction is reversible, $\left(\frac{-d[E]}{dt}\right)_r$ will counteract the rate $\left(\frac{-d[A]}{dt}\right)_d$. Under the condition when the rate of the direct reaction is predominant, the final rate will be

$$\frac{-a\,d[A]}{dt} = \left(\frac{-a\,d[A]}{dt}\right)_d - \left(\frac{-e\,d[E]}{dt}\right)_r = K_1'[A]^a[B]^b - K_2'[E]^e[F]^f$$

Consequently

$$\frac{-d[A]}{dt} = K_1 [A]^a [B]^b - K_2 [E]^e [F]^f$$

where $K_1 = K_3/a$ and $K_2 = K_4/e$

The reactions coefficients K_1 and K_2 according to classical theory simply represent certain definite constant values for the particular reaction. Just what the reaction coefficients represent ~~certainly something~~ has not yet been

197

(8)

worked out except in cases of gases. As the reaction coefficients represent certainly something very important for the chemical reactions, we shall trace out their exact values for all chemical reactions in any kind of medium. If we differentiate the above two kinetic equations for direct and reverse reactions once more with respect to time t, solve for the value of K_1 and K_2 and introduce the values of K_1 and K_2 in the original equation (1), we obtain the new equation.

$$\frac{-d[A]}{dt}=a\left(\frac{-d\ln V_1}{dt}\right)\frac{[A]^a[B]^b}{\left(a^2[A]^{a-1}[B]^b+b^2[A]^a[B]^{b-1}\right)}-e\left(\frac{-d\ln V_2}{dt}\right)\frac{[E]^e[F]^f}{\left(e^2[E]^{e-1}[F]^f+f^2[E]^e[F]^{f-1}\right)} \qquad (3)$$

where $\ln V_1$ and $\ln V_2$ mean the change of logarithm of the direct and reverse rates of the chemical reaction. This equation is obtained from the law of chemical kinetics. We shall derive a similar equation from thermodynamics. Under the condition when the solution is very dilute and when the reaction is ~~other~~ isothermic and reversible, we can write according to Van't Hoff's reaction isochore.

$$W_1=RT\ln[A]^a[B]^b$$

$$W_2=RT\ln[E]^e[F]^f$$

$$W=RT\ln\frac{[E]^e[F]^f}{[A]^a[B]^b}+RT\ln K$$

where K is the equilibrium constant, W_1 and W_2 are the chemical work due to the reactants and W is the total chemical work of the system. If we differentiate the first two equations of W_1 and W_2 with respect to time, we get by rearrangement.

$$\frac{-d[A]}{dt}=\frac{a}{RT}\left(\frac{-dW_1}{dt}\right)\frac{[A]^a[B]^b}{\left(a^2[A]^{a-1}[B]^b+b^2[A]^a[B]^{b-1}\right)}-\frac{e}{RT}\left(\frac{-dW_2}{dt}\right)\frac{[E]^e[F]^f}{\left(e^2[E]^{e-1}[F]^f+f^2[E]^e[F]^{f-1}\right)} \qquad (4)$$

Equation (4) is equivalent to equation (3). From the

198

standpoint of both physics and chemistry, we can balance equations (3) and (4). Hence we have

$$\frac{-d\ln v_1}{dt} = \frac{-dW_1}{RT\,dt}$$

$$\frac{-d\ln v_2}{dt} = \frac{-dW_2}{RT\,dt}$$

As the kinetic equation (4) is derived from the second law of thermodynamics and Van't Hoff's equation, we may denote it as the law of thermodynamico-kinetics. Equation (3) and (4) are the same except the terms $\frac{-dW}{RT\,dt}$ and $\frac{-d\ln v}{dt}$ which have been proved to be equal to each other. As the absolute T and gas constant R are not present in equation (3), we may denote it as the law of dynamico-kinetics.

From equations (1), (3) and (4), we can see that the term on the left side $-d[A]/dt$ is the same. Therefore we can balance all the three equations. If we express the products of the concentration of the reacting substances in terms of their equivalent values expressed in exponential power, we obtain the following equation.

$$\frac{-d[A]}{dt} = \frac{d e^{k_1\int(a^2[A]^{a-1}[B]^b+b^2[A]^a[B]^{b-1})dt+C_1}}{(a^2[A]^{a-1}[B]^b+b^2[A]^a[B]^{b-1})\,dt} - \frac{d e^{k_2\int(e^2[E]^{e-1}[F]^f+f^2[E]^e[F]^{f-1})dt+C_2}}{(e^2[E]^{e-1}[F]^f+f^2[E]^e[F]^{f-1})\,dt}$$

$$= \frac{d e^{-\int d\ln v_1+C_1}}{(a^2[A]^{a-1}[B]^b+b^2[A]^a[B]^{b-1})\,dt} - \frac{d e^{-\int d\ln v_2+C_2}}{(e^2[E]^{e-1}[F]^f+f^2[E]^e[F]^{f-1})\,dt}$$

$$= \frac{d e^{\frac{W_1}{RT}+C_1}}{(a^2[A]^{a-1}[B]^b+b^2[A]^a[B]^{b-1})\,dt} - \frac{d e^{\frac{W_2}{RT}+C_2}}{(e^2[E]^{e-1}[F]^f+f^2[E]^e[F]^{f-1})\,dt} \qquad (5)$$

199

where e is the base of natural logarithm, C_1 and C_2 are integration constants. Equation (5) really combines the three laws of chemical kinetics into one simple form. If we differentiate the equation with respect to time as it is shown above and *introduce* the value of the products of concentrations of different reactants into the equation, we obtain equation (1), (3) and (4). The exact steps will be given in another paper later on. If we balance the equations at state of equilibrium, we get the corresponding laws of mass action. From equation (1), we get

$$\frac{[A][B]}{[E][F]} = \frac{K_2}{K_1} = K \tag{6}$$

where K is the equilibrium constant of mass action. From equations (3) and (4), we obtain

$$\frac{[A][B]}{[E][F]} = \frac{e\left(a^2[A]^{a-1}[B]^b + b^2[A]^a[B]^{b-1}\right)}{a\left(e^2[E]^{e-1}[F]^f + f^2[E]^e[F]^{f-1}\right)} \tag{7}$$

because under such conditions $-dW_1/dt = -dW_2/dt$ and $-d\ln V_1/dt = -d\ln V_2/dt$. Equation (7) is the law of thermodynamic mass action or statics, as it is derived from the thermodynamico-kinetic equation. The same law of thermodynamic mass action was developed by Horstmann, Linie, Van't Hoff and W. Gibbs independently ~~through~~ in a different way through re-action of gases (contained in a vessel provided with pistons) with certain assumptions and longer calcula-tions. As we have shown that

$$[A]^a[B]^b = e^{\frac{W_1}{RT}}$$

$$[E]^e[F]^f = e^{\frac{W_2}{RT}}$$

we can *introduce* the values in equations (B) and (4)

$$\frac{-d[A]}{dt}=a\left(\frac{-d\ln v_1}{dt}\right)\frac{e^{\frac{W_1}{RT}}}{\left(a^2[A]^{a-1}[B]^b+b^2[A]^a[B]^{b-1}\right)}-e\left(\frac{-d\ln v_2}{dt}\right)\frac{e^{\frac{W_2}{RT}}}{\left(e^2[E]^{e-1}[F]^f+f^2[E]^e[F]^{f-1}\right)}$$

$$\frac{-d[A]}{dt}=\frac{a}{RT}\left(\frac{-dW_1}{dt}\right)\frac{e^{\frac{W_1}{RT}}}{\left(a^2[A]^{a-1}[B]^b+b^2[A]^a[B]^{b-1}\right)}-\frac{e}{RT}\left(\frac{-dW_2}{dt}\right)\frac{e^{\frac{W_2}{RT}}}{\left(e^2[E]^{e-1}[F]^f+f^2[E]^e[F]^{f-1}\right)}$$

If we balance the two reversible reactions at state of equilibrium, we obtain in both cases

$$\frac{a\,e^{\frac{W_1}{RT}}}{a^2[A]^{a-1}[B]^b+b^2[A]^a[B]^{b-1}}=\frac{e\,e^{\frac{W_2}{RT}}}{e^2[E]^{e-1}[F]^f+f^2[E]^e[F]^{f-1}}$$

It follows

$$e^{\frac{W_1-W_2}{RT}}=\frac{[A]^a[B]^b}{[E]^e[F]^f}=\frac{e\left(a^2[A]^{a-1}[B]^b+b^2[A]^a[B]^{b-1}\right)}{a\left(e^2[E]^{e-1}[F]^f+f^2[E]^e[F]^{f-1}\right)}=K \qquad (8)$$

Through rearrangement, we get

$$W_1-W_2=RT\ln\frac{[A]^a[B]^b}{[E]^e[F]^f}$$

If we add $-RT\ln K$ to both sides, we obtain Van't Hoff's equation by changing signs

$$W=W_2-W_1+RT\ln K=RT\ln\frac{[E]^e[F]^f}{[A]^a[B]^b}+RT\ln K$$

Van't Hoff's equation can be regarded as a transformed equation from the law of thermodynamic mass action.

The first new principle involved in the new laws of chemical kinetics is that the rate of the chemical reaction is not only directly proportional to the product of the momentary concentration of reactants raised to their highest powers according to law of definite and multiple proportion as formulated by Wilhemy and his followers, but also inversely proportional to the sum of the products of the concentration of the reactants raised to the highest powers except one term in each product which is only raised to one degree less than the highest power. Secondly, ~~is that~~ from the new 201

(12)

laws, we can calculate the change of chemical work or free energy of the reaction per second or change on logarithm of rate per second from the very beginning to equilibrium conditions. These facts are very important in all fields of chemistry. Take the example of inversion of cane-sugar. Based upon the old Wilhemy's law, we can only determine the rate of reaction, but according to the new laws, we can calculate the change of chemical work or free energy per second or simply chemical power either in terms of calories or ergs. Thirdly from ~~that based upon~~ the new equations, we can tell approximately when the rate of the reaction will stop, because the change of logarithm of rate $-d\ln V/dt$ and change of chemical work per second $-dW/dt$ will approach zero as the reaction reaches equilibrium. In other words, the rate of the reaction depends upon the concentration of reactants, the rate of change of chemical work as well as change of logarithm of the rate. The term $-d\ln V/dt$ may be denoted as retardation factor of the chemical reaction, because the rate of most of the reactions becomes always slower and slower until equilibrium is reached. Finally, ~~is that~~ the new principles of chemical kinetics as sown in equations (3) and (4) applied to the monomolecular reactions can be reduced ~~in~~ to Wilhemy's principle.

$$\frac{-d[A]}{dt}=K[A]=\frac{-d\ln V}{dt}[A]=\frac{-dW}{RT\,dt}[A]$$

In this case, the rate is only directly proportional to the momentary concentration of reactants for all three equations. In this way, we have proved that the classical law of chemical kinetics has become only a special

202

case in the new laws of chemical kinetics. For the bimolecular and polymolecular reactions, our principle of chemical kinetics is that the rate of the reaction is directly proportional to the product of the concentration of reactants raised to their highest powers according to the law of definite or multiple proportion, but also inversely proportional to the sum of the products of the concentration of reactants raised to their corresponding powers except one term in each product which is only raised to one degree less than the highest power, while the classical principle only states that the rate is just directly proportional to the product of the concentration of the reactants raised to their corresponding powers. For monomolecular reactions, our new principle and the classical principle are exactly the same. All these new laws are developed from the classical laws without any assumptions and therefore hold true for ~~all~~ reactions of gases and solutes.

Our second development is the electrochemical kinetics. If we have a reversible reaction of diluted solution of the following reacting substances

$$aA^{a+} + bB^{b-} + n\ominus \rightleftarrows eE^{e+} + fF^{f-} + n\oplus$$

where $\ominus$ and $\oplus$ mean the negative and positive charges, we have according to the law of mass action

$$\frac{[A^{a+}]^a [B^{b-}]^b [\ominus]^n}{[E^{e+}]^e [F^{f-}]^f [\oplus]^n} = K$$

and according to Nernst potential equation

$$E_s = E_n - \frac{RT}{nF} \ln \frac{[A^{a+}]^a [B^{b-}]^b}{[E^{e+}]^e [F^{f-}]^f} + RT \ln K$$

where E_s is the unknown E.M.F. and E_n is the normal standard E.M.F.

203

(14)

As the free protons do not exist separately in the solution, we express the concentration of positive charges in terms of decrease of electrons. Oxidation is a process which either takes up positive charges or gives off negative charges, ~~(according to th)~~ while reduction deals with taking up electrons or giving off positive charges. According to the principles of equation (2), we can write that the rate of decrease of the total concentration of all reacting substances including electrons this time is directly proportional to the product of the concentration of all reacting substances raised to their corresponding powers.

$$-\frac{(ad[A^{a+}]+bd[B^{b-}]+nd[\epsilon])}{dt}=K_1'[A^{a+}]^a[B^{b-}]^b[\epsilon]^n-K_2'[E^{e+}]^e[F^{f-}]^f[-\epsilon]^n$$

But according to the law of mass action, we know that

$$\frac{[A^{a+}]^a[B^{b-}]^b}{[E^{e+}]^e[F^{f-}]^f}=\frac{[-\epsilon]^n}{[\epsilon]^n}=K$$

Introducing this value into Nernst's potential equation, we have

$$E_s=E_n-\frac{RT}{nF}\ln\frac{[A^{a+}]^a[B^{b-}]^b}{[E^{e+}]^e[F^{f-}]^f K}=E_n-\frac{RT}{nF}\ln\frac{[-\epsilon]^n}{[\epsilon]^n}$$

From this calculation, we apparently trace out the fact that the electromotive force is a function of the concentration of the reacting substance and at the same time a function of the electron concentration.

$$E_c=f_1([c])$$

$$E_s=f_2([\epsilon]_s)$$

where E_c and Es mean the corresponding values of electromotive forces, $[c]$ and $[\epsilon]_s$ mean the total concentra-

204

(15)

tion of reacting substance and electrons. Based upon the equation, we can write

$$E_s = E_n + \frac{RT}{nF} \ln [-\epsilon]^n - \frac{RT}{nF} \ln [\epsilon]^n$$

If we put it into separate terms, we have

$$E_{(\epsilon)} = \frac{RT}{nF} \ln [\epsilon]^n$$

$$E_{(-\epsilon)} = \frac{RT}{nF} \ln [-\epsilon]^n$$

The final E_s is equal to

$$E_s = E_n + E_{(-\epsilon)} - E_{(\epsilon)}$$

where $E_{(\epsilon)}$ is the electomotive force due to the concentration of electrons for reduction and $E_{(-\epsilon)}$ is the electromotive force due to the concentration of electrons for oxidation. If we *introduce* the values into the origional kinetic equation, we obtain

$$\frac{-(ad[A^{a+}] + bd[B^{b-}] + nd[\epsilon])}{dt} = K_1 [A^{a+}]^a [B^{b-}]^b e^{\frac{nFE_{(\epsilon)}}{RT}} - K_2' [E^{e+}]^e [F^{f-}]^f e^{\frac{nFE_{(-\epsilon)}}{RT}}$$

Through simplication, we obtain the following final equation

$$\frac{-d[A^{a+}]}{dt} = K_1 [A^{a+}]^a [B^{b-}]^b e^{\frac{nFE_{(\epsilon)}}{RT}} - K_2 [E^{e+}]^e [F^{f-}] e^{\frac{nFE_{(-\epsilon)}}{RT}} \qquad (9)$$

This is the fundamental electrochemical kinetic equation. If we put it into two origional kinetic equations for the reversible reactions, we obtain

$$\left(\frac{-d[A^{a+}]}{dt}\right)_d = K_1 [A^{a+}]^a [B^{b-}]^b e^{\frac{nFE_{(\epsilon)}}{RT}} \qquad (9a)$$

$$\left(\frac{-d[E^{e+}]}{dt}\right)_r = K_2 [E^{e+}]^e [F^{f-}]^f e^{\frac{nFE_{(-\epsilon)}}{RT}} \qquad (9b)$$

where subscript *d* means derect and r means reverse reactions. If we differentiate this equation once more

205

(16)

with respect to time t, solve for K_1 and K_2 and *intro-duce* the values of K_1 and K_2 in ~~the~~ equation (9), we get

$$-\frac{d[A^{a+}]}{dt} = \frac{a\left(\frac{-d\ln V_1}{dt}\right)[A^{a+}]^a[B^{b-}]^b e^{\frac{nFE(\epsilon)}{RT}}}{n^2[A^{a+}]^a[B^{b-}]^b e^{\frac{(n-1)FE(\epsilon)}{RT}} + \left(a^2[A^{a+}]^{a-1}[B^{b-}] + b^2[A^{a+}][B^{b-}]^{b-1}\right)e^{\frac{nFE(\epsilon)}{RT}}}$$

$$-\frac{e\left(\frac{d\ln V_2}{dt}\right)[E^{e+}]^e[F^{f-}]^f e^{\frac{nFE(-\epsilon)}{RT}}}{n^2[E^{e+}]^e[F^{f-}]^f e^{\frac{(n-1)FE(-\epsilon)}{RT}} + \left(e^2[E^{e+}]^{e-1}[F^{f-}]^f + f^2[E^{e+}]^e[F^{f-}]^{f-1}\right)e^{\frac{nFE(-\epsilon)}{RT}}} \quad (10)$$

This is not the only way to derive this new equation. There is however, another way to fommulate the same kind of equation. If we denote

$$E_1 = \frac{RT}{nF}\ln[A^{a+}]^a[B^{b-}]^b[\epsilon]^n$$

$$E_2 = \frac{RT}{nF}\ln[E^{e+}]^e[F^{f-}]^f[-\epsilon]^n$$

We get through differentration of the two equations with respect to time and rearrangement,

$$\left(\frac{-d[A^{a+}]}{dt}\right)_d = \frac{a\left(\frac{nF}{RT}\right)\left(\frac{-dE_1}{dt}\right)[A^{a+}]^a[B^{b-}]^b e^{\frac{nFE(\epsilon)}{RT}}}{n^2[A^{a+}]^a[B^{b-}]^b e^{\frac{(n-1)FE(\epsilon)}{RT}} + \left(a^2[A^{a+}]^{a-1}[B^{b-}] + b^2[A^{a+}]^a[B^{b-}]^{b-1}\right)e^{\frac{nFE(\epsilon)}{RT}}}$$

$$\left(\frac{-d[E^{e+}]}{dt}\right)_r = \frac{e\left(\frac{nF}{RT}\right)\left(\frac{-dE_2}{dt}\right)[E^{e+}]^e[F^{f-}]^f e^{\frac{nFE(-\epsilon)}{RT}}}{n^2[E^{e+}]^e[F^{f-}]^f e^{\frac{(n-1)FE(-\epsilon)}{RT}} + \left(e^2[E^{e+}]^{e-1}[F^{f-}]^f + f^2[E^{e+}]^e[F^{f-}]^{f-1}\right)e^{\frac{nFE(-\epsilon)}{RT}}}$$

The final equation will be

206

(16 a)

$$\frac{-d[A^{a+}]}{dt} = \frac{nF}{RT}\left\{ a\left(\frac{-dE_1}{dt}\right) \frac{[A^{a+}]^a[B^{b-}]^b e^{\frac{nFE_{(e)}}{RT}}}{n^2[A^{a+}]^a[B^{b-}]^b e^{\frac{(n-1)FE_{(e)}}{RT}} + \left(a^2[A^{a+}]^{a-1}[B^{b-}]^b + b^2[A^{a+}]^a[B^{b-}]^{b-1}\right) e^{\frac{nFE_{(e)}}{RT}}} \right.$$

$$\left. - e\left(\frac{-dE_2}{dt}\right) \frac{[E^{e+}]^e[F^{f-}]^f e^{\frac{nFE_{(-e)}}{RT}}}{n^2[E^{e+}]^e[F^{f-}]^f e^{\frac{(n-1)FE_{(-e)}}{RT}} + \left(e^2[E^{e+}]^{e-1}[F^{f-}]^f + f^2[E^{e+}]^e[F^{f-}]^{f-1}\right) e^{\frac{nFE_{(-e)}}{RT}}} \right. \quad (11)$$

Equations (9) and (10) and (11) represent three sets of electrochemical kinetic equations just like equations (1) (3) (4) represent three sets of kinetic equations for the general reactions. If we balanced the reversible reduction and oxidation of equation (9) at state of equilibrium, we get the law of electrochemical mass action or statics.

$$\frac{[A^{a+}]^a[B^{b-}]^b e^{\frac{nFE_{(e)}}{RT}}}{[E^{e+}]^e[F^{f-}]^f e^{\frac{nFE_{(-e)}}{RT}}} = \frac{[A^{a+}]^a[B^{b-}]^b}{[E^{e+}]^e[F^{f-}]^f} e^{\frac{nFE_s}{RT}} = \frac{K_2}{K_1} = K \quad (12)$$

This equation can be transformed into Nernst's potential equation

$$E_s = E_n + \frac{nF}{RT} \ln \frac{[E^{e+}]^e[F^{f-}]^f}{[A^{a+}]^a[B^{b-}]^b} + \frac{nF}{RT} \ln K$$

207

(17)

where K is again the equilibrium constant. Therefore Nernst potential equation has been proved to be a transformed equation from the law of electrochemical statics. If we balance the reversible reaction of equations (10) and (11) at state of equilibrium, we obtain

$$\frac{[A^{a+}]^a[B^{b-}]^b}{[E^{e+}]^e[F^{f-}]^f}e^{\frac{nFE_s}{RT}}=\frac{\left(a^2[A^{a+}]^{a-1}[B^{b-}]^b+b^2[A^{a+}]^a[B^{b-}]^{b-1}\right)e^{\frac{nFE_{(\epsilon)}}{RT}}+n^2[A^{a+}]^a[B^{b-}]^b e^{\frac{(n-1)FE_{(\epsilon)}}{RT}}}{\left(e^2[E^{e+}]^{e-1}[F^{f-}]^f+f^2[E^{e+}]^e[F^{f-}]^{f-1}\right)e^{\frac{nFE_{(-\epsilon)}}{RT}}+n^2[E^{e+}]^e[F^{f-}]^f e^{\frac{(n-1)FE_{(-\epsilon)}}{RT}}}=\frac{K_2}{K_1}=K \qquad (13)$$

which is a complete electrochemical static equation for the same reaction.

Our next development is the chemical electron-kinetics. As the rate of change of electrons in reduction and oxidation bears definite relation with the rate of change of concentration of reductants and oxidants, so we can write.

$$\left(\frac{-d[A^{a+}]}{dt}\right)_d=\frac{a}{n}\left(\frac{-d[\epsilon]}{dt}\right)_d$$

$$\left(\frac{-d[E^{e+}]}{dt}\right)_r=\frac{e}{n}\left(\frac{-d[-\epsilon]}{dt}\right)_r$$

$$\frac{-d[A^{a+}]}{dt}=\frac{a}{n}\left(\frac{-d[\epsilon]_s}{dt}\right)$$

where $[\epsilon]_s$ is the total concentration of electrons $[\epsilon]_s=[\epsilon]+[-\epsilon]$ and $-d[\epsilon]/dt$ is the total rate of transference of electrons in reduction and oxidation. Under the condition when reduction is predominant, we have

$$\frac{-d[\epsilon]_s}{dt}=\frac{-d[\epsilon]}{dt}-\frac{-d[-\epsilon]}{dt}$$

The electron kinetic equations for reduction and oxidation based on equations (9a) and (9b) will be as follows:

208

$$\frac{-d[\epsilon]}{dt}=\frac{n}{a}K_1[A^{a+}]^a[B^{b-}]^b e^{\frac{nFE_{(\epsilon)}}{RT}}=K_r[A^{a+}]^a[B^{b-}]^b e^{\frac{nFE_{(\epsilon)}}{RT}}$$

$$\frac{-d[-\epsilon]}{dt}=\frac{n}{e}K_2[E^{e+}]^e[F^{f-}]^f e^{\frac{nFE_{(-\epsilon)}}{RT}}=K_o[E^{e+}]^e[F^{f-}]^f e^{\frac{nFE_{(-\epsilon)}}{RT}}$$

The final equation will be

$$\frac{-d[\epsilon]_s}{dt}=K_r[A^{a+}]^a[B^{b-}]^b e^{\frac{nFE_{(\epsilon)}}{RT}}-K_o[E^{e+}]^e[F^{f-}]^f e^{\frac{nFE_{(-\epsilon)}}{RT}} \qquad (14)$$

Substituting

$\frac{-d[\epsilon]_s}{dt}$ for $\frac{-d[A^{a+}]}{dt}$, $\frac{-d[\epsilon]}{dt}$ for $\left(\frac{-d[A^{a+}]}{dt}\right)_d$ and $\frac{-d[-\epsilon]}{dt}$ for $\left(\frac{-d[E^{e+}]}{dt}\right)_r$

in equations (10) and (11), we obtain

$$\frac{-d[\epsilon]_s}{dt}=n\left\{\left(\frac{-d\ln V_1}{dt}\right)\frac{[A^{a+}]^a[B^{b-}]^b e^{\frac{nFE_{(\epsilon)}}{RT}}}{n^2[A^{a+}]^a[B^{b-}]^b e^{\frac{(n-1)FE_{(\epsilon)}}{RT}}+\left(a^2[A^{a+}]^{a-1}[B^{b-}]^b+b^2[A^{a+}]^a[B^{b-}]^{b-1}\right)e^{\frac{nFE_{(\epsilon)}}{RT}}}\right.$$
$$\left.-\left(\frac{-d\ln V_2}{dt}\right)\frac{[E^{e+}]^e[F^{f-}]^f e^{\frac{nFE_{(-\epsilon)}}{RT}}}{n^2[E^{e+}]^e[F^{f-}]^f e^{\frac{(n-1)FE_{(-\epsilon)}}{RT}}+\left(e^2[E^{e+}]^{e-1}[F^{f-}]^f+f^2[E^{e+}]^e[F^{f-}]^{f-1}\right)e^{\frac{nFE_{(-\epsilon)}}{RT}}}\right\} \qquad (15)$$

$$\frac{-d[\epsilon]_s}{dt}=\frac{n^2F}{RT}\left\{\left(\frac{-dE_1}{dt}\right)\frac{[A^{a+}]^a[B^{b-}]^b e^{\frac{nFE_{(\epsilon)}}{RT}}}{n^2[A^{a+}]^a[B^{b-}]^b e^{\frac{(n-1)FE_{(\epsilon)}}{RT}}+\left(a^2[A^{a+}]^{a-1}[B^{b-}]^b+b^2[A^{a+}]^a[B^{b-}]^{b-1}\right)e^{\frac{nFE_{(\epsilon)}}{RT}}}\right.$$
$$\left.-\left(\frac{-dE_2}{dt}\right)\frac{[E^{e+}]^e[F^{f-}]^f e^{\frac{nFE_{(-\epsilon)}}{RT}}}{n^2[E^{e+}]^e[F^{f-}]^f e^{\frac{(n-1)FE_{(-\epsilon)}}{RT}}+\left(e^2[E^{e+}]^{e-1}[F^{f-}]^f+f^2[E^{e+}]^e[F^{f-}]^{f-1}\right)e^{\frac{nFE_{(-\epsilon)}}{RT}}}\right\} \qquad (16)$$

In equilibrium ~~conditions,~~ we can balance the reversible reactions and get the same static equations (12) and (13). From the electron kinetic equations, we can calculate the rate of transference of electrons in reduction and oxidation in terms of change of concentration of reductants and oxidants.

Our final development is the electromotive force kinetics. Based upon the electron kinetic equations, we can formulate the E.M.F. kinetic equations. According to definition

$$E_{(\epsilon)}=\frac{RT}{nF}\ln[\epsilon]^n=\frac{RT}{F}\ln[\epsilon]$$

$$E_{(-\epsilon)}=\frac{RT}{nF}\ln[-\epsilon]^n=\frac{RT}{F}\ln[-\epsilon]$$

$$E_s=\frac{RT}{nF}\ln[\epsilon]_s^n=\frac{RT}{F}\ln[\epsilon]_s$$

Introducing the value of $[\epsilon]$, $[-\epsilon]$ and $[\epsilon]_s$ in equations (14) (15) and (16), we get

$$\frac{-d[\epsilon]}{dt}=\left(\frac{-dE_{(\epsilon)}}{dt}\right)\frac{F}{RT}\,e^{\frac{FE_{(\epsilon)}}{RT}}$$

$$\frac{-d[-\epsilon]}{dt}=\left(\frac{-dE_{(-\epsilon)}}{dt}\right)\frac{F}{RT}\,e^{\frac{FE_{(-\epsilon)}}{RT}}$$

$$\frac{-d[\epsilon]_s}{dt}=\left(\frac{-dE_s}{dt}\right)\frac{F}{RT}\,e^{\frac{FE_s}{RT}}$$

It follows

$$\frac{-dE_s}{dt}=\frac{RT}{F}\left\{\frac{K_1}{a}[A^{a+}]^a[B^{b-}]^b e^{\frac{(n-1)FE_{(\epsilon)}}{RT}}-\frac{K_2}{e}[E^{e+}]^e[F^{f-}]^f e^{\frac{(n-1)FE_{(-\epsilon)}}{RT}}\right\} \quad (17)$$

$$\frac{-dE_s}{dt}=\frac{RT}{F}\left\{\left(\frac{-d\ln v_1}{dt}\right)\frac{[A^{a+}]^a[B^{b-}]^b e^{\frac{(n-1)FE_{(\epsilon)}}{RT}}}{n^2[A^{a+}]^a[B^{b-}]^b e^{\frac{(n-1)FE_{(\epsilon)}}{RT}}+\left(a^2[A^{a+}]^{a-1}[B^{b-}]^b+b^2[A^{a+}]^a[B^{b-}]^{b-1}\right)e^{\frac{nFE_{(\epsilon)}}{RT}}}\right.$$
$$\left.-\left(\frac{-d\ln v_2}{dt}\right)\frac{[E^{e+}]^e[F^{f-}]^f e^{\frac{(n-1)FE_{(-\epsilon)}}{RT}}}{n^2[E^{e+}]^e[F^{f-}]^f e^{\frac{(n-1)FE_{(-\epsilon)}}{RT}}+\left(e^2[E^{e+}]^{e-1}[F^{f-}]^f+f^2[E^{e+}]^e[F^{f-}]^{f-1}\right)e^{\frac{nFE_{(-\epsilon)}}{RT}}}\right\} \quad (18)$$

$$\frac{-dE_s}{dt}=\frac{n^2\left(\frac{-dE_1}{dt}\right)[A^{a+}]^a[B^{b-}]^b e^{\frac{(n-1)FE_{(\epsilon)}}{RT}}}{n^2[A^{a+}]^a[B^{b-}]^b e^{\frac{(n-1)FE_{(\epsilon)}}{RT}}+\left(a^2[A^{a+}]^{a-1}[B^{b-}]^b+b^2[A^{a+}]^a[B^{b-}]^{b-1}\right)e^{\frac{nFE_{(\epsilon)}}{RT}}}$$
$$-\frac{n^2\left(\frac{-dE_2}{dt}\right)[E^{e+}]^e[F^{f-}]^f e^{\frac{(n-1)FE_{(-\epsilon)}}{RT}}}{n^2[E^{e+}]^e[F^{f-}]^f e^{\frac{(n-1)FE_{(-\epsilon)}}{RT}}+\left(e^2[E^{e+}]^{e-1}[F^{f-}]^f+f^2[E^{e+}]^e[F^{f-}]^{f-1}\right)e^{\frac{nFE_{(-\epsilon)}}{RT}}} \quad (19)$$

We can measure the rate of E. M. F. from which we can calculate the final rate of change of electron concentration. We can also calculate the rate of simple cases of reduction or oxidation. For the simple reduction, we can write

$$oxd + n\epsilon \longrightarrow red$$

where "oxd" means the oxidazed substance and "red" means the reduced substance. In this case, the E. M. F. kinetic

210

equation will be

$$\frac{-dE_{(\epsilon)}}{dt}=\frac{RT}{F}\left(\frac{-d[\epsilon]}{dt}\right)e^{\frac{-FE_{(\epsilon)}}{RT}}$$

As the rate of change of electron concentration is equal to

$$\frac{-d[\epsilon]}{dt}=n\left(\frac{-d[oxd]}{dt}\right)$$

so we get by substitution

$$\frac{-dE_{(\epsilon)}}{dt}=\frac{nRT}{F}\left(\frac{-d[oxd]}{dt}\right)e^{\frac{-FE_{(\epsilon)}}{RT}}$$

If n is equal to 1, we have the simple equation

$$\frac{-dE_{(\epsilon)}}{dt}=\frac{RT}{F}\left(\frac{-d[oxd]}{dt}\right)e^{\frac{-FE_{(\epsilon)}}{RT}}$$

In this case, we can calculate the rate of reduction in terms of rate of E. M. F. very easily. According to equations (17) (18) and (19), we get three simple kinetic equations

$$\frac{-dE_{(\epsilon)}}{dt}=\frac{RT}{F}k[oxd]e^{\frac{(n-1)FE_{(\epsilon)}}{RT}}$$

$$\frac{-dE_{(\epsilon)}}{dt}=\frac{RT}{F}\left(\frac{-d\ln v}{dt}\right)\frac{[oxd]\,e^{\frac{(n-1)FE_{(\epsilon)}}{RT}}}{n^2[oxd]e^{\frac{(n-1)FE_{(\epsilon)}}{RT}}+e^{\frac{nFE_{(\epsilon)}}{RT}}}=\frac{RT}{F}\left(\frac{-d\ln v}{dt}\right)\frac{[oxd]}{n^2[oxd]+e^{\frac{FE_{(\epsilon)}}{RT}}}$$

$$\frac{-dE_{(\epsilon)}}{dt}=n^2\left(\frac{-dE_1}{dt}\right)\frac{[oxd]}{n^2[oxd]+e^{\frac{nFE_{(\epsilon)}}{RT}}}$$

where E_1 is equal to $\frac{RT}{nF}\ln[oxd][\epsilon]^n$ and v means $-d[oxd]/dt$.

At state of equilibrium, we can balance the E. M. F. kinetic equation (17) (18) and (19). From equation (17), we obtain

$$\frac{[A^{a+}]^a[B^{b-}]^b e^{\frac{(n-1)FE_{(\epsilon)}}{RT}}}{[E^{e+}]^e[F^{f-}]^f e^{\frac{(n-1)FE_{(\epsilon)}}{RT}}}=\frac{[A^{a+}]^a[B^{b-}]^b}{[E^{e+}]^e[F^{f-}]^f}e^{\frac{(n-1)FE_s}{RT}}=\frac{aK_2}{eK_1}=K \qquad (20)$$

where K is the equilibrium constant. From equations

211

(18) and (19), we get

$$\frac{[A^{a+}]^a[B^{b-}]^b}{[E^{e+}]^e[F^{f-}]^f} e^{\frac{(n-1)FE_s}{RT}} = \frac{n^2[A^{a+}]^a[B^{b-}]^b e^{\frac{(n-1)FE_{(\epsilon)}}{RT}} + \left(a^2[A^{a+}]^{a-1}[B^{b-}]^b + b^2[A^{a+}]^a[B^{b-}]^{b-1}\right) e^{\frac{nFE_{(\epsilon)}}{RT}}}{n^2[E^{e+}]^e[F^{f-}]^f e^{\frac{(n-1)FE_{(-\epsilon)}}{RT}} + \left(e^2[E^{e+}]^{e-1}[F^{f-}]^f + f^2[E^{e+}]^e[F^{f-}]^{f-1}\right) e^{\frac{nFE_{(-\epsilon)}}{RT}}} = \frac{aK_2}{eK_1} = K \qquad (21)$$

This covers a brief outline for the development of New Chemical Dynamics. So far we have formulated three sets of kinetic equations including Wilhemy's law for the general chemical reaction. The dynamico-kinetic equation is derived from Wilhemy's laws while the thermodynamico-kinetic equation is derived from the second law of thermodynamics and Van't Hoffs equation for the maximum chemical work. Based upon the new principle of chemical kinetics, we can formulate three similar sets of electrochemical kinetic equations for oxidation and reduction. As the rate of transference of electrons in reduction and oxidation bears definite relation with the rate of change of concentration of oxidants and reductants, so we formulate again three sets of electron-kinetic equations which can be transformed finally into three corresponding sets of E. M. F. kinetic equations. These kinetic equations enable us to calculate not only the rate of the chemical reactions but also the chemical power and the retardation factor of the processes.

Finally we come to the development of the dynamics of osmosis. Under the condition when certain amount of permeable and impermeable substances of very dilute possibly below one hundredth molar solution but of different concentrations separated by a semi-permeable membrane, diffusion of ions and substance will take place until equilibrium is reached. By applying the three laws of chemical kinetics, we can write the rate of diffusion from the concentrated side (1) to the diluted side (2) as follows:

$$\frac{-d\sum[C_n]_1}{dt} = K_1 \sum [C_n]_1$$

where $\sum[C_n]_1$ is the sum of the concentraions of different substances $[C_1]_1 + [C_2]_1 + \cdots + [C_n]_1$ of side (1) to side (2) and K_1 is the diffusion constant. As the solution is of side (2) becomes more concentrated, ~~(sme di),~~ some diffusible substance will migrate from side (2) to side (1)

$$\frac{-d\sum[C_n]_2}{dt} = K_2 \sum [C_n]_2$$

where $\sum[C_n]_2$ is the sum of the concentrations of different substances $[C_1]_2 + [C_2]_2 + \cdots + [C_n]_2$ from side (2) to side (1) and K_2 is the diffusion constant. The diffusion ~~or migration~~ will continue on until state of equilibrium where the rates of diffusion as well as K_1 and K_2 will be equal to each other. Therefore, we can balance the two equations

$$\sum[C_n]_1 = \sum[C_n]_2 \tag{22}$$

This is the equation for the law of osmosis which states that the total concentration of all substances of side (1) is equal is to that of side (2) in equilibrium conditions for very diluted solutions. If we differentiate the two kinetic equations once more with respect to time, solve for K_1 and K_2 and *introduce* the values of K_1 and K_2 in the original equations, we obtain

$$\frac{-d\sum[C_n]_1}{dt} = \frac{-d\ln v_1}{dt} \sum[C_n]_1$$

213

(23)

$$\frac{-d\Sigma[C_n]_2}{dt} = \frac{-d\ln V_2}{dt}\Sigma[C_n]_2$$

where V_1 and V_2 represent the total rates $-d\Sigma[C_n]_1/dt$ and $-d\Sigma[C_n]_2/dt$. At state of equilibrium, the rates will be equal to each other. We obtain again equation (22) by balancing the two kinetic equations.

We can formulate the law of osmosis through thermodynamics. According to Van't Hoff's equation, we can write

$$W_1 = RT\ln\Sigma[C_n]_1$$

$$W_2 = RT\ln\Sigma[C_n]_2$$

If we differentiate the two equations with respect to time, we obtain through rearrangement.

$$\frac{-d\Sigma[C_n]_1}{dt} = \frac{-dW_1}{RT\,dt}\Sigma[C_n]_1$$

$$\frac{-d\Sigma[C_n]_2}{dt} = \frac{-dW_2}{RT\,dt}\Sigma[C_n]_2$$

In equilibruim where the rates of diffusion and change of free energy on both sides are exactly the same, we can balance the two equatins and get again equation (22). Altogeather there are three ways to formulate the law of osmosis; namely, from the general equation of chemical kinetics, of dynamico-kinetics and of thermodynamico-kinetics.

Based upon the principles of New Chemical Dynamics, we can next discuss the dynamics of membrane potential and ionic distribution under the conditions of very diluted solutions with perfect ionization and with all ions not greatly different in sizes. If we have a sum of diffusible and non-diffusible ions of dilute solution but of different concent-

214

trations separated by a semi-permeable membrane, we can write the first two kinetic equations as follows:

$$\frac{-d\Sigma[C]_1}{dt} = K_1(\Sigma[M_n^+]_1 + \Sigma[K_n^+]_1)\Sigma[A_n^-]_1$$

$$\frac{-d\Sigma[C]_2}{dt} = K_2(\Sigma[M_n^+]_2 + \Sigma[K_n^+]_2)\Sigma[A_n^-]_2$$

where $-d\Sigma[C]_1/dt$ means the total rate of diffusion of all permeable kations or anions from side (1) to side (2) and $-d\Sigma[C]_2/dt$ means the same thing from side (2) to side (1), K_1 and K_2 are the two diffusion constants, $\Sigma[M_n^+]_1$ and $\Sigma[M_n^+]_2$ means the sum of ~~all~~ the total concentration of all diffusible ~~meable~~ ions of side (1) and side (2).

$$\Sigma[M_n^+]_1 = [M_1^+]_1 + [M_2^+]_1 + \cdots + [M_n^+]_1$$

$$\Sigma[M_n^+]_2 = [M_1^+]_2 + [M_2^+]_2 + \cdots + [M_n^+]_2$$

$\Sigma[K_n^+]_1$ and $\Sigma[K_n^+]_2$ mean the sum of concentrations of all diffusible kations of sides (1) and (2).

$$\Sigma[K_n^+]_1 = [K_1^+]_1 + [K_2^+]_1 + \cdots + [K_n^+]_1$$

$$\Sigma[K_n^+]_2 = [K_1^+]_2 + [K_2^+]_2 + \cdots + [K_n^+]_2$$

and $\Sigma[A_n^-]_1$ and $\Sigma[A_n^-]_2$ mean the sum of concentration of all diffusible anions of sides (1) and (2)

$$\Sigma[A_n^-]_1 = [A_1^-]_1 + [A_2^-]_1 + \cdots + [A_n^-]_1$$

$$\Sigma[A_n^-]_2 = [A_1^-]_2 + [A_2^-]_2 + \cdots + [A_n^-]_2$$

215

Under the condition of very diluted solutions with perfect ionization (and with all ions not greatly different in sizes,) we can balance the two kinetic equations in state of equilibrium where the total rates of diffusion of all diffusible ions on both sides as well as K_1 and K_2 are equal to each other. Therefore, we get

$$\left(\Sigma[M_n^+]_1+\Sigma[K_n^+]_1\right)\Sigma[A_n^-]_1=\left(\Sigma[M_n^+]_2+\Sigma[K_n^+]_2\right)\Sigma[A_n^-]_2 \qquad (23)$$

This is the equation for the membrane equilibrium which involves the principle of common mass action. The law of membrane equilibruim states that the product of the sum of the total diffusible and non-diffusible anions and kations of side (1) is equal to that of side (2). From this equation of membrane equilibrium, we obtain the following equation by rearrangement.

$$\frac{\Sigma[M_n^+]_1+\Sigma[K_n^+]_1}{\Sigma[M_n^+]_2+\Sigma[K_n^+]_2}=\frac{\Sigma[A_n^-]_2}{\Sigma[A_n^-]_1}=r \qquad (24)$$

where r means the distribution ratio of different ions on two sides of semi-permeable membrane. Introducing the values of different substances into the equation, we have.

$$\frac{[M_1^+]_1+[M_2^+]_1+\cdots+[M_n^+]_1+[K_1^+]_1+[K_2^+]_1+\cdots+[K_n^+]_1}{[M_1^+]_2+[M_2^+]_2+\cdots+[M_n^+]_2+[K_1^+]_2+[K_2^+]_2+\cdots+[K_n^+]_2}=\frac{[A_1^-]_2+[A_2^-]_2+\cdots+[A_n^-]_2}{[A_1^-]_1+[A_2^-]_1+\cdots+[A_n^-]_1}=r$$

Based upon the equation, the law of ionic distribution states that the ratio of the sum of the total concentration of all diffusible and non-diffusible kations of sides (1) to that of side (2) is equal to the ratio of the total concentration of all diffusible and non-diffusible anions of side (2) to that of side (1). If we separate the total ratio into single ratio of diffusible ions, we

216

~~shall~~ have

$$\frac{[K_1^+]_1}{[K_1^+]_2} \gtreqless \frac{[K_2^+]_1}{[K_2^+]_2} \gtreqless \cdots \gtreqless \frac{[K_n^+]_1}{[K_n^+]_2} \gtreqless \frac{[A_1^-]_2}{[A_1^-]_1} \gtreqless \frac{[A_2^-]_2}{[A_2^-]_1} \gtreqless \cdots \gtreqless \frac{[A_n^-]_2}{[A_n^-]_1} \gtreqless r \qquad (25)$$

which comes out to be either greater or smaller than one another or possibly equal to each other. The value of ratios of the diffusible ions on both sides of semi-permeable membrane depends entirely upon expermental results. It is impossible to predict what ratios will be equal to each other for the complicated cases. There are however, two other methods to formulate the law of membrane equilibrium and of ionic distribution. If we differentiate the two kinetic equations once more with respect to time, solve for the values of K_1 and K_2 and introduce the value of K_1 and K_2 into the original kinetic equations, we obtain

$$\frac{-d\Sigma[C_n]_1}{dt} = \frac{-d\ln v_1}{dt}\frac{(\Sigma[M_n^+]_1+\Sigma[K_n^+]_1)\Sigma[A_n^-]_1}{(\Sigma[M_n^+]_1+\Sigma[K_n^+]_1+\Sigma[A_n^-]_1)}$$

$$\frac{-d\Sigma[C_n]_2}{dt} = \frac{-d\ln v_2}{dt}\frac{(\Sigma[M_n^+]_2+\Sigma[K_n^+]_2)\Sigma[A_n^-]_2}{(\Sigma[M_n^+]_2+\Sigma[K_n^+]_2+\Sigma[A_n^-]_2)}$$

where $v_1 = -d\Sigma[C_n]_1/dt$ and $v_2 = -d\Sigma[C_n]_2/dt$ mean the total rate of diffusion of permeable ions either cations or anions. At equilibrium, we can balance the two equations

$$\frac{(\Sigma[M_n^+]_1+\Sigma[K_n^+]_1)\Sigma[A_n^-]_1}{(\Sigma[M_n^+]_2+\Sigma[K_n^+]_2)\Sigma[A_n^-]_2} = \frac{\Sigma[M_n^+]_1+\Sigma[K_n^+]_1+\Sigma[A_n^-]_1}{\Sigma[M_n^+]_2+\Sigma[K_n^+]_2+\Sigma[A_n^-]_2}$$

According to the law of osmosis, we can write

$$\Sigma[M_n^+]_1+\Sigma[K_n^+]_1+\Sigma[A_n^-]_1 = \Sigma[M_n^+]_2+\Sigma[K_n^+]_2+\Sigma[A_n^-]_2$$

It follows

$$(\Sigma[M_n^+]_1+\Sigma[K_n^+]_1)\Sigma[A_n^-]_1 = (\Sigma[M_n^+]_2+\Sigma[K_n^+]_2)\Sigma[A_n^-]_2$$

This is equation (23) for membrane equilibrium from which equation (25) for ionic distribution can be derived. 217

The third way to develop the membrane equilibrium and ionic distribution is through thermodynamics. Under the assumption that the reaction is isothermic, we can write according to Van't Hoff's equation:

$$W_1 = RT \ln(\Sigma[M_n^+]_1 + \Sigma[K_n^+]_1)\Sigma[A_n^-]_1$$

$$W_2 = RT \ln(\Sigma[M_n^+]_2 + \Sigma[K_n^+]_2)\Sigma[A_n^-]_2$$

where W_1 and W_2 are the total free energies for side (1) and side (2). We can differentiate the two equations with respect to time. Through rearrangement, we obtain

$$\frac{-d\Sigma[C_n]_1}{dt} = \frac{-dW_1\,(\Sigma[M_n^+]_1 + \Sigma[K_n^+]_1)\Sigma[A_n^-]_1}{RT\,dt\,(\Sigma[M_n^+] + \Sigma[K_n^+] + \Sigma[A_n^-]_1)}$$

$$\frac{-d\Sigma[C_n]_2}{dt} = \frac{-dW_2\,(\Sigma[M_n^+]_2 + \Sigma[K_n^+]_2)\Sigma[A_n^-]_2}{RT\,dt\,\Sigma[M_n^+]_2 + \Sigma[K_n^+]_2 + \Sigma[A_n^-]_2}$$

In equilibrium ~~condition,~~ we can balance the two equations as before and again obtain the equations for membrane equilibrium and ionic distribution.

Donnan developed the law of ionic distribution on basis of change of free energy through tranferences of one kind of permeable ions from one side to another. According to Donnan's principle, we can write.

$$\frac{[K_1^+]_1}{[K_1^+]_2} = \frac{[K_2^+]_1}{[K_2^+]_2} = \cdots = \frac{[K_n^+]_1}{[K_n^+]_2} = \frac{[A_1^-]_2}{[A_1^-]_1} = \frac{[A_2^-]_2}{[A_2^-]_1} = \cdots = \frac{[A_n^-]_2}{[A_n^-]_1} = r$$

which can hardly be regarded as a special case in our equation (25), as the ratios will be most likely greater or smaller than one or another. The chances for the distribution of diffusible ions in unequal ratios is very much greater than that in equal ratios, since the chemical properties of different diffusible ions such as migration velocity, combining power with certain impermeable ions especially proteins and so on are different from one another.

As donnan's law is for membrane equilibrium and ionic distribution, it does not hold true for all cases according to our new equations. The law of membrane equilibrium is derived from the laws of chemical kinetics, while the law of ionic destribution is derived from the law of membrane equilibrium. For a simple case of very diluted non-diffusible substance M^+ with only two kinds of diffusible ions K^+ and A^-, Donnan's law may be regarded as a special case in the new general law of ionic distribution

$$\frac{[M^+]_1+[K^+]_1}{[K^+]_2} \geqq \frac{[A^-]_2}{[A^-]_1} \geqq r$$

When $[M^+]_1$ is negligibly small, we have

$$\frac{[K^+]_1}{[K^+]_2} \doteq \frac{[A^-]_2}{[A^-]_1} \doteq r$$

which is practically Donnan's equation. When the diffusible ions are more than two kinds, Donnan's equation can hardly be accepted as a general equation for membrane equilibrium and ionic distribution.

Concerning the practical value of the new laws in chemistry, they will be just as useful as the classical laws. The new laws predict certain important facts which the old laws cannot explain. For instance, the distribution ratio of different diffusible ions between red cells and serum according to the new principle will not be equal to one another. Through the new electrochemical and E. M. F. kinetics, we can explain the chief reactions between quinhydone components and blood. We can further formulate the principal equations for the buffer

219

regulation of the reduction and oxidation of quinone-hydroquinone with blood or serum. Besides this, we can also develop the thermokinetic equations for the effect of temperature upon the reduction and oxidation of quinone and hydroquinone with blood.

In conclusion, I may say that in New Chemical Dynamics, we have developed three sets of fundamental kinetic equations including Wilhemy's law for ~~four kinds of processes, namely~~ the general reactions, oxidation ad reduction, electronic and E. M. F. kinetics. These twelve sets of kinetic equations can be transformed into twelve sets of static equations of mass action. This will include the classical theory and classical laws of chemical dynamics in several instances as special cases. Based upon this development, we can exactly postulate and formulate the fundamental laws of chemical kinetics and mass action in addition to the old laws which are ~~been ser-~~ the working basis for all fields of chemistry.

Literature:

W. Ostwald: Chemie II 2, Verwandtschaftslehre erster Teil. 1911, 2 Auflage.

W. Nernst: Theoretische Chemie 1926

M. Trautz: Lehrbuch der Chemie. 3 Bd. 1924

R. Toleman: Statistical Mechanics with Application to Physics and Chemistry. 1927.

G. N. Lewis & M. Randall: Thermodynamics and the Free Energy of Chemical Substance. 1923

L. Michailis: Die Wasserstoffionenkonzentration Teil 2 Oxydation and Reduction 1929.

W. M. Clark: Studies on Oxidation & Reduction Hygienic Laboratory Bulletin, 1928

220

(50)

W. Schotlky: Thermodynamik 1929.

F. G. Donnan: The theory of Membrane Equilibrium. Chemical Reviews Vol. 1 1924 and 1925.

F. G. Donnan: Theorie der Membrangleichgewicht und Membranpotential bei Vorhandsein von nicht dialysierenden Elektrolyten. Zeitschrift für Elektrochemie 572, 1911.

C. N, Hinshelwood: The kinetics of Chemical Change in Gaseous Systems 1929.

A. Eucken: Grundlage der physikalischen chemie 1924

Jeans: Dynamical Theory of Gases. Cambridge Press:.

221

FORM 8097

THE JOHNS HOPKINS HOSPITAL

Ward........................ Unit History No........................

NAME........................ Ophthalmological No........................

"Trachoma our Great Scourge"*

Eugene Chan, S.B., M.D.
(陳耀真)

It is not without hesitation that the writer ventures to present such a topic before a group of scientists who are specializing in widely separated fields. Nevertheless, he feels that there are a number of reasons which justify him in engaging the attention of his most intelligent audience on this important subject.

You all who are citizens of the Chinese Republic should naturally be interested in the affairs of China. During the present period of Reconstruction, you should especially take to heart any program which is a prerequisite in the building of a strong & powerful China.

You must still recall when you left China, you had your eyes inspected & lids everted by a doctor, either over there or at a port of entry in this country. Your scientific curiosity must have been aroused as to the necessity of such an obtrusive investigation. When foreigners go to our country, they do not have to be examined. Is that fair?

From a mere personal standpoint, anyone with a pair of eyes cannot but have some concern about his ocular health. That delicate visual mechanism enables you to appreciate the beauty of Nature & to acquire

*From Wilmer Ophthalmological Institute of Johns Hopkins University & Hospital

230

FORM 8097

THE JOHNS HOPKINS HOSPITAL

2

Ward........ Unit History No........

NAME........ Ophthalmological No........

your profound erudition. How priceless it is! Can you afford to have it impaired by that treacherous disease, trachoma — or any disease for that matter?

Trachoma is a contagious disease which gives rise to granulation or roughness of the conjunctiva, the smooth conjoined lining membrane of the eyelids. It is by no means a new malady. It probably existed in Egypt as early as the nineteenth century B.C. The disease described by our Sun Ssu Miao (孫思邈) of Tang Dynasty (唐朝) known as Lien Sheng Feng Li (臉生風栗) in the famous ophthalmologic treatise, Yin Hai Ching Wei (銀海精微) apparently signifies trachoma. Horace & Cicero suffered from this infirmity. When Shakespeare make Lancelot Gobbo say that his father was "more than sand blind — he was gravel blind," this great English writer was mindful of the widespread ocular affliction in his days.

That trachoma is contagious is well established. Treacher Collins, recording his experience as an ophthalmic surgeon to the London ophthalmia schools, portrayed the following dramatic incident: "Some of the children when their eyes are cured are very loth to depart from these pleasant surroundings to return to their parish barrack schools in London. Various tricks are played by them to keep up discharge from their eyes, or to make them injected, so that they may not be sent away. One child, whose name peculiarly enough was Sly, was admitted with marginal blepharitis & slight conjunctivites; this

281

FORM 8097

THE JOHNS HOPKINS HOSPITAL

3

Ward......................... Unit History No.........................

NAME......................... Ophthalmological No.........................

was cured & all treatment was stopped preparatory to her leaving the school. She was then caught by the nurse taking discharge from another child's eye who was suffering with trachoma & deliberately putting it into her own. The symptoms of acute mucopurulent ophthalmia rapidly set in, & two months later typical trachoma follicles on the tarsal conjunctiva were recognized. After a year's treatment the trachoma was cured."

During the World War hundreds of conscripted soldiers in the armies of the Russian & of the Austro-Hungarian Empire infected themselves with trachoma in order to avoid active military service. They accomplished this by placing within their conjunctival sacs bits of cotton soaked in the secretion of trachomatous patients. We certainly have ample evidence of the facility with which this horrible disease can be transferred from one person to another.

As you know, America is the land of opportunity for the downcast & depressed in Europe. A vast number of immigrants flock to U.S.A. from Ireland following the Irish famine, then from Italy & other countries around the Mediterranean Sea & later from Poland & Russia. They bring with them more than their strong bodies, their hopes & ambitions — often an eye disease. Perceiving the imminent danger, the American Ophthalmological Society in 1897 urged their Government to take immediate steps against the further importation of trachoma. The Government was quick to respond. In a very short time, the

232

FORM 8097

THE JOHNS HOPKINS HOSPITAL

4

Ward.................. Unit History No..................

NAME.................. Ophthalmological No..................

Surgeon General of the U.S. Public Health Service officially proclaimed the disease as "dangerous contagious." An alien, suffering from it, is excluded from admission to the United States. The alertness with which the American Government attempts to stamp out a contagious disease should incite our National Government to make similar efforts."

Generally, the onset of trachoma is insidious. In the incipient stage, the victim may have no knowledge of his disaster. Later on, there may be ocular discomfort, redness, lacrimation, photophobia, pain, discharge, drooping of the lid, rapid loss of vision, etc. The patient may go through untold suffering until finally he becomes totally blind. Trachoma mutilates the lovely organ of sight; it causes misery; it interferes with education; it diminishes one's working capacity. Who can guess what great possibilities are installed for the unfortunate one, had his vision not been destroyed? Furthermore, trachoma not only depresses the economic & social status of the individual, it frequently involves that of his family. It is thus a link in the vicious cycle of ignorance, poverty, & disease, each being the result as well as the cause of the others.

Trachoma is widespread in the world. All races would suffer equally from it, if exposed to conditions which favor its spread. It was very prevalent in England. By careful control, it has become practically extinct there. The percentage of infection in Egypt is extremely high. Over

223

FORM 8097

THE JOHNS HOPKINS HOSPITAL

5

Ward........ Unit History No........

NAME........ Ophthalmological No........

90% of the Egyptian population is infected. The accompanying diagram will give you some idea of this pandemic.

Let us focus our attention on the number of victims in China. At the Jones Child Welfare Exhibit in Canton, Y. P. Chan & Frank Oldt participated in the examination of 1602 persons. They found the incidence rate of trachoma to be approximately 15%. S. P. Chang examined 1843 students in ten different schools in Peiping. He discovered 416 cases of trachoma, i.e. 22.2%. C. H. Chou's study showed that among the 4,150 new eye patients treated in Peiping Union Medical College Hospital from May 1, 1928 to April 30, 1929, 1,393 patients or 33.56% were suffering from trachoma in one phase or another. H. J. Howard's investigation near Paotingfu gave the following results: "In one school which represented the children of school age from seven adjoining villages, 47.2% of the boys & 66.7% of the girls, or 56.5% for both, were found to have trachoma. In that village 90% of the adults had trachoma, which made an average for that village, including both children & adults, of 67.5%. In another village a school maintained by the Presbyterian Mission showed 68% of the children with trachoma. Two more villages were visited, & in one 79% & in the other 80% of the people had trachoma." Howard further stated: "From statistics I had gathered, I had come to the conclusion that fully one hundred million of Chinese people have trachoma, & that probably five million new cases, mostly children, develop

234 each year. I had estimated that not less than one

FORM 8097

THE JOHNS HOPKINS HOSPITAL

6

Ward.................... Unit History No.....................

NAME.................... Ophthalmological No.....................

million Chinese are blind in both eyes, & that three or four million are blind in one eye; further, that not far from twenty million have had their vision so much impaired by inflammation & the formation of scar tissue, due to trachoma, that they are able to eke out only the barest kind of existence."

You may wonder what the etiology of this loathsome disease is. Unfortunately it is still undetermined. Numerous eminent workers have sought for the causative agent during the last half a century. Now & then, we hear an announcement about the discovery of the specific cause. But, none of the claims were substantiated. The latest piece of research which may shed some light on the etiology of trachoma was performed by the brilliant Japanese scientist, Noguchi. However, his untimely death cut short his valuable service to humanity. While there are reports which confirm his labor, other able investigators, among whom is F. F. Tang of National Central University, Woosung, fail to verify it.

It would be beyond the scope of this paper to discuss the technical methods of treatment & the medications administered in cases of trachoma. Nevertheless, I want to remind you of the gospel of scientific medicine. The good result derived from a proper course of therapy is nothing short of a miracle. Too great a stress, however, cannot be laid on the importance of early treatment. It would be a folly to expect too much from any remedial measure after irreparable damage has occurred.

235

FORM 8097

THE JOHNS HOPKINS HOSPITAL
7

Ward.................. Unit History No..................

NAME.................. Ophthalmological No..................

I cannot condemn too strongly the old school of Chinese medicine as it is practised today. Let me note here two prescriptions from an authoritative textbook of medicine:—

At sunset, the patient travels to a bush where there are birds. While scaring the poor creatures, he has to mutter the following words:

紫公！紫公！
我還汝盲；
汝還我明.

Having repeated the above for three consecutive evenings, he is expected to find his vision improved!

An alternative:

赤眼神！赤眼神！
我今知道你緣因.
你是相公前掃街人！
只因灰塵吹入目,
至今留下赤眼人.

You may say these are superstition. Read Pillat's two articles in National Medical Journal of China. They describe vividly the injuries done to eyes which were mildly afflicted with trachoma. Just imagine the self-styled "eye-specialists," some of whom are old women, with absolutely no knowledge of anatomy or physiology, performing operations on the delicate visual organ! Acupuncture without the least aseptic precaution is the usual method of choice! Other times, medical treatment in the form of 珍珠散, 撥雲散, or 靈光丹 is employed. Buy any of

236

FORM 8097

THE JOHNS HOPKINS HOSPITAL

8

Ward........ Unit History No........

NAME........ Ophthalmological No........

these drugs from a Chinese drug store, apply it to the eye of an experimental animal, & observe the result yourself. It is simply inconceivable that in the twentieth century & in a civilized country such outrageous atrocities could have been committed ad libitum.

Preventive medicine is gradually taking the place of curative medicine. To combat trachoma or any other diseases, prophylaxis should be the first consideration. The slow development of our public health system & the gross neglect of the simple rules of hygiene & sanitation among the majority of our people have let all kinds of infections flourish throughout the entire country. The indiscriminate use of the common towel, basins, & various household utensils constitutes the chief factor in the dissemination of trachoma. The lack of physical examination in schools, factories, & other public institutions also promotes the diffusion of this malady. "An ounce of prevention is worth a pound of cure." You, too, play an important part in the revitalization of our national health.

In conclusion, may I be allowed to quote the challenging remarks of our noted ophthalmologist, T. M. Li?

"Trachoma is undoubtedly the greatest single cause of the economic losses that are occurring in China today. But it truly appalls one to find that so much apathy exists concerning a disease which has made millions of people blind & several times that many nearly

237

FORM 8097

THE JOHNS HOPKINS HOSPITAL

9

Ward......................... Unit History No..............................

NAME......................... Ophthalmological No..............................

blind. It seems as though the people have come to look upon it as a necessary evil. The duty devolves upon us who know that trachoma is not a necessary evil to lay the foundation plans for eradicating it from our land. Are we ready & willing to give ourselves to this service, or shall we leave it to those of nobler spirit & of greater zeal, — to those of a generation yet to come?"

The eradication of trachoma is indeed a gigantic problem. But we can declare with confidence that it is not an impossible task. England did it. We will!

238

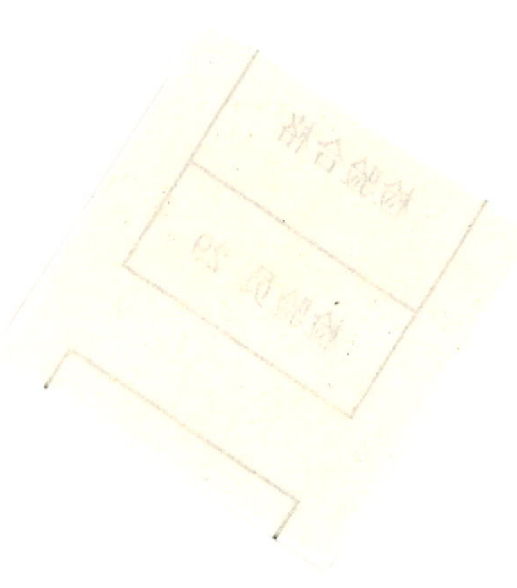